# THE UNMAKING OF GOD

William F. Nietmann

UNIVERSITY
PRESS OF
AMERICA

Lanham • New York • London

**Copyright © 1994 by**
**University Press of America®, Inc.**
4720 Boston Way
Lanham, Maryland 20706

3 Henrietta Street
London WC2E 8LU England

**Library of Congress Cataloging-in-Publication Data**
Nietmann, William F.
The unmaking of God / William F. Nietmann.
p.    cm.
Includes bibliographical references and index.
1. Hermeneutics—Religious aspects—Christianity.   2. Philosophy
and religion.   3. Language and languages—Religious aspects—
Christianity.   I. Title.
BR118.N54      1994      231—dc20      93–49437 CIP

ISBN 0–8191–9435–2 (cloth : alk. paper)
ISBN 0–8191–9436–0 (pbk. : alk. paper)

 The paper used in this publication meets the minimum requirements of
American National Standard for Information Sciences—Permanence
of Paper for Printed Library Materials, ANSI Z39.48–1984.

*to my mother*

**Grace**

*and my first philosophy teacher, my father,*

**William D. Nietmann**

# Contents

# Preface

The religious concepts of Christianity have a checkered pedigree, essentially because its framers moved beyond authentic religious concerns to seek philosophical legitimation. Philosophy added its visions to the language of Christianity, resulting in a "dehancement" of religious life. The issue of God's existence focuses our concern. Whether God is born in metaphysical necessity or inductively allowed because of the reasonableness of a "God hypothesis," philosophical interest in God remains part of the context of uncovering objective truth. However, objective truth is double edged. Critics of "proofs for God's existence" seek ways to display the shortcomings of such existence claims. Clever people who saw "God" everywhere were matched by their equals who denied that God was implicated in reality. Their argumentation was enabled by their agreement that the meaning of words must be grounded in an objective state of affairs. With the driving force of inquiry being a concern for objectivity, failure of the word "God" to refer to something makes religion a matter of indifference should one see religious life in terms of the worship of God—we leave out those cases where nothing thoughtful has an effect on those who are temperamentally dedicated to the concept of God.

Two opinion surveys reported in the newspapers of the early 1990s agreed that nearly all people in the United States (considerably in excess of 90%) believed in the existence of God. However, the everyday lives of people would seem to belie the importance of this belief despite an emotional attachment to it. Practically speaking, nothing much seems to hang on it. Were I to guess, I'd speculate that belief in God's existence is not a matter of religious faith but of philosophical faith. People offer philosophical reasons for believing in the existence of God which are tied to human drives to explain things, arrange things, and sustain things. Superficially, God's existence explains why things are, arranges and makes sense of the ordinary life and death affairs of our lives, orders and sustains events and happenings to suit the divine will. A "God" idea can unify a theory of reality, thereby providing a ground for the ultimate truth of knowledge. Truth then becomes the conduit to God's mind instead of being pragmatically grounded in human activity. The hermeneutic of "objectivity" organizes our conceptualization of "world" and concurrently of "God," presumably to unify the religious and philosophical mind. Instead of an expression of religious piety, however, the hermeneutic of "objectivity" reflects philosophical piety. Sadly for religious life, the religious establishment exists in and condones this state of pious confusion leading to superstitious uses of the idea, "God."

When authentic religious language is inauthentically expressed in terms of objective truth, it perpetuates a view of religion which leads ultimately to religion's intellectual dismissal.[1] Those unsympathetic with religion see the difficulties of religion's claims at the point of what can be allowed objectively to be true. Some modern thinkers who claimed that the demands of objectivity require religions' abandonment include David Hume (1711-1776), Karl Marx (1818-1883), Sigmund Freud (1856-1939), and Bertrand Russell (1872-1970). Religious apologists agreed with the demands of an objectivist philosophy for scientifically valid intelligibility, but concluded that religion was in fact objectively viable.

The debate which ranged over the nature and requirements of objectivity was formidable, but (to my thinking) irrelevant for religion. My reasoning has three sources. (A) One is the general persuasiveness of the arguments in what is called "contemporary continental philosophy" which show the idea of objectivity to be a hermeneutical tool. (B) The second is Anders Nygren's *Agape and Eros*. His exposition of the first-century idea of *agape* completes a twentieth-century analysis of human existence which began with Soren Kierkegaard's *Concluding Unscientific Postscript* and was extended by Martin Heidegger's *Being and Time*. (C) The third source reflects the analyses of language formulated from viewpoints in contemporary continental philosophy, especially those of Maurice Merleau-Ponty's *Phenomenology of Perception* and Georges Gusdorf's *Speaking*.

(A) Continental philosophy portends a revolution on the way that philosophy may come to be understood—at least this is a claim made by those who have followed Martin Heidegger's work. A starting point for the work of contemporary continental philosophy, however, begins with the work of Soren Kierkegaard (1813-1855). In *Concluding Unscientific Postscript* he drew the problem this way:

> Whether truth is defined more empirically as the conformity of thought and being or more idealistically as the conformity of being with thought, it is, in either case, important carefully to note what is meant by being.[2]

This Kierkegaardian remark reports historical philosophy's division over the procedures for objectively determining truth. Either knowledge resulted from an enumeration of objective, experiential structures which conveyed their own inherent meaning—thinking conformed itself to this objectivity; or knowledge resulted from an identity between the ideal structure of reality and mind which reflected being's essence. These were the opposing desiderata of "being." For "being" to be what empiricists or rationalistic idealists claimed for it (meanings objectively and inexorably effected in sensation or by reason), the impossible occurred. Persons viewed themselves as expressions of the broader realities of reason and experience when these very interpretations of existence were themselves the creations of an existing individual. In Kierkegaard's reorientation of concern and focus on the subject who thinks, we were to consider what we mean by "being." We were to probe the implications of being a person able to ask questions. Questions and context establish each other as both are invested with the sense of being which emerged from one's living. Meaning was something humanly produced, a configuration of reality which came alive in human living and inquiry. One's sense-making activity, as Kierkegaard says, "is effected through a resolution of the will, essentially in the strength of faith."[3] The meanings which become the world are human projects. As we intellectually constructed the world we live, the results were of such intimate importance and so definitive of our being that the conceptual form of our life was simultaneously taken to be life's truth as well. Practical success in the "livableness" of our ideas was sufficient to establish the parameters of truth. But the objective truths thus achieved and the understanding of the truth of a person's existence were not the same truth.

The expression of one's finitude seeks a language to give sense to being as this erupts in human existence. "Subjectivity" is a word used by Kierkegaard to get at a distinction between objective explanations of existence and a logic of finitude implicit in being a subject, the grounding for which ultimately is beyond justification. This latter, "subjectivity," is not to be confused with its psychological correlate, "subjective," meaning "emotional" or "emotive." The former deals with a universal concern with human existence—its capacity to evoke purpose and meaning; the latter points to matters of feeling, taste, inclination—the particulars which mark an individual's psychological states. *Subjectivity* is the focus of religion: "what it means to exist as a person, a subject" is its concern. A better word for this inquiry, were one to be coined, might be "subjectology."

The effect of this Kierkegaardian adjustment in the theory of knowledge, of course, makes the philosophical quest for objectivity itself a form of human existence. I join cause with Kierkegaard to argue that religious language has stumbled into alien territory when it makes objective knowledge its cause. When religion becomes permeated with the concerns of philosophical objectivity, it ceases to have religious meaning—worse, it becomes superstitious. This book aims to show why nothing essential to religious language need lead it down the path of objective concerns. Happily, that road followed has escape ramps from philosophy's influence.

(B) Religious language is absorbed in the implications of human finitude. It is the language of human existence. It is used in the context of confession, not representation; and the verification of religious language is to be found in its capacity to address human existence and not in whether its propositions conform to an objective state of affairs. Nygren's work is instructive on this point. Although his concerns were focused on Christian history and incidentally on its philosophical entanglements, he lays open a concept of *agape* which (to my thinking) concretely addresses the issue of human finitude. He (inadvertently for his purposes) shows how one's being comes into focus through Christian religious language. I am impressed with how the idea of *agape* addresses human finitude, both to reflect and explore the limits of human existence. To make religious language serve other purposes distorts it. Specifically, religious language is not intended to depict objective truths about the universe. To focus on such matters disguises or hides, sometimes obliterates, the human finitude which religious language is meant to address.[4] Nygren's development of the notion of *agape* is especially well suited to the analysis given here of religion's essence. With rare exception I leave the word "*agape*" untranslated. The familiar rendering of *agape* as "love" or "charity" becomes problematic when compared with the use of *agape* in the first-century discourses in which it occurs. Its nuances extend into poignancy and dread, abandonment and despair. It is a desperate hope in the absence of value. It is not fulfillment but emptying. A careful study of the historical and sociological climate surrounding first-century Jewish culture makes clear that the Biblical writers chose the word *agape* to grate in the ear of the hearer. Its use upset the ordinary and objectivist notions of human existence. I leave it to the reader to investigate Nygren's work. Though some of its scholarship may be dated, the careful analysis of *agape* is the book's purpose, and the radical quality of this early Christian idea, it seems to me, only now can be brought to full measure because the domination of philosophical objectivity in self-understanding is under such severe and convincing attack. Hopefully, in the final two chapters I make clear the connection between *agape*, finitude, and the unmaking of God.

Nygren focused on how *agape* fared in its exposure to philosophy. But the voice of philosophy overwhelms, snuffs out, *religious* life. This Nygren did not clearly see (as some of his other theological writings seem to show).[5] The typical view of philosophy as all-encompassing was subscribed to by religious thinkers. Nothing, including religious thinking, was to exist outside the limits thought to be objectively established by philosophical investigation. I contend, however, that religious life and philosophy exist in two irreconcilable realms. Nevertheless, Christianity's superficial similarities with philosophy caught the attention of Christian thinkers, and unique religious concern succumbed to philosophical hope. The religious language of Christianity invested in *agape* and the meaninglessness of human existence became transformed by philosophical excitement about meaning and the nature of things. *Agape* and its religious context was uninviting.

(C) Knowing "objective reality" occupied the attention of historical philosophy. The demonstration of the ultimate meaning of all existence, including the meaning of human existence, is a goal of objectivist thinking. This theme of ancient times spilled over into the modern thinking of Hume and Kant with respect to the different ways they paid attention to the role of consciousness and language in shaping what is known. Older views thought of consciousness as a location for a linguistically unencumbered thinking.[6] That is, there were things, the mind's recognition of them, and the sounds (words) assigned to indicate the latter's recognition of the former. The Wittgensteinian, John Cook, calls this position the "Meaning Assumption," a phrase used to indicate the common and naive urge to think of words as standing for or naming things.[7] Cook represents the more contemporary view that words and thought are inextricable—there is no consciousness independent of one's capacity for its articulation.[8] From "objectivity" and a mind free to observe it, a center of philosophical concern after Hume and Kant focused on the subject and language.

This movement in philosophy is explained by Richard Rorty in his *Philosophy and the Mirror of Nature*.[9] Chapter VII, "Epistemology to Hermeneutics," treats the transformation of traditional philosophical concerns by contemporary ones. The notion of "hermeneutics" points the way. This word was actively used in Biblical interpretation from the turn of the nineteenth century. In the twentieth century it took on a broader, more profound sense. It became the analysis of the unspoken interpretive expectations which we place on understanding the ordinary aspects of our everyday lives. Our urge to interpret life in terms of *proof, data, facts, information, findings, evidence, confirmation, substantiation, reasonableness, objectivity, believability, probability, plausibility, likelihood, encounters, experiences, verification, results, knowledge* reflects a hermeneutic which falls prey to the epistemological objectivity of philosophy. Hermeneutics is the interpretive measure of what is regarded as intelligible, an attitude in which (according to Rorty) there are no presuppositions respecting truth's final nature. Said another way, what counts as truth depends on the interpretive form by which the sense of world is established. In this regard, Rorty notes that philosophy found a symbol in "the Platonic philosopher-king who knows what everybody else is really doing whether *they* know it or not, because he knows about the ultimate context (the Forms, the Mind, Language) within which they are doing it."[10] Rorty continues:

> For epistemology to be rational is to find the proper set of terms into which all the contributions should be translated if agreement is to become possible. For epistemology, conversation is implicit inquiry.[11]

The challenge to objectivist epistemology is found in a more subtle investigation of understanding which evolved into a modern understanding of "hermeneutics." There are ways of understanding experience which do not lend themselves to those analyses which are collected under an objectivist theory of knowledge. Says Rorty,

> For hermeneutics, to be rational is to be willing to refrain from epistemology—from thinking that there is a special set of terms in which all contributions to the conversation should be put—and to be willing to pick up the jargon of the interlocutor rather than translating it into one's own.[12]

Rorty mentions Ludwig Wittgenstein and Martin Heidegger as having shown how "unthought" (Heidegger's charge) conceptual commitment closes an understanding of human existence.

*The Unmaking of God* is a book on religious hermeneutics. I argue that the objectivist hermeneutic (which people like Kierkegaard, Nietzsche, and Heidegger attack) has become a pervasive interpretative mode of being which destroys religious life. The urge toward "grounding" or "objectivity" is widespread. In Christendom it spans the gamut from fundamentalism through liberalism. The ironic consequence is that as much as each side thinks the other ignorant and heretical, nothing in principle separates these two "isms." Their disagreements are over what shall count as the objective warrant for Christianity. Bound together by a hermeneutic of objectivity, they both make themselves irrelevant to a religious life.

The first centuries of the Christian church itself faced the hermeneutics of objectivity in gnosticism. The deeply entrenched cultural perspective of Hellenic culture, philosophically expressed in the thinking of Plato (c. 427-347 B.C.) and Aristotle (384-322 B.C.), confronted an alien world view in the religious hermeneutic of Judaism's subjectivity. First- and second-century Christian thinkers fought off gnosticism as best they could, but given the overwhelming commitment to "objectivism," it was a losing battle.

Caught early by the philosophical mind of Platonism, Christianity shared its interest in the reality and nature of divine being. Heidegger cited the ancient philosophical question: "Why are there essents ['Essents' = 'existents,' 'things that are'] rather than nothing?" as the source of philosophy's genesis.[13] From the perspective of ancient philosophy the being of anything remained a source of wonder. The question: "Why is there something?" yielded metaphysics and its heir, science. The philosophical task was conceived as fathoming divine information and assessing its consequences for daily life. Christianity adopted Platonism's scientific mood where the "why?" of something was answered by a "how?"

Little was changed by the modern spirit. We likewise submitted eagerly to the long tradition of offering descriptions and looking for causes of things and ideas. The metaphysical world of philosophy became the scientific world of things and their arrangements. Whatever made sense was grounded in thingness. Rational structures represented in logic and mathematics became the ultimate stuff of being. Thinking became a technology, and thoughts became things, Ideas. Words especially were things standing for things in the relationship of sign to signified; and the logical force of a language merely reflected the general force of deeper logical relationships. Thingness molded being in its terms. God was shrouded in thingness which produced its own technology: theology.

Relying on Platonism, early church fathers found the divine mind in Reason and conspired to sanction faith in Reason's terms. God only need be brought to light objectively in the various proofs for his existence to legitimize religious belief. Theologians produced "proofs for God's existence" thereby making "God" accessible. No need to produce a tangible God: logical being was sufficient to placate the requirements of objectivity associated with "what is." A non-physical "thingness" grounded the being of physical things in an ultimate cause which produced the necessity of divine existence out of cosmological and design arguments about reality. This spirit of philosophical objectivity forced aside any authentic religious sense to human existence.

Though attempted in periods of Christian reformation, dislodging the objective philosophical viewpoint which so thoroughly shaped religion's intelligibility was a nearly impossible task—until contemporary times. Kierkegaard began to forge the tools of analysis which could breech the bastion of objectivity. Twentieth-century thinkers such as Martin Heidegger or Hans-Georg Gadamer showed how interpretative structures regulated our outlooks.[14] Accordingly, the contemporary "deconstruction" of historical philosophy forces us to rethink a religious life which had depended on philosophy's theories. The attack alleges that from Plato forward, philosophy has misconstrued its tasks and abused its limits. The call is to purge philosophical tradition of its impossible or misleading tasks, to regenerate it in hermeneutical and linguistic analysis, and to follow out the implications of human finitude for our lives together as persons—in ethics, political relationships, religion.

To defeat a skepticism with respect to religious language religion must once again investigate its own genesis. No longer can the religiously motivated person legitimize religious language by something factual. No longer can the philosophical mode of the day be employed to satisfy its demands for intelligibility. Where "feeling" once was reckoned a legitimizing source of meaning, where emotive complements to the idea of "God" were spawned by sentiment, wonder and awe, where aesthetics inspired by logical perfection fixed a sense of well-being and moral ordering of life, of Holy Spirit, all such veneration of religious life must be rethought, for they are all the progeny of a philosophical hermeneutic and themselves are religiously barren.

To unmake the religious edifice which was constructed by philosophical ideas is no small task. We are so absorbed in a philosophical culture that it will be difficult to enter into the task of freeing religion from philosophy. We will feel uneasy if nothing philosophical warrants making sense of the idea "God." Yet, the season is right to begin such a discussion. Philosophy finds itself at a crossroad in self-understanding. Philosophy as it has been practiced historically seems to be coming to an end, and the religion which depended on it will likewise disappear in due season—unless a philosophically unadorned religiousness regenerates itself from its own resources.

My thesis, then, is this: though inadvertent, the hermeneutic of the philosophical tradition annihilated religious insight, effecting the metamorphosis of the varieties of Christianity into cultural reminders of various philosophical intuitions. I join with other contemporary thinkers to understand the limits of philosophy and in this light to reconsider what the Christian life is about.[15] I am persuaded that traditional philosophical descriptions of human experience were misleading. Uncoupled from philosophical tradition, a literate Christianity once again struggles with the question of what it is. Philosophical analysis can reveal the differences, but no commitment to a philosophical theory need be prerequisite to religious life. My attempt to reformulate religious authenticity, to deny it philosophical attachments, will show that human existence is essentially religious.

Recognitions of who was helpful in the development of the book include my wife, Betty. As encouraging as she is, however, she likes to stay away from philosophy. It creates dissention, and she believes in living in peace with others. Over the time of the book's development, my colleague, David Sherry, has been most generous with his advice, both stylistic and philosophical. Though he is not especially interested in religion, his interest in philosophical history and his demand that philosophy not lapse into jargon has kept him at my heels. I may not achieve the expectations he would have for my work, but his help and encouragement have been much appreciated. I especially appreciate the proof-reading work of Louella Holter. Finally, I thank the students in my Philosophy of Religion classes who have endured the "test runs" of this book. Their practical advice has been helpful.

# Notes

1. The popularity of religion is not the issue here nor is the ordinary use of the word. Whatever is ideologically put forward as Christianity indeed can influence people's state of mind, changing people's perceptions of their life—this is well known. The banner of "religion" has been made to extend from performing religious circuses to somber, dusky cathedral. The psychological fixtures which make up religion even become part of the debate as to the relative popularity of fundamentalism vis à vis the so-called "liberal" churches. Such trends are neither here nor there in this analysis.

2. Trs. Lowrie and Swenson (Princeton: Princeton University Press, 1941), p. 169.

3. *Ib.*, p. 169.

4. There are other responses to finitude which mark the differences between the world's religions. Some religions address human finitude by prescribing a path to meaningfulness (Judaism, Buddhism); others see the concern with human finitude and its implicit meaninglessness as itself the essential problem of self-consciousness and take steps to ignore or obliterate that consciousness of self which is at the core of the problem (Zen Buddhism, Hinduism). This book focuses on Christianity. It nicely demonstrates my contention that religious language is the language which frames the finitude of human existence. This interpretative motif works for various of the world's religions as well.

5. See for instance his *Essence of Christianity; two essays*, tr. Philip S. Watson (London: Epworth Press [c. 1960]).

6. There is a difference between language and speaking. The latter is what persons do; the former is derivative from speaking. Maurice Merleau-Ponty describes the intimacy between speaking and world as follows: "The denomination of objects does not follow upon recognition; it is itself recognition." (See Chapter 6, "The Body as Expression, and Speech," in *The Phenomenology of Perception* [tr. Colin Smith [New York: The Humanities Press, 1962].) Speaking is like a gesture: "Here the meaning of words must be finally induced by the words themselves, or more exactly their conceptual meaning must be formed by a kind of deduction from a *gestural meaning*, which is immanent in speech. . . . I begin to understand the meaning of words

through their place in the context of action, and by taking part in a communal life" (*op. cit.*, p. 179). It is a common theme in the existential variety of continental philosophy to affirm the intrinsically human quality of speaking and its derivation, language, in contrast to seeing meaning as independent of the lived world, somehow imbedded in things, and merely attended by their signs—words.

7. John W. Cook, "The Fate of Ordinary Language Philosophy," *Philosophical Investigations* (Spring, 1980, 3:2), esp. p 20f.

8. See also Georges Gusdorf, *Speaking*, tr. Brockelman (Evanston: Northwestern University Press, 1965) which likewise captures the sense of intrinsic unity between world and speaking.

9. New Jersey: Princeton University Press, 1979.

10. *Op. cit.,* p. 317f.

11. *Ib.*, p. 318.

12. *Ib.*

13. *Introduction to Metaphysics*, tr., R. Manheim (New Haven: Yale University Press, 1959), p. 6. The book reworked a 1935 course and was first published in 1953.

14. The history of what is here called "contemporary continental philosophy" can be found in books such as Robert C. Solomon's *Continental Philosophy Since 1750: The Rise and Fall of the Self* (Oxford/New York: Oxford U. P., 1988). The names of "the movement" include Edmund Husserl, Martin Heidegger, Jean-Paul Sartre, and Maurice Merleau-Ponty, along with many others.

15. In Part II, I note that contemporary continental philosophy has brought the tradition of philosophy to an end. For instance, part of Martin Heidegger's work from Vol. II of his book *Nietzsche* and a chapter of his *Vorträge und Aufsätze* is published in English under the title *The End of Philosophy* (tr., J. Stambaugh, New York: Harper and Row, 1973). Techniques in the analysis of language and argument developed by Jacque Derrida (called "deconstruction") bring him to a concluding remark in his essay "White Mythology" that "Metaphor . . . always carries its death within itself. And this death is also the death *of* philosophy" [in *Margins of Philosophy* (tr. A. Bass, Chicago: University of Chicago Press, 1982) p. 271]. What I find intriguing about the insights which lead to such conclusions is that religious insight (and here specifically, the insights of the Judeo-Christian tradition) turn out to be more fundamental to understanding human existence, more so than those of philosophy.

# Acknowledgments

The author thanks the following for giving permission to quote from the works mentioned:

Passages from GWF Hegel, *Reason in History*, reprinted with the permission of Macmillan College Publishing Company from REASON IN HISTORY by Hegel, Robert S. Hartman, trans. Copyright ©1953 by Macmillan College Publishing Company. Inc.; Martin Heidegger, *An Introduction to Metaphysics*, tr. Ralph Manheim (New Haven, Yale University Press, ©1959); passages from Immanuel Kant, *The Critique of Practical Reason*, reprinted with the permission of Macmillan College Publishing Company from THE CRITIQUE OF PRACTICAL REASON by Immanuel Kant, Lewis White Beck, trans. Copyright ©1956 by Macmillan College Publishing Company. Inc.; Immanuel Kant, *Grounding for the Metaphysics of Morals*, J. W. Ellington, tr. (Indianapolis, Hackett Publishing Co., 1981), all rights reserved; passages from Immanuel Kant, *Prolegomena to Any Future Metaphysics*, reprinted with the permission of Macmillan College Publishing Company from PROLEGOMENA TO ANY FUTURE METAPHYSICS by Immanuel Kant, Lewis White Beck, trans. Copyright ©1956 by Macmillan College Publishing Company. Inc.; Soren Kierkegaard, *Concluding Unscientific Postscript*, trs. David Swenson and Walter Lowrie (Princeton, Princeton University Press, ©1941); James Russell Lowell, "Once to Every Man and Nation," *The Book of Hymns*, copyright ©1964, 1966 by Board of Publication of the Methodist Church, Inc. Used by permission.

Except as noted, scripture quotations are from the *Revised Standard Version of the Bible*, copyright 1946, 1952, 1971 by the Division of Christian Education of the National Council of the Churches of Christ in the USA. Used by permission.

# Chapter I

---

# Introduction

> [A] faith that does not perpetually expose itself to the possibility of
> unfaith is no faith but merely a convenience: the believer simply
> makes up his mind to adhere to the traditional doctrine. This is neither
> faith nor questioning, but the indifference of those who can busy
> themselves with everything, sometimes even displaying a keen interest
> in faith as well as questioning.[1]
>
> *An Introduction to Metaphysics*
> *Martin Heidegger*

In the epilogue of Dostoyevsky's *Crime and Punishment* Raskolnikov, the antihero of the novel, has a dream in which persons become
infected by a dread disease, a philosophical disease. These "plague-
ridden creatures" were infected by their essential humanity: "reason
and will." Dostoyevsky makes the disease come "from the depths of
Asia." It must be Greece, the cradle of Western Civilization. From
Plato onward, "reason and will" were believed to comprise human
nature. Those infected by this disease claimed truth for their ideas; self-
righteousness and arrogance were natural to their character. Said
Dostoyevsky, "Each one propounded his own theories" and "wrung his
hands" if others should imagine that they instead possessed truth. The
cure for the disease of reason and will is as yet unknown. How can
persons set aside reason and will—their natures?

And yet, Sonia, the character whose healing presence intimated
Christian love, vitalizes life. She is neither self-righteous nor arrogant.

No objective truth directed her life. Rather in the truth of human finitude, she lived a life of *agape*. Though Dostoyevsky concluded the novel by saying that her portrayal of human existence was a story for another occasion, it was not a story he ever told. Still, his sensitivity to the difference between the philosophical life represented by Raskolnikov and the nearly invisible Christian life of Sonia was prescient. It becomes the theme of our concern.

The philosophical seduction of religious life is so thoroughgoing that more often than not what is taken to be religious faith is no more than the extension of philosophical beliefs. The connection is not easily broken. The two have become so intertwined into a fine fabric of thinking that the separation of the warp from the woof of these differing ideas requires careful and extended examination. Our propensity is to cultivate "reason and will." Applied to the various meanings of religious life, philosophical thinking was able to shield us from religion's poignancy. It transformed religious language into philosophical language, which eradicated the necessity of living with the truth of our mortality. The erasure was never complete, however, for no putative "intrinsic to human nature" could shield it from an essential meaninglessness dispensed to existence by its finitude. This claim is sustained in the opinion found in the earliest literature of Christianity where existence stood in need of redemption.[2] This voice was muted and distorted, however, by the context into which it was born.

The cultural/intellectual setting of first-century Christianity was that of ancient Greece. Alexander the Great's Hellenization of the ancient world three and a half centuries earlier had effects that reached into Hebrew culture and with this, the development of Christianity during the first and second centuries. In his book, *Bandits, Prophets, and Messiahs,* Richard A. Horsley reconstructs the social and intellectual history of this period of time. He writes:

> The Hellenistic empires of Alexander's successors brought a systematic program of increased economic exploitation and a general policy of cultural imperialism that threatened the Jews' traditional ways of life. The ruling priestly elite, who maintained their privileged social position, attracted by the glories of Hellenistic civilization, began to compromise themselves culturally, religiously, and politically.... Alexander and his successors founded numerous Hellenistic cities in Palestine, with the Greek-speaking citizens and their local gentry in control of the indigenous population, who had no citizenship rights in

the cities proper.[3]

By the time one can speak of "Christendom," the Jewish religious commitments of the first century had taken into account the *philosophical* world views of Platonism and Aristotlianism, with their attendant concepts of "the divine." An intellectual tension existed between Jewish *religious* concepts and Greek philosophical ideas. Christianity's outreach into the broader Hellenistic culture eventually found a Platonic philosophical idealism sanctified and made a part of Christian religious beliefs. Chapter I of this work gives an account of this transformation. The thinking of Plato and Aristotle intruded itself into Christianity at its inception, especially as it grappled with Gnosticism. Four hundred years later St. Augustine's (354-430) Platonism, then still later St. Thomas Aquinas's (1225-1274) Aristotlianism, were explicitly used in the formulation of Christian theology. Medieval thinkers pronounced the necessity of God's existence in the cause of explaining being.

Philosophy is unceasing. The divine optimism of medieval thinking faded as antiquity's durable philosophical ideas were reevaluated two thousand years later. With the onset of scientific rationalism and empiricism of the seventeenth century, the need for a logically necessary god faded, though not the plausibility of a divine mechanic. With a presumably disinterested scientific eye, apologists for religion wanted objectively to ground possible meanings for the word "God" in observable nature. After all, "observation" was the watchword of scientific thinking. Thus, in order to authenticate religious faith, some sort of objective truth, free from parochial confines, was sought in order to make the God idea plausible. The philosophical passions of the modern age ensnared the religious body. The evolution versus creation debate remains a remnant of such concern where both Christian liberalism and fundamentalism, each from its own quite different point of view, attempt to find elements in experience, clues, which point to God's existence. How scientific objectivity effected a change in the focus of Christian thinking is the subject matter of Chapters II and III.

The inadequacies of rationalism and empiricism provoked Immanuel Kant's idealism. His thinking influenced the nineteenth century's religious moralism, especially through his rationalistic doctrine of "the inherent dignity and worth of every person." This is the topic of the fourth chapter. The fifth chapter focuses on the nineteenth century's Hegelian idealism. Georg Wilhelm Friedrich Hegel (1770-1831) bound God into time and nourished the thinking of what was to become social science and its religious expression: contemporary "liberal" Christianity and the social gospel. The scientific spirit of the nineteenth and twentieth centuries with respect to social reality found liberal religious thinkers agreeing in the name of God to the adjustments needed for social harmony, itself a matter of scientific calculation.

From Plato through Hegel, theories of knowledge and reality were developed to bring the true nature of reality to light, each one hopefully being the final word, but each merely becoming the occasion for further explorations. One correctly anticipates that these persistent quests for objective truth had their parallel transforming effects on the idea of God and religious life. After all, shouldn't truth's demands be equally binding on religious life? It is with some wonder, then, that one hears my answer: I argue that matters bearing on the objective truth of reality are incidental to religion and the religious life—illegitimate for religious concern.

The reformers of Christian thought (e.g., Luther, Zwingli, Calvin, and later, Wesley, or twentieth-century thinkers like Barth, Bultmann, or Tillich) struggled in certain respects to put philosophy aside in favor of concern for human existence; but they were not always clear about how to sustain a Christian indifference to philosophical founda-tions—historical Christianity had always depended on philosophy's enthusiasms to give it cogency.[4] I argue that the philosophical dedica-tion to objective truth forms a barricade to authentic religious life, that the widespread concern with the objectivity of God's existence is irrelevant for religious life and its practice, that the familiar philosophi-cal uses of "God" for purposes of explanation have no religious value, and the effect of this approach to religion is sanctimonious superstition. It seems to me, rather, that the beginning point for religious life is a person's address to finitude. The foundation for the analysis of religious life is laid whenever one contemplates the limits of one's life. Religious life emerges from an essential meaninglessness identified with finitude. In such a context the idea "God" and its attendant implications emerges.

In Christianity the intricacies of being a finite subject evoked humility, a forgiving, unrelenting care, what is called *agape*. *Agape* used in conjunction with the idea "God" enabled a placement of human existence. *Agape* is itself logically rooted in finitude. (I believe but will not demonstrate that what is true of Christianity is true also of other religions.) The use of the idea of divinity enables the reality of finitude to become articulate. But these religious matters were compromised by the philosophical world of the Occident in which Christianity flourished. The context for seeing the changes in Christian thinking is the philosophical world: from ancient Greece through the subsequent rush of changing outlooks which erupted during the sixteenth through twentieth centuries.

We should not wonder that Christian thinking attached itself to philosophy. Philosophy housed an understanding of all reality. Even the use of the word "God" in philosophy becomes enough to establish a kind of pious sympathy for philosophical thinking among religious thinkers. A philosopher's use of "God" is religiously seductive—but also destructive of religion. In intent, religious uses of "God" are different from philosophical uses. *The Unmaking of God* puts forward a view of what authentic religious language does, how it has a force which is independent of philosophically produced visions of truth, reality, and humankind's place in it. Part I of this book, then, shows how religious belief about God is grounded in philosophical thinking. Part II delineates the difference between religious and philosophical life to show wherein religious authenticity lies.

## Aculturated Religion

The project is innocent enough. "However," someone asks, "doesn't the title of the book belie such innocence? Surely there is more to the notion of 'unmaking' than mere separation." Controversy lies in the offing. The questioner continues: "Implicit in the title is the suggestion that *all* ideas of 'God' are artifacts, human creations, things *made*." It is a charge I cannot deny. The capacity to put the universe together in such a way that God is necessitated in its understanding is a philosophical task, *whatever guise it takes*. To imagine "God" as a thing awaiting discovery is a human vanity, a pleasant philosophical conceit in which some specific conceptualization of "world" and concurrently of "God" provided a principle for the unification of being. Because both philosophical and religious minds can believe in God, presumably they come together. Thus began a parade of thinkers who attempted to unite religious faith with philosophical truth. The author of the Gospel of John, a person with philosophical insights inherited from Platonism, saw a pre-existent *logos* as the origin of being. This reliance on Platonism continued in the thinking of early church fathers. For them the truth of divine reason sustained the normal purposes of understanding; faith was a remainder, something left over to serve the incapacity to pronounce the last word in matters of belief. It was a remainder, too, for later theologians who were able to produce "proofs for God's existence" and make "God" accessible, though not quite reveal the quintessential god. Nevertheless, this divine *thing*, this God, would come close to discovery through the intensities of reason and spiritual discipline. As visible things were the effects of invisible laws, so all Being, visible and invisible, was to be dependent on the invisible God as highest being. A non-physical "thingness" grounded the being of all existence. An ultimate cause posited in cosmological and design arguments yielded God's existence.

Philosophical tradition has argued that "God" can be reasonably believed to exist because of features in the natural order which require an ultimate explanation. Popular culture reflects this contention in its remark that "It is no accident that..." (now fill in the blank) "trees grow," "planets orbit," "babies smile," and so on. The rhetorical "where did it all come from, if not God?" hopes to make obvious that design and causality are sufficient reasons to believe in the existence of God. People transport a philosophical fascination with design and causation into religion, and neglect to notice that these same ideas slice the God hypothesis from objective explanations as well. Such questioning also infects the dogma that God stands just over the horizon causing events. Quantum philosophy, for instance, introduces questions about traditional notions of causation and the ordering of the universe.[5]

If at one level abstract arguments from the order of nature hold a fascination for people, at another there is the more practical hope that divine powers can structure everyday life. Some look at divinity as something like possessing a lucky rabbit's foot. God is invoked for guidance and control—events are understood as acts of the supernatural. Others appeal to divine reality for purposes of moral control: God's "eye in the sky" with the warning of divine reproach. Religious belief is used to invoke social stability; "God" becomes a shibboleth of socialization.

Karl Marx, Emile Durkheim, or Sigmund Freud each produced a version of this latter explanation of religious commitment. The human need to survive enriched by a collaborative division of labor led to the development of a kind of common sense marked by productive cooperation, called moral rectitude. However, it took a religious belief in divine authority to give teeth to common sense. Thus, religion and morality (according to these social thinkers) merged in the cause of communal harmony. In these times of modernity where social science promises an understanding of human behavior, if not human existence, each of these thinkers called for a scientifically conceived "objective truth" which alone would provide the eventual basis for an ultimate human happiness. Thus, Marx and Durkheim conceived of thought as responses to the material conditions of life; Freud argued that religion was a confused amalgam of pseudo-causes aimed at the control and understanding of life. All agreed that no philosophically derived religious machinations would be adequate to the empirical task of producing human happiness. Happiness required a configuration by objective science and its pragmatics. Thus the need for religion would fade as mankind learned of the natural operations of the psyche and the social order. As the social sciences demystify religion by explaining its causes and effects, no longer was a supernatural being required for what in fact they see as natural human responses.

In the face of such analyses, progressive religious thinkers understood what was required to regain credibility. The social sciences would themselves become effective tools to promote what in religious circles was called God's will to "meet the needs of people." It would be a morality which harkened back to the first-century Jewish appeals for God's justice in (from the viewpoint of a Jewish peasant people) an unjust and hostile social environment. If "justice" required them to overthrow authority alien to Jewish rule and life, it now would entail passive resistance in the name of "peace and justice" in a "kingdom of God on earth." Morality was not personal but social, and the tie between morality and religion came at the point of the just cause.

However, it takes little imagination to note that no divine imperative is needed to "do good in the world." After all—what could be added by "God's way" to the happiness promised as part of the adjustment of the social order? Nevertheless, the religious liberal hoped scientifically to respond to human demands for psychological and social stability, thus providing some semblance of a connection between effective religion and daily life. The elements of religion became a participation in God's natural social order, scientifically defined, and the personal moral life functioned only as a natural effect in the economy of human affairs. As we shall see in Chapter IV, such commitments to explanation and social harmony are built from philosophical positions.

The prospects are seductive: philosophical methodology is exploited on behalf of religious concerns to make the existence of God, the purpose of nature and history, the nature of mankind, and so on, believable. It is not so curious, then, that the explanatory power of the sciences proved influential in religious circles: a hermeneutic of

objectivity proportioned to "the natural outlook" of science spawns a
hope for information which hopefully will confirm faith. We see it in
far-ranging matters made over into religious concern—the meaning and
purpose of the universe (at least this particular corner of it); the
machinery and paraphernalia needed to effect "God's will" (should
there be such). As Christian thinkers adopted each new outlook of
objectivity and made their religious outlooks conform to the best
thinking of the age, their thinking was soon displaced by the inevitable
revisions in thought which characterize objective thinking. Philosophy
and its scientific progeny are quite willing to conform to each new
requirement of objectivity. Philosophical explanations move toward
closure when they overcome what is false. Hope for a rationally
regulated human existence is created. Philosophy is easy to tolerate and
reassuring in its results. Philosophical objectivity shields people from
life's uncertainty. It is palatable, expansive; people like its objectivity.
As history demonstrates, whenever a theory of reality or knowledge
was devised, a "God" idea soon became connected to the theory and
made a part of religious language. It is especially embraceable by
religion. However, the context of living that creates what each intends
by "God" is not the same. To ignore this difference is to undo religious
concern. When defined by philosophical interests, the unintended
consequence for religion is that it becomes unessential to life. Religion's concerns are not with objectivity. In fact, the language of
religion must remain indifferent to philosophical visions of truth and
reality.

*Baptized Philosophy*

The urge to investigate God objectively, like the urge scientifically
to unpack the secrets of nature, is understandable—the presumption of
an essential objective meaning to Being spawned philosophical
traditions. It is also without religious merit or interest. The nature of
knowledge, the "I" which knows, truth, the parameters of that which
is ultimately real—this is the stuff of philosophy, not religion. People
who think divine objectivity proper to religious discourse are a
testimony to the power of philosophy to infiltrate and dominate
religious interests, eventually usurping them. The quest for "God,"
which might pass for a religious concern, has nothing to do with
religion but plays to our philosophical desires and the enhancement of
our intellectual prowess. People love philosophical ideas—they can use
them to compose God—and thus (unwittingly) regard philosophy as the

occasion for religious piety. Nevertheless, even if philosophy argues in behalf of the reality of God, authentic religious life shares *no* intimacy with the creative expressions of philosophy. Thus, to *unmake* the baptized gods of philosophical piety is the beginning point to uncovering an essential religiousness. Put another way, the philosophical uses of the word "god" lend themselves to superstition. Precisely the opposite occurs with the religious uses of "God." Religious uses of "God" begin at a polar opposite from the philosophically derived ideas of "god" debated in theism and atheism. A Christianity unraveled from philosophical commitments does not evanesce but regains its uniqueness.

Religious concerns would not be proved or referenced. In religious life God would have no plans for the rational ordering of being. There would be no pretense for deciphering God's plans, for no objective truth would be of religious concern. Biblical stories (Adam and Eve in Eden, the Red Sea crossing, Virgin Birth, turning water into wine, resurrection) would not be understood as events to be verified but would have their religious force provided by a quite different hermeneutic. Faith would not be the weigh station for what we are almost, but not quite, sure of.

The qualities of objectivity should never have been taken up as decisive for Christianity and religious life; more to the point, the believer who is caught up by objectivity subverts the force of the religious life. Unfortunately, too often what people take to be religious talk is simply the application of one or another philosophical positions to life. A philosophically reshaped idea of religion obfuscates the religious sense of life. To make this accusation stick, I show that religious language does not depend on fathoming its sense through philosophical theories. It is Heidegger who says:

> Only epochs which no longer fully believe in the true greatness of the task of theology arrive at the disastrous notion that philosophy can help to provide a refurbished theology if not a substitute for theology, which will satisfy the needs and tastes of the time. For the original Christian faith philosophy is foolishness.[6]

Religiously one turns one's attention not to "God" but to the searcher for God, there to see persons perpetually existing in error. When one speaks to the state of human finitude, one draws on the name of God. One's own helplessness finds one throwing oneself into the abyss. It is Peter plunging into the water.

The religious use of the concept of "God" is the special language which addresses this human nothingness. The Psalmist gives expression to the sense of finitude when he says[7]

> My god, my God, why hast thou forsaken me?
> Why art thou so far from helping me, from the words of
>     my groaning?
> O my God, I cry by day, but thou dost not answer; and by night, but
>     find no rest.
> Yet thou art holy, enthroned on the praises of Israel.
> In thee our fathers trusted; they trusted, and thou didst deliver them.
> To thee they cried and were saved; in thee they trusted, and were not
>     disappointed (Ps. 22:1-5).

These words give life to the petitioner's despair of existence and place an awesome silence over what is given voice. God exists in this silence. "God," enunciated, reflects the speaker's mortality and reflects its constraining effect through the confession that he cannot transcend his finitude. Given the silence of God, one's own being is thrust out upon the "seventy thousand fathoms," unable to be the master of one's fate. There is "nothing" left but hope in the power of divine deliverance. In this religious utterance "God" is not a thing or even the condition for the being of things. This form of religious language finds the use of the idea of "God" framing one's manner of existence. Religion is a sphere of existence rather than the effect of discovery. It is the confrontation of nothingness.

The philosophical god is unmade while the religious god remains silent. We posit no discovery, no argument, no reason for the existence or non-existence of God. God is neither an assumption nor a conclusion. The purge of philosophy from religion presumes that religious language has its own proper sphere of concern, and the task of *The Unmaking of God* is to show this.

## Notes

1. Heidegger, Martin, *Introduction to Metaphysics*, tr., R. Manheim (New Haven: Yale University Press, 1959), p. 7.

2. Although the language of the early church is that of eschatological mythology, if demythologized, this language speaks to the issues of finitude. The hermeneutical context for sustaining demythologization, that is, for claiming that religious language is not a language of objectivity and referentiality, is developed in the concluding chapters of the book. Here is a typical

passage from Paul's letter to the Romans (8:18-25) which points to the broader context of meaninglessness.

> For I reckon that the sufferings we now endure bear no comparison with the splendour, as yet unrevealed, which is in store for us. For the created universe waits with eager expectation for God's sons to be revealed. It was made the victim of frustration, not by its own choice, but because of him who made it so; yet always there was hope, because the universe itself is to be freed from the shackles of mortality and enter upon the liberty and splendour of the children of God. Up to the present, we know, the whole created universe groans in all its parts as if in the pangs of childbirth. Not only so, but even we, to whom the Spirit is given as firstfruits of the harvest to come, are groaning inwardly while we wait for God to make us his sons and set our whole body free. For we have been saved, though only in hope. Now to see is no longer to hope: why should a man endure and wait for what he already sees? But if we hope for something we do not yet see, then, in waiting for it, we show our endurance. (*The New English Bible with the Apocrypha* [Oxford University Press; Cambridge University Press, 1970])

3. Richard A. Horsley (with J. S. Hanson), *Bandits, Prophets, and Messiahs: Popular Movements at the Time of Jesus* (San Francisco: Harper and Row, Publishers, 1985) p. 10, 11.

4. This is a book which works with ideas, their implications and connections. Philosophy defined Christian thinking. As interesting would be a companion study, an empirical demonstration of what historical theological figures read and studied. The connections between the philosophical and religious motifs are logically persuasive. Historical detail would cinch the claim. Regrettably, this detail lies beyond my expertise.

5. See John Horgan's essay on "Quantum Philosophy" in the July, 1992 (267:1) issue of *Scientific American*. As part of the whetting of appetite for the article, he says "... quantum theory has deeply disturbing implications. For one, it shattered traditional notions of causality" (p. 95).

6. *Introduction to Metaphysics, op. cit.*, p. 7.

7. Unless otherwise indicated, all quoted Biblical material is from *The Holy Bible: Revised Standard Version* (New York: Thomas Nelson & Sons, 1953).

# Part I: Philosophical Objectivity And Its Religious Impact

## Chapter II

---

# God and Reality

### Introduction—Rational Perfection

Divinity was a concept appropriate to the life of Greek philosophy, especially metaphysics. The idea of "the divine" or "divinity" is not used by Biblical writers. Instead, the Jews used political language to speak of God. God was majestic. God commanded. People were subject to God's will, a will which may be difficult to fathom and even capricious. Jews believed that if God said something, it was so because *God* said it. God was not a rationally perfect being but a volitional one, not a divine being but one who was involved in the affairs of the Jews. God's justice and mercy sufficed for a people in need.

In contrast, Plato argued that God looked to what was right for his commands. As envisioned by Plato, things divine flourished in the context of an ordered, rational, absolute and ultimate reality. The forms (the Ideas which ordered reality) and the Good (the cogency which ordered the realm of Ideas) were required if things were to exist at all. All lesser being was dependent on this necessary, divine reality. The difference is important. As early Christian thinkers came under the influence of Platonic philosophy, they reconstructed the Jewish understanding of God to fit divine things. They transformed religious life into a celebration of philosophical thinking. In the evolution of

Christian thinking, "God" became divine being, the God of pure principle. Divine principles, the logic of God's being, determined the natural order, including the requirements for the moral and social order. One purified one's own divine nature through contemplation on the divine. Striving toward the divine, the highest one knew, became the fulfillment of a religious life.

Other differences emerged. The religious perceptions of the Hebraic mind allowed for God's personification. Divine perfection ruled out personification. This was because the philosophical tradition began with the fullness of being in its rational ordering and was quite unlike the incompleteness inherent in personhood. In the Hebrew tradition one was dependent on God as on the sovereign ruler. The natural order and the requirements of the social order would be regulated by God to serve human need and life. In this Jewish tradition, one gave thanks to, paid homage to, was obedient to, served God.

Though in different senses, it obviously could be said that both Hebrew and Greek cultures recognized that all existence depended on "God." Further, in both, a relationship with God, whatever that might be, was of special concern. In Christianity, these superficially parallel religious languages about God (one seeing God as a sovereign and the other as divine) merged into an amalgam, a conflation of religious languages. The fact remained that what was meant by "God," "dependent," and "relationship" differed.

It is not surprising that *divinity* and *sovereignty* became merged. Christian thought early fell under the influence of the varieties of Platonistic thinking, especially in its Stoic and Gnostic forms.[1] Philosophically acute religious thinking dismissed the volitional, politically fashioned, Jewish God. Christian thinkers such as Valentinus and Marcion thought the Jewish god inferior to the sublimity of that divine perfection from which Jesus was sent. Gnostic Christian beliefs about "God" reflected the ineffable properties of a divine rationality diffused throughout all reality. Life was to be focused by the reality of *divine* being found in the divine spark within ourselves. An ineffable god of rationality, a divine presence, made the idea of union with God a purpose of Christian worship. Worship became a ceaseless meditation on divinity—hence the life of the monk—rather than obedience to the more pragmatic demands of the Judeo-Christian God. Jesus was thought to have revealed the divine information necessary for union. He was thus necessary for salvation as one strove to reintegrate one's own (divine) being with God, the ultimate source of all being. One learned divine truth, disciplined life to its requirements, and thereby fulfilled one's divine nature. Feelings of awe and wonder, positive feelings evoked (supposedly) in the contemplation of Being, were inspired by God. Religion reflected reality and that form of life compatible with perfection's requirements. What would be more humanizing than to get in tune with reality?

It may strike one as strange to think that the ancient philosophical world is sustained in our own desires for the harmonious ordering of Being, oneness, unity, for overall rational cogency—the stuff of a rational life. Early Christianity struggled with these philosophical desires, eventually to define itself in their terms. After all, philosophy was the "science" of that time. Everything would center and depend on divine reality, including religious life. Thus begins the tale of Christianity's love affair with Greek philosophy; specifically, Plato and Aristotle, in which all ideas must ultimately be harmonious, unified, with a divine God as their source. Our intellectual heritage in religious matters turned on the thinking of Plato and Aristotle with respect to divine things.

Plato (427?-347 B.C.) and Aristotle (384-322 B.C.) each formed a theory to explain change as well as an explanation as to why there was anything at all. They each argued for an ultimate reality in which changelessness was its natural state of being. Divine being was the reason why lesser things changed. They were drawn to an Ideal perfection inherent in Being. They changed. The changeless Ideal was itself perfect (changeless) because there was nothing on which it was dependent or could strive for. Thus, ultimate perfection must be "divine" or "God." The divine, God, explained the being of the universe—why there was anything at all.[2]

The question "Why do things change?" thus called for causal explanation; but unlike the eighteenth-century view of causation which required that we determine the components of objects in their temporal ordering, antiquity understood cause as that in the absence of which nothing could be. Appeals to divinity as a causal explanation for Being may sound odd to our scientific ears. Yet because of the idea of absolute rational perfection, change could be explained. It was not so much that a thing's immediate causation was sought as it was that without God, there could be no reason for the being of anything. Any explanation of change presumed the changeless, the perfect, by which change could be measured. To be sure, one cause of things was the proper admixture of the elements—fire, earth, water, and air in the ancient "periodic table." Yet, the simple presence of elements was insufficient to account for the being of an object. Something more was needed—a structure or design—which was the essence of that thing. The intrinsically chaotic nature of stuff had to be ordered through the imposition of its essence from an ordered, divine realm of being—for Plato, these essences were Ideas.[3] When Ideas were infused into matter, their intelligibility permeated the material order of being; they structured existence, making it rational, experiential, and knowable.

The nature of this fusion was an ancient debate. For Plato the combination of matter and idea was unnatural. These two causes of things were so utterly unlike one another that in order for each to be true to its own nature, they attempted to separate themselves from each other, each returning to its own natural home. This "return" explained why things change. Matter decayed into an inert, chaotic lifelessness while ideas flew to their proper home in a divine realm. Since matter could defile the Ideal world, it was of some consequence that Ideas remain pure, or else they would become unworthy of returning to their true, heavenly, state of being. The practical effect of corruption of human beings was that one's soul would have to be purified by the fires of hell, if it did not keep itself free from the desires of the flesh. At death—the separation of soul from body—a pure soul would return to heaven, a corrupt soul be sent to hell.

Plato's dualistic explanation was rough hewn, lacking in explanatory elegance, when compared to the more cogent picture of reality his student, Aristotle, provided. Aristotle argued that there was a natural unity between the intelligible and the material. Idea and matter were aspects of a harmonious Being. The beauty of a thing's defining Idea motivated it to fulfill its nature. Only insofar as something actualized its highest potential did it realize its highest reality. Unfulfilled, an idea remained latent in a thing, its potentiality awaiting actualization. It would change—become what it was—by striving to actualize its Idea.

Plato and Aristotle gave the idea of divinity added force through the assumption that change required ultimate Ideas. Early Christian thinkers capitulated to the philosophical impulse, to make the divine central to being. Thus the ideas of Plato and Aristotle became the foundation for the proofs for God's existence and the Christian worship of divine things. A study of the persuasive detail of their thinking shows why.

# Plato

The *Timaeus* was influential in the development of Christian theology. Here was presented a well-developed argument that distinguished between two orders of being: form and matter. Plato stated that an Idea, form, was "that which always is and has no becoming" and matter was "that which is always becoming and never is." The distinction between change and perfection being given, Plato notes that

> That which is by intelligence and reason is always in the same state, but that which is conceived by opinion with the help of sensation and without reason is always in the process of becoming and perishing and never really is. Now everything that becomes or is created must of necessity be created by some cause, for without a cause nothing can be created.[4]

Context now established, Plato asks about creation:

> was the world ... always in existence and without beginning or created, and had a beginning? ... Which of the patterns had the artificer in view when he made it...?[5]

His concern focused on the "stuff" of existence. The cosmic elements of form and matter always existed. They were the pre-existent agent and substance of all existence. But a motive force was needed to bring them together, an "artificer," a necessary but secondary fixture in the explanation to bring existence about. He created to make existence accord with

> the eternal, for the world is the fairest of creations, and he [the artificer] is the best of causes. And having been created in this way, the world has been framed in the likeness of that which is apprehended by reason and mind and is unchangeable, and therefore of necessity ... be a copy of something.[6]

The motive of the artificer for combining form (the perfect and changeless) with matter (the unthinkable, because in its changeableness it could not remain "quiet" or fixed and hence be thinkable) was that of introducing as much order as it permitted into the chaotic aspect of reality:

> God desired that all things should be good and nothing bad, so far as this was attainable. Wherefore also finding the whole visible sphere not at rest, but moving in an irregular and disorderly fashion, out of disorder he brought order, considering that this was in every way better than the other. Now the deeds of the best could never be or have been other than

> the fairest, and the creator, reflecting on the things which are by nature
> visible, found that no unintelligent creature taken as a whole could ever
> be fairer than the intelligent taken as a whole, and again that intelligence
> could not be present in anything which was devoid of soul [Form]. For
> which reason, when he was framing the universe, he put intelligence in
> soul, and soul in body, that he might be the creator of a work which was
> by nature fairest and best.[7]

The terms of creation were "intelligence/soul" and "visible/body,"
brought together by an artificer. The artificer, however, was not the
source of being. He merely put together what was found to be "fairest
and best" as this was displayed in "intelligence/soul," the ultimate
motive for motion. The artificer imposed eternal rationality—intelli-
gence/soul (Ideas)—on an otherwise unwilling and chaotic material
order of being (visible body). Design and order (intelligibility) were
forced into the chaos of matter, and thus became the condition for its
knowable existence. The presence of Idea moved matter to conform to
what was perfect; yet as matter, its urge was to fall back to its unintelligible nature. The unnatural merging of the visible and the intelligible
explained motion. These two opposing parts of a thing desired to return
to their native states—the visible to material existence, the Ideal to
heavenly existence. In desire, motion occurred.

Plato's cosmology offered a framework for positing divine reality.
The intelligible, present in a thing because of a divine act, transcended
the changeableness of the temporal world, yet permitted the thing to
exist. Essentially, intelligibility (unlike visible things) remained closed
within its own essential being—outside motion, change, and being
caused. In itself, it was complete, and thus had nothing outside itself
to strive for. The idea of "completeness" was important. It augured the
idea of divine perfection. Completeness was analogous to the completeness of a logical or mathematical system. In such systems the rules
or axioms which governed the system were precise—any additional
rules or axioms would be superfluous, and any fewer would render the
system incomplete and ineffectual. Rational completeness possessed a
kind of aesthetic elegance. Plato understood absolute being as complete,
self-sufficient, effective, lying outside time and motion. It was the
ultimate, infinite cause of existence. Such vision portended what would
become the early Christian and medieval notion of God.[8]

Platonic causes, Ideas, were the stuff of rational completeness which
existed independently of one's capacity to discover them in observation.
The contrast between modern thinking (exemplified, for example, by

the eighteenth-century David Hume) and Plato found the former locating cause within temporality and the latter locating cause outside temporality. Plato's rationalistic urge for completeness relegated ultimate cause to that which was not itself caused—ideas standing outside of time, having no beginning or end. Perfect and eternal being, the divine, was the cause of all that is.

The perfection of any created thing was an approximation of the Ideal it imitated. Thus the entire order of being was of divine proportion. This innate goodness of being, this rational harmony, was the source of creation's natural intrinsic divinity. As fixed in metaphysical urges, one saw the divine everywhere. This rhetoric had its religious effect: meaningfulness was guaranteed in the metaphysical ordering of Being. The difficulty, of course, was that the theory was itself disputable.

Plato's explanation of motion suffered the metaphysical awkwardness of dualism. Two ultimate realities were proposed: the (1) Ideal was required for the configuration of (2) material existence. To bring the two together, a divinity, a creator, was required. The mistaken belief that the Hebrew and Platonic notions of God were compatible gained its force at the point of God's creative activity. However, the total sovereignty of the Jewish God contained in the idea that he created out of nothing is to be contrasted with the Platonic god who was an "artificer" who put together stuff already on hand. It was the Ideal aspect of this stuff which was fully divine. Another contrast is at the point of creation. The Hebrew God created it "good." The artificer forced together opposing things, each type to remain unreconciled to the other. The ramifications of these contrasts show up at points where self-understanding is at stake. For instance, nothing could become an occasion for possessing an immortal soul in Hebrew thinking. There was no need to escape this world. One believed God would be faithful to His promises (eventually) to establish heaven on earth as His culminating act for His people.

## Aristotle

Aristotle preserved Plato's metaphysical urge for completeness and finality; but unlike Plato, Aristotle developed a unified picture of reality. He proposed that the two apparent aspects of Being—form and matter—were really aspects of the same reality. Although his theory of reality was more elaborate, it was also more elegant and metaphysically simple. Aristotle argued that nothing in experience suggested that two distinct realms existed; moreover, the postulation of these realms as existing did not help us understand reality.[9] Without rejecting the elements which comprised the Platonic dualism, Aristotle envisioned an order of being integrated by unified, rational design. Though form and matter were distinguishable in analysis, in fact they were interdependent.

Particular things strove to actualize their potential, their ultimate reality. Their motion was explained by their striving. The growth of an acorn illustrates Aristotle's theory of reality. The acorn, integrated as a combination of form and matter, exists only as the potential to become what it truly is, an oak tree. The ideal oak tree in the acorn becomes an actual oak tree in reality as the material of the acorn strives to become actual through its Idea. The form of 'oak tree' is a defining rational presence for the acorn, and the fullest rationality of the acorn is in its becoming an oak tree. It becomes what it actually is; it achieves its true nature or perfection.

What "oaktreeness" was to the acorn, rational perfection was to the whole of being. The tree could not exist without a defining rationality, the "oaktreeness" present in the acorn. Matter actualized its potential in fulfilling its idea. Concurrently, "oaktreeness" was nothing without the being of the matter of the acorn. Rationality required a vehicle for its expression. Form and matter (plus proper nutrition and climate) caused acorns to become oak trees. This model applied to all change. Rocks fell to achieve that perfect state of rest natural to them, and minds became educated to satisfy the rational life. Each thing strove for that state of being which was natural or appropriate to it. Once reached, it was at rest or peace with itself. It had become what its formal essence, its nature, demanded.

What was true of particular things was true of existence. Imagine a primordial scene of undifferentiated matter. Intrinsic to this material stuff was the rationality of form. Anything that could ever exist has from the start been within the capabilities of that matter to become. Latent in a state of pure potentiality and intrinsic to the stuff of existence, form existed within matter. The rationality of "stuff" beckoned forth its presence, evolving eventually into the self-conscious rationality by which we know ourselves. The potentialities in the material order were fulfilled; new possibilities materialized. A sense of progress toward the fullest possible actualization of being emerged.

Existence could not be without the presence of a rational perfection by which being was motivated to became what it was; an ultimate reality attracted being to fulfill itself in existence.

For Aristotle, nothing material could be motivated to actualize its existence were there not something which possessed ultimate completeness, rational perfection. In other words, the existence of an absolute perfection, something changeless and complete, was a necessary condition for the being of anything whatever. Whether this presence be called "God" or the "absolute final cause" or as with Aristotle, the "prime mover," its presence was the condition of all existence. Perfect rationality was necessary to being. This ultimate cause of change is identified in Book XII of Aristotle's *Metaphysics*.

> ...there is something which moves without being moved, being eternal, substance, and actuality. And the object of desire and the object of thought move in this way; they move without being moved.[10]

> For the final cause is (a) some being for whose good an action is done, and (b) something at which the action aims; and of these the latter exists among unchangeable entities though the former does not.

> Now if something is moved it is capable of being otherwise than as it is. Therefore if its actuality is the primary form of spatial motion, then in so far as it is subject to change, in *this* respect it is capable of being otherwise—in place, even if not in substance. But since there is something which moves while itself unmoved, existing actually, this can in no way be otherwise than as it is.... The first mover, then, exists of necessity; and in so far as it exists by necessity, its mode of being is good, and it is in this sense a first principle.[11]

Rationality itself had nothing further to strive to become; it was already complete. Were this not so, it would not be fully rational. It was precisely this completeness which caused all of existence to rouse itself to achieve the particularities of its being. In such striving, change and motion were explained.

> The first principle or primary being is not movable either in itself or accidentally, but produces the primary eternal and single movement. But since that which is moved must be moved by something, and the first mover must be in itself unmovable, and eternal movement must be produced by something eternal and a single movement by a single thing, and since we see that besides the simple spatial movement of the universe, which we say the first and unmovable substance produces, there are other spatial movements—those of the planets—which are eternal...,

each of *these* movements also must be caused by a substance both unmovable in itself and eternal.[12]

So far as an explanation of motion was concerned, there must be a changeless perfection to which all existing things were drawn and by which they actualized their potentiality. Attracted by perfection, things moved, aiming at rest or completion. When speaking of the nature of this perfection, Aristotle said

> ...there is a substance which is eternal and unmovable and separate from sensible things. It has been shown also that this substance cannot have any magnitude, but is without parts and indivisible (for it produces movement through infinite time, but nothing finite has infinite power; and, while every magnitude is either infinite or finite, it cannot, for the above reason, have finite magnitude, and it cannot have infinite magnitude because there is no infinite magnitude at all). But it has also been shown that it is impassive and unalterable....[13]

The Aristotelian solution to 'why things move' was adapted to religious theorizing, especially as this pertains to a conception of God. Though the Aristotelian Prime Mover and the Christian God were scarcely relatable (recall: the perfection of the Prime Mover meant that it could not direct attention outside itself; it could not love), the attributes of perfection seemed philosophically desirable to ascribe to God. God, too, was a perfect being, changeless, divine, on whom all existence depended and whose existence was necessary. It was natural, then, that the metaphysical foundations laid by Plato and Aristotle, the notion of striving to reach perfection, achieving one's highest potential, "becoming at one with God," were adopted into Christian life for their explanatory power and presumptive objective truth. These expressions of philosophical theorizing which presumed divine perfection yielded a religious *eros* which became foundational for subsequent theological development in Christianity.

## Theological Implications of the Idea of Perfection

Plato and Aristotle developed philosophical ideas which became promoted in Christianity centuries later. They provided an explanation of reality and an attractive account of human existence based in a value system. The religious meaning of human existence was defined in terms of that special part of creation which is conscious of its own rationality.

By contemplation on the divine, persons participated in the life of holiness. The soul which strove to fulfill its own highest nature cultivated perfection's divinity. Ultimate human happiness lay in making life harmonize with rational perfection. A picture emerged in which reason was the necessary condition for the existence of both the temporal and spiritual orders of being.

Theological edifices were built on these foundations. Because divine perfection, the fully actual, was necessary for existence, St. Anselm can introduce his ontological proof for God's existence by quoting scripture: "Only the fool says in his heart, 'There is no God'" (Ps. 14:1). Christianity came to depend on metaphysical speculation.[14] What many regard as relevant issues for religion: does God exist? what is the nature of God? what does God require of people—what is the nature of human responsibility and the quality of human life? could be answered through a concept of the divine, revealed in the ideal and changeless condition of being itself. The speculative fascination with ultimate reality organized thought about the divine. Theology used the metaphysical notion of perfection to develop its ideas of God into what has become a familiar "catalog" of divine attributes.[15] Here are several.

(1) God is omnipotent.[16] The notion that God is all powerful found superficial reinforcement in the religious traditions spawned in the Judeo-Christian tradition. The Hebrew God acted as he willed, out of absolute power. But in the Judeo-Christian concept of God, there need be no rational account of why He might act as He did. God's purposes remained his own.

The metaphysical God of Hellenistic philosophy was much more palpable. In the rational order of being, divine Idea was that by which existing things received their being. Rational necessity pervaded existence, including the Ideas themselves. The essential nature of this rational substance could be called "God." As the condition for the being of any existing thing, God was all powerful. Rational perfection was the occasion of God's power, and all existence was bound to the demand of an eternal rationality as the *sine qua non* for its being. Nothing could be without God.

The apparently paradoxical challenge to divine omnipotence, "Could God make a rock so large he could not lift it?" was actually like asking "Can something be red and green all over?" It was a nonsense question, incompatible with rational thought. Lifting was a physical action, itself dependent on those rational laws which give intelligibility to a universe; thus, God was the condition for the possibility of lifting but not something which itself lifts. "Making," likewise, was misunderstood as a possibly divine act of a physical sort. Rather, were it not for rational principles in terms of which rocks become rocks, they could not be. God's power, then, was reflected in the universe's conforming itself to the divine "plan."

(2) God is omniscient. To call God all-knowing was not to say that God was smart, has an infallible memory, could not make mistakes, and so on. Such attributes, while appropriate to human beings, were irrelevant to God's omniscience. Rather, as perfectly rational, divinity must be complete. There are no gaps in God—he was "omniscient."

(3) God is infinite.[17] Infinity was inherent to an Idea. To seek God's beginning or end would make as much sense as asking *when* $1+1=2$ *became* true, or *when* it could *cease* making two. Ideas have no beginning and no end. Another way people have looked at the timelessness of Ideas is found in *our* view of discovery. We view ideas as things to be discovered. Thus, when Robert Boyle (1627-1691) developed the gas law relating pressure, volume, and temperature, it was evident that the law prevailed in spite of his discovery of it. Though the circumstances of the seventeenth century permitted the enunciation of the law, time was not a factor in its truth. Truth has no beginning and end; it is infinite. As in Plato where an Idea had no specific form but was the essence of all specific manifestations of that Idea, so God became the overall unity of the Ideas necessary for existence in its perfect wholeness. Pure rational cogency, the condition for existence, was itself not bounded by the particulars of this existence. Infinite rational substance and its transcendence over time was equated to God.

(4) God is changeless. If the perfection of God was the condition of all that exists, then to add anything to God would be redundant or superfluous. To take anything away would make God incomplete and thus imperfect—something less than God. Thus, the necessary completeness of perfect rationality meant that God cannot be changed or change and still be God.

(5) God is a unity. According to Aristotelian metaphysics, things that must strive to fulfill their natures changed as potentialities became actualities. Multiplicity was implied in the idea of change. Were potentiality applicable to God, there would be something God was not and a higher perfection to which he must strive. God would be incomplete and as such, less than perfect; and were this the case, it could not

be God. Thus, the perfection of God required his completeness, oneness, or unity.

(6) God loves. This last concept is not entailed by divine perfection. It is mentioned only because New Testament writings attribute love to God. The idea of a loving God is otherwise inappropriate to the God of philosophical perfection. Here is why.

If God is changeless, he cannot direct attention to anything other than himself; to love, that is, to strive after that which would complete or fulfill one's own being, would suggest that God was lacking in something. Put in another way, were God to have something other than himself to which he directed attention, then God's own perfection would be compromised. Things move to fulfill themselves. For God to attend to something other than himself suggests that there is something lacking in the divine nature. But if God is perfect, he lacks nothing; therefore, there is nothing (but himself) which he could love. Of the Prime Mover, Aristotle says that it is "thought thinking on itself."[2]

As perfect, God loves only himself. How, then, could God be said to love mankind? Philosophically influenced church theology rescued this claim of Christian dogma by allowing him to love in the following two ways. First, divine creation made the world "the best of all possible worlds," a world designed to accommodate human happiness (despite any appearances to the contrary).[18] As such, God's love could be spoken of without seeing God as having effected some sort of action, for God's self-love was a love which blessed all.

Second, the rational quality of human existence was itself something divine. God could care for his own nature in man. By loving the spark of the divine in each person, God loved himself.[19] Because it was an aspect of God's nature, persons cultivated their "spark of the divine," thereby authenticating their being.

In summary, God's attributes of perfection included his omnipotence and omniscience, infinity and changelessness, unity and completeness. Likewise, a notion of "love" as *eros* could be deduced from metaphysical perfection. Such perfection is assumed as well in the traditional proofs for God's existence.[20] Here are four such proofs.

## Perfection and Arguments for God's Existence

(1) St Anselm's (1033-1109) ontological argument began by asserting that God was a completely perfect being. A mark of perfection was that

it possessed the property of "existence"; for as he argued, that which does not exist or exists only in imagination has less perfection than that which exists in fact. If perfection required existence as part of its conceivability, as perfect, God must exist.

(2) The concept of rational perfection also appeared in cosmological proofs for God's existence. Since the cosmos—all material things—was contingent, it not only could be other than it was, it was conceivable that there could be nothing at all. Mere undifferentiated materiality was insufficient to initiate being, and the material order of being was incapable of providing for its own being. In other words, since matter which existed in a state of pure potentiality could not *necessarily* exist, it could not be the cause of itself. Thus, there must be something whose being was both completely sufficient and necessary which was the cause of dependent things. Only that which was rationally perfect could possess such being, and this was what was meant by God—at least so St. Thomas Aquinas argued.

(3) Another way of developing a cosmological argument is to note the perpetual dependence of things on antecedent conditions. Logically, the idea of things causing things has no beginning point. However, respecting material existence, there was irrationality in not being able to posit a start of *things*. To escape an infinity of antecedent causes, one must posit a first cause, itself uncaused—an independent, antecedent state. This sort of thing could not be in the material order of being because of the inherent nature of matter to be dependent. However, it was in the nature of an Idea to be uncaused, as ideas were timeless, having no beginning or end. The idea of perfection (God) became necessary for the being of the cosmos.

(4) Expressions of purpose, design, or adaptation in the natural order had to be deliberatively patterned in order to express the rationality inherent in design. The notion of perfection also fueled teleological arguments for God's existence. If nature exhibited purpose, there must be a "mind," God, which provided it. Otherwise, from inert matter one derived only chaos and non-being, the antithesis of perfection. Nature was possible only insofar as it exhibited design and purpose; and since nature does reflect such rationality, a supreme, divine intelligence must be posited as its cause.[21] Philosophical theology hypothesized God as the origin of design and purpose.

The philosophical requirements of metaphysical perfection became imposed on religious discourse. Competition in the arena of divinities found the Judeo-Christian monotheistic tradition well served by the elegance of metaphysical perfection and its necessity of the existence of one ultimate God. In the midst of a world populated by gods who served every purpose, the theological elegance of a supreme rationality inspired awe and wonder. Metaphysical teachings about the nature of reality and man's place and purpose in it reinforced a religious spirit. God became the source of religious emotion. In a prefatory remark to reading St. Anselm's proof for God's existence, John Hick says,

> To feel religiously is therefore to presume surpassing greatness in some object: so much characterizes the attitudes in which we bow and bend the knee, and enters into the ordinary meaning of the word 'religious.'

> [W]e are led on irresistibly to demand that our religious object should have an *unsurpassable* supremacy along all avenues, that it should tower *infinitely* above all other objects. And not only are we led to demand for it such merely quantitative superiority: we also ask that it shouldn't stand surrounded by a world of *alien* objects, which owe it no allegiance, or set limits to its influence. The proper object of religious reverence must in some manner be *all-comprehensive*: there mustn't be anything capable of existing, or of displaying any virtue, without owing all of these absolutely to this single source.[22]

"The one true God" who vied with other gods for power and the God who "should tower infinitely above all other objects," were tied together by the demands of metaphysical perfection. This philosophical God of reason, in love with eternity, indifferent to day-to-day concerns, became conceptually tied to the monotheism of the Judeo-Christian tradition.

## Perfection and Human Existence

*Morality and Human Responsibility*

Perfection pervaded all of being, from an underlying rational substance in which everything was true to its own nature to the rational nature of the whole in which individual pieces conspired toward their own being. There was nothing in existence which could be said to be without purpose. By a design intrinsic to rationality, meaning penetrated existence. When extended to human affairs, the results were obvious: respect for self, others, and nature was the only rationally viable posture for human beings. Since "man is a rational animal," one should harmonize one's own life with moral attributes befitting the good, the true, and the beautiful.

A distinction between good and evil was built into the concept of rationality. The divine focal point of human existence was the soul, the agency of divine rationality. Divinity was the objective source of ethical truth and the occasion for value in life. Divine perfection permeated the whole of being, imparting meaning and worth to it. One drew oneself into a unity with God, the source of value, through moral striving. Eternal values order life to a rational design.

What stood in the way were "the desires of the flesh." The soul, "the spark of the divine," struggled against "the flesh." Reject the "desires of the flesh." Purify life. Be magnanimous instead of licentious, charitable instead of envious, generous instead of greedy, benevolent instead of exploitative, kind instead of abusive—the Platonic formula for spiritual well being. Unlike the body which doted on the elements of chaos, the soul found fulfillment in striving for that which was like itself: good, true, and beautiful. Though the shroud of flesh tempted a person, the spark of divinity fanned into its godly fire saved one. The fulfillment of one's highest potential brought forth an authentic, rational human nature.

## The Quality of Human Life

Ancient Greek philosophy and its progeny laid claim to discerning the true nature of reality. First-and second-century Christianity eventually accommodated itself to ideas grounded especially in Platonic thinking. It was almost impossible for it to have done otherwise. To have retained a Jewish hermeneutic in a Hellenistic world would have defied outlooks which (for them) comprised common sense. Soul and body, the divine and the world, harmony and diversity—these became the context of being's possibilities, not a simple Jewish materialism invested with the despotic but benevolent rule of an Oriental potentate. To be viable at all, Christian thinkers would have to be cognizant of Platonism—the "science" of the ancient world. In Plato, a person strove for perfection by blending the ideal into the soul. One became fitted for heaven. Aristotle likewise saw human happiness achieved when persons fulfilled their rational essences.

The religious models of the ancient world were driven by Platonic thinking in which a theory of ultimate reality imputed religious meaning to life. Salvation was the state of being in which persons became united with the divine.[23] Caught between chaotic, insatiable desire and a satisfying unity with the changeless realm of the rational life, the holy longings of the soul were fulfilled by striving for a unity with divine perfection. In this regard, St. Augustine's Platonic heritage shows itself in an opening remark to *The Confessions*. "For Thou hast made us for Thyself and our hearts are restless till they rest in Thee."[24]

Equally, the Aristotelian state of rest, enunciated in a religious charge to achieve "oneness with God," allowed one to "find peace within oneself." The true state of human happiness—salvation—was achieved by actualizing one's potential and thus being in harmony with the divine. Lesser states of transitory happiness served by material, fleshy desires competed for human commitment. However, given a person's spiritual essence, to succumb to a lesser desire could not match the satisfaction and rest achieved in the purity of divine contemplation.[25]

In the early centuries of Christian history, Christian gnostics "discovered" hidden meanings, the secrets of Being, in the words of Jesus. Salvation was to be found either in yearning for purity in life by making it conform to the divine light or participating in worldly affairs and matters of "flesh" in a spirit of indifference borne of one possessed by life's secrets. Persons in harmony with God would be saved from their carnal nature and realize the perfection of their highest selves. The human spirit (soul) can approach divinity precisely because it was modeled after the rationality of God.[26] People made their lives conform to that ultimate truth which Christianity, too, wanted to reflect.

The writer of the Gospel of John assumed the language of gnosticism as his context when presenting the teachings and person of Jesus. He attempted to display the meaning of *agape* in a language that was fundamentally antithetical to it. The limits of the human intellect forbad one's knowledge of the divine mind. So, to make Jesus exemplify a divine and redemptive love, the author (unadvisedly) resorted to the machinery of gnosticism to make this revelation intelligible. Its themes of light and darkness, flesh and spirit, this world and the heavenly world became a part of church tradition. For instance, the writer has Jesus say: "I am the light of the world; he who follows me will not walk in darkness, but will have the light of life" (8:12). Jesus was accorded a superior position over others who claim knowledge of divine truth. Jesus' teachings became the correct way to truth: "I am the door; if any one enters by me, he will be saved, and will go in and out and find pasture" (Jn. 10:9). Persuaded that metaphysical truth determined the force of an idea, this early Christian writer permanently

enshrined gnostic language in the Christian church. At least superficially, this gospel fell into the concerns of gnostic thinking so that it would
conform to its theory of reality.

Insofar as Platonic realities can be made to dominate religion, their
rationality lent authority to the religious insistence that "divine law"
was inescapable. Human happiness was contingent on one's faithfulness
to the truth; and though an apparent happiness might accompany
whatever was "less than divine," such happiness was ephemeral. Ignore
the divine commands, and one's self-indulgence returned its own
reward in sorrow. Though they came naturally, such lives portended
nothing of merit. Only life disciplined by divine law, God's teachings
revealed by the person of Jesus, as the writer of John has it, brought
human existence to a proper sense of fulfillment. By this account, the
religious life could be taught and learned. It required discipline and
work to reach the goal. As the source of man's eternal happiness, such
information was highly prized: "Jesus then said to the Jews who had
believed in him, 'If you continue in my word, you are truly my
disciples, and you will know the truth, and the truth will make you
free'" (Jn. 8:31-32).

Why, then, would one ignore the truth if one could know it? The
Gospel of John formulated the question this way:

> Jesus said to them, "If God were your Father, you would love me, for
> I proceeded and came forth from God; I came not of my own accord, but
> he sent me. Why do you not understand what I say? It is because you
> cannot bear to hear my word. You are of your father the devil, and your
> will is to do your father's desires. He was a murderer from the begin-
> ning, and has nothing to do with the truth, because there is no truth in
> him.... If I tell the truth, why do you not believe me?" (Jn. 8:41-45).

One devoted oneself to the divine "words of God." Lack of devotion
revealed a lack of character.

> He who is of God hears the words of God; the reason why you do not
> hear them is that you are not of God (Jn. 8:47).

But unlike Plato who averred that salvation went through the maieutic
of philosophy to a vision of truth and its enlightenment of the human
soul, the author of John appealed to divine revelation in a person: "As
long as I am in the world, I am the light of the world" (Jn. 9:5). He
commented elsewhere that "...whoever believes in him should not
perish but have eternal life" (Jn. 3:16). In both cases, truth, immedi-

ately grasped, opened life to its meaning, though they would disagree on what the "truth" entailed. Ambiguity on this point opened the door to Christian mysticism.

## The Otherworldly Life

Mysticism became an important branch of Christian tradition. Cloistered in the rationalistic thought of the ancient world, the mystic contemplated divinity in order to redeem an otherwise meaningless life. Lifted to divine heights through the inspiration of goodness, truth, and beauty, mystics strove to become at one with the universal truths of reason—God. In this way, Plato's and Aristotle's influence on the development of Christianity was reducible to the belief that genuine human life was produced by divine value. The "infinite worth of the human soul" or the "spark of the divine in each person," "eternal values," are samples of rationalistic ideas which came to have a religious force in Christendom. Thus, mystical striving to live up to the highest one knows found one attracted to the divine ideal.[27]

# Conclusion

Plato and Aristotle produced a conceptual (metaphysical) answer to the question: "Why do things change?" An ultimate, changeless state of being, pure in its harmony, perfect in its completeness, answered the question of change. Reason, the source of being, was reified into "God." Embedded in a fabric of Platonic rationalism, Christian ideas, including the idea of "love" as striving toward the beauty of perfection, were given credibility. A picture of religion unfolded, transformed to accord with the idea of reason, the proper beginning point in the ancient world for proper human understanding and activity.[28] Philosophy provided the metaphysical framework for all understanding. Any unique sense of "religion" was dispersed by the demands of universal reason. Although it was a confused religion which imagined that speculations about the nature and origin of things were relevant to its task, nevertheless this spirit prevailed in the next major portion of intellectual history. Philosophy exists through criticism and revision; it refigures itself. The events of the last four centuries on the intellectual front evoked a substantial revision in ancient philosophical outlooks and correspondingly in the sense of "religion." What early and medieval church thinkers took seriously by way of understanding reality would have to be abandoned, if religion and the new visions of reality were to remain compatible. The next case we look at sees philosophical notions of experience becoming the condition for knowledge—and the occasion for revising religious thinking. We turn to this development.

## Notes

1. See Rudolph Bultmann's *Primitive Christianity in Its Contemporary Setting*, tr. R. H. Fuller (New York: Meridian Books, 1956).

2. Regarding a motivation for developing the idea of divinity, we see one revealed in Aristotle's opening remark to Book Alpha of the *Metaphysics*: "All men by nature desire to know" (*The Basic Works of Aristotle* [ed., R. McKeon, New York: Random House, 1941], p. 689). Here the issue is that of discovery—uncover the objective truth and one will know what life requires. I suggest in Chapter VI that the religious life does not begin with philosophical concern for knowledge, but with the incapacity of knowledge to provide for life's meaning.

3. In spite of David Hume, the temptation remains to think of the laws of nature as immaterial, invisible commands which make matter conform to their requirements. See n. 8.

4. *The Collected Dialogues of Plato*, eds. Edith Hamilton and Huntington Cairns (New Jersey: Princeton University Press, 1961), p. 1161 (27f.).

5. *Ib.*, p. 1162, (28).

6. *Ib.*, (29).

7. *Ib.*, p. 1162f., (30).

8. For us to appreciate what will unfold, we must shift our thinking about the nature of causality away from its delineation by David Hume (1711-1776). He saw cause as the actions between events which were temporally prior but persistently juxtaposed to each other. In his presentation of the idea of cause, the question of the necessary conditions for the existence of things does not arise. Necessary causation is beyond one's observational capacities, for one is limited in observation only to what one sees; and one could not observe the necessity of a necessary cause. Thus, Hume closed the door on the traditional rational proofs of a divine existence. Causal matters pertained purely to the pragmatics of experience, not the plausibility of God.

9. The relevant passages in Aristotle are found in the *Metaphysics*, Book I, especially Ch. 9 (990b-993a), and in Book XII. Frederick Copleston, in *A History of Philosophy* (Vol. I, "Greece and Rome," [Westminster, MD., The Newman Press, 1950, orig., 1946], pp. 292-310), points out that Aristotle argues that the Platonic theory of subsistent forms is useless for our understanding of things, impossible logically, and insufficient to our understanding

of mathematics. In appraising Aristotle's arguments, Copleston says that

> it would appear that there is an ultimate substratum which has no definite characteristics of its own, but is simply potentiality as such, [something] which is found in all material things and is the ultimate basis of change (*ib.*, p. 307).

This means that prime matter never exists precisely as such—as bare prime matter, we might say—but always exists in conjunction with form, which is the formal or characterizing factor. In the sense that prime matter cannot exist by itself, apart from all form, it is only logically distinguishable from form; but in the sense that it is a real element in the material object, and the ultimate basis of the real changes that it undergoes, it is really distinguishable from form (*ib.*).

Applying this general position to the case of human existence, Aristotle defines persons as rational animals, whose proper life lies in approximating rationality. For Aristotle, this meant a life which required analytical reflection on each act in order to measure its rational appropriateness for the good life, the temperate life.

In church theology, the idea of rationality allowed for beings freed from material bonds. The approximation of ideal rationality in an evolutionary sequence points to souls as well as "angels, archangels, and all the company of heaven." These in their purity approached the throne of divine being itself.

When translated into the modern era, the philosopher Immanuel Kant argued that immortality was required if persons were to make sense of moral perfection. If absolute perfection was the goal of morality, and temporal desire waylaid even our best intentions, the moral individual must envision the soul's immortality as the condition for the possibility of becoming perfect.

10. *Metaphysics, op. cit.,* Bk. XII, Cha. 7, ln. 24ff., p. 879.

11. *Ib.*, p. 879f.

12. *Ib.*, Ch. 8, p. 881f.

13. *Ib.*, Ch. 7, p. 881.

14. So far as early Christianity was concerned, it made its way in an intellectual climate dominated by the philosophical ideas which harked back to Plato and Aristotle. By the second century, the early church was in the grip of philosophical ideas—especially those generated in gnosticism. The Apostles' Creed, for instance, is an attempt to separate Christian belief from the philosophical commitments of gnosticism especially through the concepts of creation and incarnation. God and Jesus Christ were interpreted in gnosticism in terms of matter/spirit distinctions. Marcion (c. 85-159), for instance, denied the appropriateness of such a distinction for Christian faith and understanding. Suffice it to say, St. Augustine (354-430) and St. Thomas Aquinas (1224-1274) fell victim in a most forceful manner, respectively, to the ideas of Plato and Aristotle, and the theologies of each reflected the theories of reality demanded

by their philosophical legacies.

The language of philosophy overwhelmed theological thinking, and seldom was Christianity able to distance itself from philosophy. It became difficult to articulate a religious sense of life. Sputtering attempts to move away from philosophical concerns and language occurred in the Reformation. Even so, philosophical concerns quickly returned to become substitutes for religious ones.

15. Philosophical theories of reality shaped theological thinking rather than anything distinctively religious and, I claim, has become destructive of anything religious.

16. The point of the discussions that follow is not to enter into them, but to illustrate how philosophical ideas were pursued. For instance, our thought that things have other things as their cause leads us to wonder whether God could create something from nothing, an apparent demand of the creation account in Genesis. The Biblical notion of God's purported creation out of nothing is perplexing. "Nothing" can be only the "cause" of nothing, so creating something out of nothing strains our causal sensitivities. The Greek tradition was not plagued with this question, for as Plato construes the nature of reality, both the Idea realm and the material realm are eternal, without beginning and end, so there is no need to discern their cause. They are eternal substances (although uncaused material substance is not without problems).

I would argue that scripture is not interested in astronomy but in the logic of God's sovereignty. I hold that Genesis 1 is mistakenly seen as a creation story; it rather is a religious story whose existential bearing places human existence in absolute dependence as this is juxtaposed with the absolute sovereignty of God. Hence it is a confusion to equate the mechanistic notion of God's creative power with the religious idea of his sovereignty. The focus of the first is on what nature means; the second is on what being God means.

17. An issue might be raised as to whether God's infinity is the same as his eternality. The eternal god need not be aloof from temporality; the eternal God simply never ends. This God could become involved in temporal affairs and is not tightly merged with rationality's perfection. The idea of an infinite God gains its force by transcending time. The difference between "infinite" and "eternal" is one of metaphysical proportions, one of proximity to human existence.

18. Gottfried Wilhelm Leibniz (1646-1716) proposed the metaphysical idea of "the best of all possible worlds." The doctrine of emanation found in the writings of Plotinus (205-270) would suffice as another historical example of this position. Like the perfume in the bottle which emanates without the perfume being moved, so God's creation is the product of his own perfection. In the love of himself a loving existence is made possible.

19. Both Gnostics and Stoics adapt the Platonic notion of a divine soul to these ends. Early church theology makes use of the notion of the divine spark in every human breast.

20. Stories about the relationship of persons with the Biblical God did not begin with an investigation into the nature of divine being and, subsequently, mankind's involvement with it.

21. An easily accessible formulation of this argument is found in William Paley's (1743-1805) *Natural Theology* (Frederick Ferré, ed., [Indianapolis, 1964]) in which he rhetorically asks us to imagine the details of a watch in its intricate fabrication. No more than we could conceive of it not having a designer could we conceive of the overwhelmingly more complex universe as not having a designer.

22. John Hick, *The Existence of God* (New York: MacMillan Publishing Co., 1964), p. 24.

23. The heavy emphasis on the role of God in the explanation of reality lent credence to thinking that metaphysics and religion had something to do with one another. Quite often in contemporary times, attacks on metaphysics are taken simultaneously to be attacks on religion. Although both are seen as having a bearing on one's ultimate happiness, the claim of this book is that religion and metaphysics are in fact independent of one another.

24. *The Confessions of St. Augustine*, tr. F. J. Sheed (New York: Sheed & Ward, 1942), Book I, p. 3.

25. Though early Christianity was influenced by gnosticism, contemporary Christianity has not succeeded in escaping these gnostic snares. If one views Biblical remarks as revealing the secrets to an eventual divine life, such prized knowledge reflects the urges of gnosticism. If the point of religion is to provide the formula to salvation, direct persons in their quests, and promote a continuing search for "god" or "god's will" through divine enlightenment, those likewise were the goals of gnosticism.

Besides gnosticism, early church writers were influenced by Stoicism (e.g., St. Paul makes remarks which smack of Stoic ethics) and Neoplatonism (e.g., St. Augustine [354-430]).

Although Aristotle shared the motifs of Platonism (not the detail), his direct influences on western religious thinking had to await his utilization in the thirteenth century. St. Thomas Aquinas develops a Christian theology predicated on Aristotle's metaphysical views.

26. At this point one might quote the scriptural verse: "So God created man in his own image, in the image of God he created him; male and female he created them" (Gen. 1:27). When looked at through the eyes of Platonic forms, man's rationality is the image of God. However, insofar as this same writer goes on to distance God from man, it is more likely that what transpired in the mind of the Biblical writer was no more than an earthy comment on why we look the way we do—and not the metaphysical one of being divine 'chips off

the old block.'

27. Immanuel Kant is closely aligned with the notion that one's true nature requires that we respect other people. For him, all rational being possessed intrinsic worth, because a rational nature alone "sets itself an end." In a moral universe such a capacity points to the "dignity of human nature," "above all price." (See *Grounding for the Metaphysics of Morals*, section 434-436.) Though for Kant value was not structured into being by a divine mind, the reality of man subject "to his own, yet universal, legislation" imparted a dignity to man which required all being treated "as an end." Kant humanized the ancient tradition which demanded Absolute Reality as a justification for value.

28. The Bible or Koran, the Upanishads or sayings of special persons such as Confucius, likewise could be made to illustrate the contention that religious understanding commonly thinks in terms of a special, divine knowledge, thought to be creative of life. But this may not be enough.

Devotion to religious truth is vulgarized in notions of being rewarded for belief. The hypothetical stance, 'If one does this (e.g., confess Jesus as Lord and Savior), beneficial results follow (e.g., one gains entry into heaven)' reflects the rational expectations of existence in a causal order.

The issue is whether characteristics taken to mark religious life aren't in fact marks of a philosophical life. Later I argue that religious language is disinterested in anything philosophical. Nevertheless, as we begin to think about religion, our philosophical assumptions prejudice us to think in terms of a theory or reality or knowledge that opens life to the logical requirements embedded in their conceptual machinery.

# Chapter III

# Religious Experience

Plato regarded sense impressions as an inferior foundation on which to establish knowledge. It's not that the senses were irrelevant for knowledge of a world external to consciousness; they simply could not give us knowledge to which the idea of 'truth' was applicable. Since experiences were changeable, how could one choose between experiences to fix the truth of an idea? Even Aristotle, who spoke of the delight we have in our senses to produce knowledge, believed with Plato that knowledge finally required an underlying rational structure, inherent in being. Reason was the cause of being, and sense experience was a supplement to our knowledge of the absolute truth of this perfection. Rational perfection remained the condition for anything's cogency. True knowledge needed something fixed, stable, rational, a standard, an Ideal, to judge any particular experience. Subsequent thinkers substantially agreed with Plato's and Aristotle's arguments: sense experience gave us the illusion of knowledge in the form of opinion. Access to divine *truth* required reason.

Ancient Greek philosophy held the religious thinking of the West substantially in its grip until the seventeenth century. Religious thinkers in Christendom delighted in the wisdom of those philosophical claims which presumed surely that the existence of God was demanded by (what for them was) 'scientific' thinking. The innocence of two thousand years of philosophical inquiry into the natural order was jolted to its foundations in the 1600s. Views on reality, and correlatively, religion, were to change.

It was not that philosophy wasn't ready for these changes. Always lying close at hand were views which posited that nature could reveal itself through sense experience. It came into its own, however, in the writings of people like Francis Bacon (1561-1626), Galilei Galileo (1564-1642), John Locke (1632-1704), or Isaac Newton (1642-1727). This is not to say that older rationalistic notions disappeared; they continued—and do so to this moment. But they were transformed. Those sensitive to the power of the new thinking found it necessary to revise their understanding of reason. Instead of its representing the mind of the divine, it reflected the mind of man—but this is a story for the next chapter. The power of *experience* to yield knowledge received a serious hearing in the seventeenth century. This change was not simply due to a casual change of heart about the sources of knowledge. The new science burst the bonds of ancient thought. To remedy its shortcomings, philosophy rethought its traditions and changed—and if philosophy, could religion be far behind?

"Experience" was of the material world; and by the time David Hume (1711-1776) refined the idea of empiricism, the sphere of divine rationality was relegated to pure speculation, to be placed beyond knowledge at the nether end of the spectrum of curiosity. The idea that 'all knowledge comes from experience alone'[1] had overcome the long-standing rationalistic prejudice of both philosophy and theology. We focus on the advent of the new science in the seventeenth century and the emerging empiricism, as these portended the coming revolution in thinking and (more especially) religious understanding.

Among the various threads which became woven together as science, we begin with the same question which we saw posed in ancient philosophy: why do things move? In ancient philosophy, one would study the "science" of being, metaphysics, to answer this question. Plato and Aristotle penetrated the mystery of motion by appealing to perfect rest to explain motion. They settled the matter on the basis of how reality *ought* to work, were it to accord with their rationalistic metaphysics. Motion was explained by divine necessity. The religious mind agreed: no source of knowledge that appealed to experience could show the necessity of divine being.

It was not until the new science with its revisionary account of motion that metaphysical explanations of being were made irrelevant. It is no wonder, then, that religious thinking became divided, some to stay with ancient tradition, others to fall into step with modern times.

The former rested secure in a certain knowledge of divine reality. The latter knew that with the new thinking, perfection could no longer be viewed as the natural cause of the order of being; divine necessity could no longer be sustained; and reason could no longer be the source of human confidence for knowledge of God. Modern religious thinkers joined their thinking to the new measure of authentic knowledge: "experience." Experience would justify religious life. We begin with the work of Galileo Galilei and Isaac Newton to show why divine perfection could no longer suffice for understanding motion. We then examine what the idea 'experience yields knowledge' means for religion and, more especially, Christianity.

## From Reason to Experience

In a rational universe, why did things change? Plato's metaphysical explanation spoke of the unnatural connection between form and matter, each moving to return to its own true nature. Aristotle showed that the diversity of motions were unexplained by this simple account. He proposed a more reasonable explanation, characterizing motion in terms of objects' moving to achieve their natural perfections—things strove to actualize their true natures and thus moved. Since all of finite being was in motion, an ultimate, infinite perfection was required to evoke the existence of everything. Things structured themselves to accord with the requirements of this necessary perfection.

In both Plato and Aristotle ultimate perfection transcended mere existence. *Things* exist; perfect *being*, the divine, transcends existence and truly *is*. It was no wonder, then, that the power of perfection became transformed into the image of God in Christian tradition. As perfection, a fully actual God (of the proofs for God's existence) was ultimately necessary to explain motion in the temporal world.

The thinking of Galileo and Newton worked against this metaphysical tradition of philosophy. Instead of that which was perfect (at rest) explaining that which moves, motion was natural to the universe, "a given," used to explain all phenomena. In his *Dialogues Concerning Two New Sciences*, Galileo argued that if the Aristotelian idea were true that each thing possessed an essential nature which it strove to fulfill (thus putting it in motion), we should expect that a rock weighing twice that of another to fall at a greater rate of speed. Rocks had a natural desire to seek rest in the center of the earth (so it was said)—that's why they fell. Thus, a rock weighing twice another should have twice the desire to reach the center. This was so because there was twice the potential within the rock to draw it to its natural state of rest. Now, suppose the smaller rock were tied to the larger one. Would not the smaller one impede the larger one in its falling? Galileo conjectured that

> if a large stone moves with a speed of, say, eight, while a smaller moves with a speed of four, then when they are united, the system will move at a speed less than eight; but the two stones when tied together make a stone larger than that which before moved with a speed of eight. Hence the heavier body moves with less speed than the lighter; an effect which is contrary to your supposition.[2]

With this bit of ingenious reasoning a new idea emerged: motion was *not* the expression of something's state of alienation from its true nature. The motion of objects reflected considerations which were quite independent of the rationalistic idea that things possessed ideal natures that they strove to fulfill. The doctrine of actuality/potentiality was irrelevant to understanding motion. Galileo's achievement initiated a reversal of ancient metaphysical thought and our understanding of nature.

Sir Isaac Newton made explicit what Galileo began. His laws of motion stated:

I.  Every body continues in its state of rest, or of uniform motion in a right [straight] line, unless it is compelled to change that state by forces impressed upon it.

II.  The change of motion is proportional to the motive force impressed; and is made in the direction of the right line in which that force is impressed.

III.  To every action there is always opposed an equal reaction....[3]

These laws assumed that the natural state of matter was to be in motion. Even rest was understood as an aspect of motion, as is revealed in Law III. Thing X rested on Y. Y pushed up with a force equal to X's downward force. Nothing shifted position because there was a balance (a standoff) in the motion between the two objects. The universe naturally was in a state of motion, not rest, and the understanding of existence was to be shaped in terms of the laws of motion.

Historian of science, Herbert Butterfield, summarized some implications of this turn in thought about the nature of motion.

A universe constructed on the mechanics of Aristotle had the door half-way open for spirits already; it was a universe in which unseen hands had to be in constant operation, and sublime Intelligences had to roll the planetary spheres around. Alternatively, bodies had to be endowed with souls and aspirations, with a "disposition" to certain kinds of motions, so that matter itself seemed to possess mystical qualities. The modern law of inertia, the modern theory of motion, is the great factor which in the seventeenth century helped to drive the spirits out of the world and opened the way to a universe that ran like a piece of clockwork.[4]

Dismissing essences from nature made a metaphysical God unnecessary. Given matter in motion, our knowledge of nature required no more than discerning and describing its movements. Inquiry was direct, and explanation simply pointed to particular interactions—when this happens, that happens. No general cause such as divine rationality was required. Ultimate explanations were unnecessary.

## Reason versus Cause

Without ever intending to do so, Newton brought about a conflict between science and the religion which depended on ancient metaphysics. Instead of God becoming an ultimate explanation, matter was explained by its natural motion. Those with rationalistic religious inclinations were not assuaged. It seemed reasonable to ask whether there must be an ultimate beginning point beyond which there was no matter in motion, a first cause which both created the matter and set it in motion, a first cause which was God. The question of causes is natural to our curiosity.

Approached from the context of an older rationalism the prospect of an unending regression of causes invites a stopping point in a "first cause," something itself uncaused but which was the cause of all else. From a modern perspective we ask a nonsensical question if we ask about first causes. Cause is something empirical, immediate. The empirical thinker, then, explains what is meant by "cause" by pointing to antecedent conditions verifiable in an observation. "First cause" disappears as an issue, because one could never identify what counted as "first." To understand how the ideas of reason and cause became modified, we turn to the work of the eighteenth-century empiricist, David Hume.

Hume explained our idea of causation in the same way that he explained the origins of all ideas. Sensation generated meanings which became our ideas. Sense impressions gave rise to knowledge. Thus, sensation must be the source for our idea of cause as well. In this regard, successive events juxtaposed to one another in time created a sense impression of connection. When juxtaposed events could be similarly repeated in a new time framework, the idea of "cause" and "effect" identified the temporal relations between the ideas. An anticipation that when "A" happens, "B" will follow became that habit of mind we called "causal relationship." Accordingly stated Hume, "causes and effects are discoverable, not by reason but by experience."[5] The idea of "cause" arose in the context of matter in motion. Where events repeatedly appeared in constant relation to one another over time, cause became the report of this persistence. Since one could not know if the future would be like the past, it was conceivable that the causal order of being could change. Unlike the demand of rationalistic theories, causal relationships were not necessary, according to Hume. They were contingent.

Rationalism saw cause as something embedded in nature, with God as the likely first cause. Ultimate reason stood behind the phenomena of experience. Hume countered by showing that causal relationships could not be known to structure being. A necessary, internal structure could never be an object for observation. The rationalistic idea of an invisible, internal cause of things, the sort of cause generated by perfection, was a speculation beyond our ability experientially to know. Reason was the faculty of the mind devoted to identifying similarities and differences in our experience. In the process of creating knowledge, it related sensations, logically ordering them, abstracting from them, generalizing, and arranging the things that people know. It produced no knowledge by its own light except that of logical relationships. Honesty demanded that one live in those terms which the limits of our knowledge provided us. Thus, religion that would place its hope in a rationality claimed for the universe and echoed in the proofs for the existence of God became gibberish. Only a dishonest person who exaggerated what in fact could be known would suggest that there was knowledge of God. True to his inquiry into the limits of knowledge, Hume remained skeptical of theological and metaphysical speculation.

The two ideas before us, matter in motion and cause defined by experience, made the idea of God extraneous to the requirements of explanation. Matter in motion as an assumption about the nature of reality required no explanation as to its beginning or end—matter and motion were themselves conceived as eternal. First cause or uncaused cause became logically inconceivable inasmuch as the idea of "cause" was our response to the habitual way we experience events.

Nevertheless, the question of ultimate beginnings does not easily disappear. Suppose one could probe the distant past of the universe with as-yet-unknown exploratory tools, and witness stuff in one instant and nothing in the previous moment.[6] Even were this possible, we need not conclude that "God must have done it." Instead, physics would turn attention to how[7] something could appear to come out of nothing. If one "saw" something preceded by nothingness, the best one could say is that one didn't understand it. Although conclusions about the cause could be hypothesized, none could be legitimated without confirming observations—and how will "God" be observed? What could "God" even mean? A fundamental inconceivability then arises at the point of trying to specify what would count as a supernatural first cause, when cause is defined in naturalistic terms by juxtaposition and repeatability. A godly first cause would be unrepeatable as well as unobservable. Moreover, in thinking in terms of "cause," nothing stops one from asking what preceded the godly cause. In the natural world, one cannot leap from natural events to the juxtaposition of a natural event with a supernatural one. God as the first cause is thus excluded from knowledge precisely because such a unique hypothetical event extends experience beyond all possible knowledge. It seems, then, that there is no empirical way in which the truth of "God created" could be meaningful, let alone true. Religion could not be a source of information about the universe or human existence. Empiricism prospered. The notion of absolute rational perfection no longer needed, its notion of divine being became superfluous.[8] Though religion may have served the humanization of life, morality alone sufficed for the post-religious world. As experience revealed the natural sense of the world, so it justified moral life by a utilitarian analysis of a good life.[9] One doesn't have to be religious to be moral.

However, religious ingenuity was not idle. New religious thinking would mend a fractured religion and make it intellectually respectable. Religion sustained its case by adjusting its thinking to the new philosophical requirements. Religion need not be legitimated by reason; it, too, could appeal to experience.

## Experience and Religion

Instead of grounding religion in speculation and the lofty perspective of absolute certainty sought by Plato and Aristotle, theological thinking moved toward the new atmosphere of empiricism where metaphysical arguments for God's existence were not required. Lifted by the philosophical winds of the seventeenth century, religion would be sought in experience. Experience demanded no metaphysical correlate. Divine reality would be revealed in *human* consciousness, in aesthetic and moral experience, in self-understanding,

The words "religious experience" sound natural enough.[10] Anxious to validate religion within the context of sensation, people with religious commitments looked to their inner states for signs of a special experiential something, a religious something. A philosophically viable religion would be based on experience—but what sort of experience? What sensations could justify religious matters? Empiricism's naturalistic tendencies allowed for psychological realities. Thus, to be compatible with the new philosophy, religion would have to look to the human psyche for religious experiences which would fuel theological imagination—awe and wonder at being, the inexplicable sense for beauty, the mystery of life, moral sensitivities. In feelings such as these, realities were brought forward which were thought to point beyond the immediacy of sensation to something greater and unknowable, something divine. Fascinated by feelings, people endowed them with "value." Empirical feelings of value built the road to divine reality and moral responsibility. F. R. Tennant developed this point in his *Philosophical Theology*.

> Aesthetic values are closely associated, and often are inextricably interwoven, with ethico-religious values. God reveals Himself, to such as have differentiated these valuations, in many ways; and some men enter His Temple by the Gate Beautiful. Values alone can provide guidance as to the world's meaning, structure being unable to suggest more than intelligent power. And beauty may well be *a* meaning. That is the element of sense contained in the romanticist's paradox, beauty is truth, or truth is beauty.... Theistically regarded, Nature's beauty is of a piece with the world's intelligibility and with its being a theatre for moral life; and thus far the case for theism is strengthened by aesthetic considerations.[11]

Within the world of inert matter in motion, we experience the sublime.

Whereas the material configuration of nature should be indifferent to value, we encounter its presence. Thus it was argued that value experiences were a form of divine revelation. Or more carefully, the God known by experience could be inferred from the presence of value in the world. However, if feelings of the sublime pointed to God as the cause of value, in any direct way God lay beyond description. God was not a sensation—no one could imagine what sort of sensation could count as God. Still, subject to certain kinds of emotions, we are to take them as pointing beyond themselves to an ineffable divinity to which we give the name, "religious experience."

In a 1948 radio debate with the renowned philosopher and religious critic, Bertrand Russell, the noted historian of philosophy, Father F. C. Copleston, enlisted Russell's empiricism against him to argue that "when you get an experience that results in an overflow of dynamic and creative love, the best explanation of that, it seems to me, is the actual existence of an objective cause of the experience."[12] From inner experience—experience asserted to be incapable of being explained solely on naturalistic grounds—we were to be led to God or religious life.

We shall explore two directions of religious thought enamored with the idea of experience: first, the blatant appeal to sense experience; second, a more sophisticated and theologically suggestive moral striving said to characterize religious experience.

## Religious Feelings and Emotions

For the empiricist, "experience" meant that sensations meaningfully inserted themselves into consciousness. The source of a sensation could be internal or external, either the physiological product of the stimulation of one of the five senses or an inner feeling (pleasure or pain, for instance). Sensations were experienced in immediacy and vividness. They formed an indelible image (idea) on the mind. We kept track of these meanings by assigning sounds (words) to our sensations as their identifying marks. Thus when we heard the word (a sound), it caused us to bring the meaning forward to consciousness, associating the sound with the idea. The meaning of the word, then, was an image in the mind placed there by a sensation.[13]

Accordingly, for there to be religious knowledge, there must be religious experience—sensations appropriately identified as religious sensations. If appeal could be made to feelings of the sublime (internal sensations), the special set of words associated with these sensations would become the substance of religious (as well as moral) language.[14] Since religious words were not like words which refer to material things, sublime experience was necessary if religious language was to have legitimate referents. The religious appeal of empiricism was that sensations could be made appropriate to religion.

Religious experience was immediate. As feeling, it was indisputable. In some way, the feeling of sublime aesthetic intensity was to form the foundation of religion—the glow of awe and wonder when immersed in natural beauty (the mountain-top experiences), the warmed heart, confidence built by positive thinking, feelings of love, social urges toward brotherhood, a relationship with a personal, loving savior, feelings of the presence of a departed person, meditations of various sorts which give "peace of mind" or "feelings of security," the catharsis of confession and forgiveness. Also included would be self-induced neurotic longings, a vivid wishful thinking, mass hysteria, feelings of being visited by the Holy Spirit as manifested, for example, in glossolalia,[15] voices from on high, trances, dancing fits, drug-produced consciousness.[16] All these and more initiated a catalog of sensations thought to qualify as "religious" experiences. Religious difference arose at the point of a person's interpretation of inner sensation. The earnestness of the believer in claiming an authentic religious experience was more important than correct belief. Insofar as religion was grounded in sensation, no particular religious claim could be the superior of another. An appreciation for difference became the proper attitude toward religion, not truth. Given that no individual's sensations could be said to be more laudable or truer than another's— they all belonged to the psycho-physical constitution of a human being—all religious and moral language possessed fundamental, humanistic equality. Religious life was legitimized by the emotive experience of others with similar "religious" feelings. The fact that people converted to a religion or from one religion to another demonstrated only the search of inner feeling for a suitable expression. Religious truth was not a proper category for religious understanding. Psychological "meaningfulness" was. "Cultural awareness" was. In its insistence that knowledge come from experience, empiricism fashioned a criterion for what would count as meaningful (ideas based in experience) and meaningless (ideas with no logical or experiential correlate—empty of content). It was a tough-minded requirement. Religious thinkers who understood empiricism's force of necessity would reform their ideas to withstand the onslaught of an empiricist rejection of rationalistic religion. As religion joined in the new philosophy's standards for intelligibility, it gained philosophical respectability. The sublime—the source of religious phenomena, an internal sensation in the neurological system—reoriented religious understanding. Religious phenomena were explained as sensations.

A critical problem emerged when attempting to tie human feelings to something which could be called religious experience. Each person's sensations were unique, known to others only by analogy.[17] What one person experienced could not be known to be identical to the experiences of others, nor could the words used in reference to the unique experience be known to mean the same as the words used by another. Thus we hear, "each person has his or her own idea of God," a cliche summarizing the idea that what I mean by a word could not be known to be the same as what you mean, because our experiences are different. (There is a kind of satisfaction in knowing that the other person is forbidden from a challenge to your experiences—there can be no authority in religious or moral matters.) Religious experience was pliable respecting the interpretations which informed it, and alternative interpretations were possible for those sensations thought to be religious ones. Why should any specific sensation be identified as a *religious* sensation? Why would one choose a religious explanation for that experience over (say) a psychological one? Though persons could not know with absolute certainty that their sensations were indicative of religious experience, they felt their lives transformed or enriched by the experience and understood their lives in its terms, resisting other explanations. Though emotional satisfaction lent weight to the explanation of experience as "religious," religious experience was accepted "on faith."

There might be equally plausible, non-religious explanations for the sensations experienced. The experiences from which religious faith was derived had its skeptical challengers. Sigmund Freud in his *The Future of an Illusion*[18] presented a view, widely held in non-Freudian circles as well, which argued that religious experience was to be interpreted singularly in terms of human, psychological causes.

The natural drives for survival and security involuntarily caused persons to devise psychological means to achieve a sense of accommodation to the hostility of the natural environment. Prompted by the experience of family security, sustained by the benefits of social accommodation, our earliest ancestors projected a supernatural family with rules for social interaction (morality) and, irrespective of the vicissitudes of life, guarantees of ultimate happiness (immortality). A natural, innate desire for security (a survival instinct) triggered these psychological inventions and produced morality and religion. Deities were devised to hypostatize these psychological functions.

For instance, moralistic Christianity invented a stern father with a heavenly family. Besides God, the law-giving but loving father, there was Virgin Mary, mother symbol with feminine influences, and Jesus, the son, representative of and advocate with the father. The terrors of life were exorcised by the heavenly family. Death was not real but a gateway to a family reunion for the deserving, an eternal life in which ordinary human worries no longer held sway. Religion was a haven against the troubles of life. As natural fathers loved their children and sought what was best for them, so the Heavenly Father willed the best for His children. Such faith psychologically allowed a person to endure hardship. Thus, in the name of religion persons became advocates of happiness, security, of a justice which overcame human suffering. The children had a responsibility to cooperate in the divine plan for human happiness by seeking out the causes of human suffering, correcting them, and promoting the plan of God for his kingdom on earth: "God calls people to repentance and obedience."

Though the same rules for living might be devised by some individual, when put in the mouth of God, the restrictions on life gained psychological acceptability. God's power stood behind them, not that of a challengeable individual. Freud postulates that individuals possessed insatiable appetites and were grasping and selfish. It was the individual which threatened society. Thus, society's weaker elements defended themselves against the individual through regulative procedures and the institutions required to enforce them.[19] The individual had to be repressed for the good of all. In view of this threat, only more perceptive people could see the advantage in giving up their individuality and conforming to group requirements. The "half a loaf" of cooperation, understanding, and harmony was better than wanton expressions of individuality. These privileged people therefore were willing to subdue the satisfactions of individuality—aggression, conquest, exploitation—in favor of a rational control over human existence. Since the fiat of another human being carried no special weight for the individual bent on self-aggrandizement ("No person has the right to tell me what to do!" is the oft heard rejection of conventional behavior), a god was required to utter the word of constraint.

It's not as if divine purpose in fact justified human happiness. Rather the religious system was generated by the need to strengthen human socialization. However, argued Freud, religion's long history has been only modestly successful; it did not produce the satisfactions in life the masses desired. With the advent of social science, it was time to exercise a more rational control.[20] As the race matures, people should be honest enough to recognize the need for self-control, and remove the excess psychological baggage of god and religion. Freud became an advocate for social engineering. There was nothing intrinsically religious in the task of bringing people to a better life. The good life didn't need religious trappings to give it force; it needed a scientific understanding of social and psychological processes.[21]

Freud's naturalistic concept of human existence depended on experience as a grounding source for knowledge. Mankind's overarching concern was to achieve a feeling of satisfaction with life. Social relationships and value structures were in part determined by economic reality. As earlier mankind determined and controlled its collective life by a rationalizing appeal to God and the haphazard manipulation of social value, so in the maturity of the race a scientifically produced belief structure would create satisfying human relationships. Plan rationally; control the environment (social and natural); and knowledgeable people can bring about a happy citizenry—the secular counterpart of "the kingdom of heaven on earth." At worst religion was socially counter-productive; it was the "opiate of the people." At best it was a harmless social diversion aimed at maintaining a set of values which were themselves created by economic forces.[22] The psychological effort to bolster moral resolve by a religious supplement could be abandoned in the humanistic appeal to social harmony through rational control.

Freud's recommendations for the achievement of human happiness may be realistic. Happy individuals might be produced by social engineering and the administration of psychological techniques. The first halting step may fail—scientific experimentation learns from its mistakes. But in time, Freud suggests, people will discover how to create happiness. Morality's meaning will change from something having absolute demands to something which evokes a practical concern for social equality, a satisfying distribution of wealth, justice, fair play—the rules for achieving the goals of happiness.

Must there be a religious sense to life? Traditional religion produced social control through the device of the omnipresent eye of God who found out immoral behavior and consigned the offender to torment! This sense of religion was unnecessary to achieve the goals of human existence. It provided illusions of security, but chance and unscientific attempts to devise rules of behavior which produced the good life rarely, and then inadvertently, succeeded. It failed to achieve actual social progress.

A Christianity updated by empiricism felt compelled to join forces with those promoting social well-being. It joined that realism advocated by Freud which looked for security achieved by scientific control of the factors of living. Modern Christianity was forward looking. Cognizant of the workings of the social world, this mature Christianity cultivated feelings of concern for the well-being of mankind. Its "religious activity" encouraged stability and justified social, political, and economic reform. Scarcely any of the godly trappings of religious life seemed necessary; or rather, they were necessary only to the degree that religious life introduced psychological motivation and reinforcement "to bring about God's will." Even the atheist could think of these as legitimate goals. However, a modern, scientific, rational person (a social scientist) moved straight to the cause of value structures—the economic system—and argued that the fulfillment of a person's life must finally be achieved through an equitable distribution of wealth. Religion may motivate action but was essentially superfluous to the deep structures of economic life.

One edge of the empirical sword cut in favor of religion when it carved the divine from otherwise inexplicable experience. The side that cut against religion reduced human experience to something completely natural. In the grappling between different explanations of the same experiences, the one which was simpler and empirically testable was preferable to the one less so. In this respect, Freud's thesis of survival through rational control both explained religious fervor in naturalistic terms and explained so-called moral elements of experience thought to be the domain of religion. If religious experience was to be more than the mere invocation of divinity into an otherwise purely psychological realm, a richer notion of "religious experience" was needed than one that could be psychologized away.

## Moral Feelings

Jeremy Bentham (1748-1832), an ethical apologist for empiricism, saw feeling as the experiential condition for morality. Thus, moral life became a matter of calculation. What degree of intensity of pleasure or pain would be induced by an act or policy? Bentham imagined that one could measure the increase of pleasure over pain for the greatest number of people. When pleasure weighed more heavily in the scales, the act or policy was desirable; if pain, the act was undesirable. Commitment to the claim that "all knowledge came from experience" made moral life an expression of subjective feelings. Morality was seen as an objective reflection on long-run and collective pleasure and pain. The moral theory of utilitarianism was the logical outgrowth of empirical philosophy. To establish a satisfying life was a scientific matter. Thus it was for Freud that reason and experience, not religion, fixed felicitous moral limits to human existence.[23] Modernized morality was a function of useful social processes.

The theory of utility attempted to derive moral sensitivities from the inner sense of pleasure and pain, broadly conceived. Its empirical bias favored sensation as the source for ideas—neural responses to environmental stimuli. Those with religious commitments argued, however, that feelings of moral approval or revulsion could not be rooted in naturalistic forces and retain the sense of moral obligation. The inert chemical elements and physical processes that make up the natural world function independently of value considerations, and nature's biological forces appear indifferent to moral considerations. Why think the sense one has for good and evil is materially based? Suppose moral feelings were themselves particular sorts of sensations, that they shaped life instead of were shaped by it. If so, another hypothesis about morality would be forthcoming: the spiritual presence of moral value in human experience would transcend utilitarian calculations for establishing human happiness.[24] Their naturalistic account of moral life as something promoting civilization wouldn't do justice to moral reality. The religious person could agree with the utilitarian that moral life reflected human sensitivities rooted in the natural world but insist that morality itself remained a spiritual phenomenon.

As people have a natural sense for harmony and beauty so likewise they recognize the naturalness of moral feelings. The pull of conscience toward doing what is right, just, good, the feelings of guilt when these inclinations are not followed, like sensitivity to beauty and harmony, are recognized for their facticity. Care has moral value; concern and charity are morally desirable. Lust and greed are morally repulsive and viciousness morally reprehensible. The explanation of these feelings, it is argued, cannot singly appeal to the natural realm. Value seems less an expression of a survival instinct than the presence of the feelings of moral worthiness with its own intrinsic attractiveness, despite personal inclinations. Contrary to Freud, it wasn't that one recognized a general state of well-being enhanced by a civilized attitude of self-sacrifice for the common good. Were this so, we couldn't explain a society's ready ability to rationalize its evil propensities as something good (witness Adolph Hitler's and Germany's rationalizations of "the Jewish question"). When people sensed value in a material universe that ought to be indifferent to value, they concluded that such feeling is an empirical index of a spiritual reality which transcends material processes. Objective value existed in addition to the interactions of matter in motion.

Feelings of morality seeded religion. An internal experience yielded a moral impression. Inner feeling justified our saying that moral experience was simultaneously divine experience, that God was the objective source of moral harmony and aesthetic beauty. One example of the claim that the divine was experienced through moral longings is developed by John Baillie in *Our Knowledge of God*.[25] He wrote,

> That life finds its only beginning in the revelation of our finite minds of One whose transcendent perfection constitutes upon our lives a claim so sovereign that the least attempt to deny it awakens in us a sense of sin and shame....
>
> (T)he knowledge of God first came to me in the form of an awareness that I was "not my own" but one under authority, one who "owed" something, one who "ought" to be something which he was not. But whence did this awareness come to me? Certainly it did not come "out of the blue." I heard no voice from the skies. No, it came, without a doubt, from what I may call the spiritual climate of the home into which I was born.... I know [my mother] had a right to ask of me what she did; which is the same as to say that I knew that what she asked of me was right and that my contrary desire was wrong. I knew, therefore, that my mother's will was not the ultimate source of the authority which she exercised over me. For it was plain that she herself was under that same authority.
>
> It was, then, through the media of my boyhood's home, the Christian community of which it formed a part, and the "old, old story" from which that community drew its life, that God first revealed Himself to me. This is simple matter of fact. But what I take to be matter of fact in it is not only that God used these media but that in using them He actually did reveal Himself to *my* soul.[26]

Baillie experienced divinity in moral awareness. Matter should produce no moral sensitivity; and yet, we end products of matter's evolution have awakened to right and wrong as revealed in life experience. Surely, then, there is a divine element to reality, morally expressed, as well as a material one.

# Conclusion

Freud appealed to morality as the setting of survival rules. Utilitarians provided a naturalistic account of moral behavior. However, empiricism need not be non-theistic. There are other plausible empiricist explanations of morality where features of human existence can be seen as aspects or revelations of divine reality.[27]

The traditional rationalistic idea of what was involved in being religious was transformed by the new perspective of "religious experience." One looked to inner experience. In contrast to rationalistic views which saw God's necessity as part of Being, moral experience would point to God. One contemporary church publication illustrated the point: people should seek "a personal awareness of God" or "the experience of Christ in one's own life." The clergy should be "a facilitator of the experience of God's forgiveness and love to His people." Such phrases indicate a concession to the primacy of experience. Inner feelings of moral rectitude, social justice, and beauty point toward divinity for those religiously committed persons whose religious energies became directed by the logic of empiricism.

Once again, a religious viewpoint was constructed to conform to philosophy, this time through the activities of identifying and cultivating sensations which counted as warranting one's being religious. The accession is not without risk. The religion fed by empiricism could also be starved by it. And to be sure, the appeal to religious experience was met at every point with explanations of the experienced phenomena which were non-spiritual. More damningly, religious ideas remained superfluous to explanations of natural events, and seemingly supernatural events could be understood as well in naturalistic or humanistic terms. At best, an intellectual stand-off was the result, and religion remained without an intrinsic sense of its own. As philosophy created its history, so religion followed. Change or destroy philosophical empiricism and its religious expression must be correspondingly changed or destroyed.

The next study in this account of the influence of philosophy on religious thinking focuses on Immanuel Kant, for Kant's account of knowledge transformed the idea of what the world external to consciousness meant. Kant resolved the conflict between rationalism and empiricism by rethinking what "reason" and "experience" meant. The results of Kant's analysis became religion's new cause.

## Notes

1. "Whence has it all the materials of reason and knowledge? To this I answer, in one word, from *experience*; in that all our knowledge is founded, and from that it ultimately derives itself" (John Locke, *An Essay Concerning Human Understanding*, Book II, Chap. I, No. 2 [New York: E. P Dutton & Co., Inc., 1961, p. 77]).

2. *Dialogues Concerning Two New Sciences*, tr., H. Crew and A. deSalvio; in *Great Books of the Western World*, ed., R. M. Hutchins (Chicago, Encyclopaedia Britannica, Inc., 1952), Vol. 28, p. 158.

3. *Mathematical Principles of Natural Philosophy*, tr., A. Motte; rev., F. Cajori; in *Great Books of the Western World*, ed., R. M. Hutchins (Chicago, Encyclopaedia Britannica, Inc., 1952), Vol. 34, p. 14.

4. *The Origins of Modern Science, 1300-1800* (New York: The Free Press, 1965), p. 19.

5. *An Inquiry Concerning Human Understanding*, ed., C. W. Hendel (New York: The Liberal Arts Press, 1955 [orig., 1742]), p. 42. Italics deleted.

6. This statement itself reveals problems with the notion that all knowledge comes from experience alone. It mentions "instant" and "previous moment." Problems will arise here in the idea of "time." What could "time" mean in the presence of nothingness? Since repeatability is required for an event to become a "habit of thought" (and thereby a cause), unique events are problems for empiricism. But then, these speculations are posed for the purpose of getting at Hume's idea of causation.

7. Lest one think that a different question "why?" would introduce a different dimension to our thinking, I hasten to point out that "why?" and "how?" are the same questions in empiricism, given that nature is understood as matter in motion.

8. Bishop George Berkeley (1685-1783) in his *Principles of Human Knowledge* offers an argument for the existence of God by making God a requirement of empirical epistemology. He argued that matter is a metaphysical fiction; things are therefore built of "idea" stuff (some of which are hard and some soft); that because the being of a thing requires that it be perceivable and only ideas are perceived, things must therefore be perceived by an infinite mind "who neither slumbers nor sleeps" in order that they not fade from being. This argument appears to most people to fetch hypotheses from too far afield in order to save God. Put another way: it's easier to deny that God exists than that matter exists.

9. For an extended argument from the empiricist viewpoint of how morality fits into the requirements of empiricism, see Hume's, *An Enquiry Concerning the Principles of Morals* (e.g., J. B. Schneewind, ed. [Indianapolis: Hackett Publishing Co., 1983 orig., 1751] esp. p. 16). He shows moral sentiment to be rooted in the inner experiences of pleasure and pain and puts forward a "scientific" program for determining true morality, based in its utility and in pleasure/pain distinctions. Value was naturalistic, requiring no Divine Being for its authentication.

10. William James's, *The Varieties of Religious Experience* (1902) attempts to validate religion through various sorts of experiences. Although he attributed such feelings to psychological causes, their persistence in human affairs and general social usefulness authenticated religion.

11. *Op. cit.*, Vol. I, 1928, Vol. II, 1930 (Cambridge: The University Press, and New York: The Cambridge University Press). Quotation from Vol. II, p. 93.

12. "'The Existence of God,' A Debate Between Bertrand Russell and Father F. C. Copleston, S. J.," in *Classical and Contemporary Readings in the Philosophy of Religion*, ed. J. Hick (Englewood Cliffs, N. J., Prentice-Hall, 2nd ed., 1970) p. 291. (1948 Third Programme of the British Broadcasting Corporation.)

13. See David Hume, *An Inquiry Concerning Human Understanding*, Chap. II for his description of this process. Though this philosophical theory of meaning is motivated by an intellectual concern to oppose rationalism, it is even today widely thought to describe a factual process. Contemporary philosophical analyses confute these empiricist claims. See, for example, Maurice Merleau-Ponty's *Phenomenology of Perception*, esp. Chap. 6, "The Body as Expression and Speech," (London: Routledge & Kegan Paul and New York, Humanities Press, tr. 1962, orig. 1945) or Georg Gusdorf's monograph, *Speaking*, (Evanston: Northwestern University Press, tr. 1965, orig., 1953). Ludwig Wittgenstein's *Philosophical Investigations* (tr. G. E. M. Anscombe (New York: The Macmillan Co., 1953) likewise fought against such theories. Though it is beyond our scope to develop the views of these authors respecting language and perception, the remarks about how language works from images can be addressed. The assumptions to be challenged are that words are sounds standing for images in the mind and that what gives words their meanings are sensations.

Consider this: if words are meaningless until they are associated with their images, then the sound made by the letters symbolizing (say) the word 'cat' is meaningless until it is associated with the image of the feline. As the ear picks up the sensations produced by the vibrations in the air, set initially in motion by the word's utterance, that meaningless sound begins a trek about the labyrinth of the mind seeking an image to which it may be associated and thereby shed itself of its meaninglessness. There is no way of knowing in advance whether the meaning-imputing image will be forthcoming. It is done by "association."

Suppose, then, as the empiricist claims, that some image were in fact associated with the sound-experience. How could association with any specific image be known to be a correct association? In this case, in order to verify correctness, the meaning of the word would have to be known prior to its association with the image, in which case the image was unnecessary for the meaning of the word.

To push this criticism to cases, imagine by some mental quirk that the image of a cow became associated with the word 'cat,' so that when the sentence "My cat climbs and descends trees easily and is an excellent mouser" was uttered, a bovine image would be associated with such exploits. If the meaning of a word is an image in the mind, there is no way of knowing that the image was correctly identified, either by the speaker or the hearer, for the word in itself has no meaning independently of the image. Not only would we not know what the other person said, we could never know for sure what we ourselves had said. This is as reduction to the absurd, for we know full well about the tree climbing merits of cows; there could never be a mistake of the sort described.

To reiterate, the possibility of making a mistake of the sort indicated, and not knowing it, is inescapable in the empiricist theory of language. If one knows the meaning of a word, however, so that one also knows the appropriateness of images attached to that word (and here it should be noted that not all words have images—merely consider the words in these parentheses—this in itself is an additional critical detail), then the images are superfluous to our understanding language. The empiricist account of language is simply wrong.

Incidentally, if this criticism is valid for hearing a word, it is also valid for speaking. If the listener has to know the meaning of the word prior to knowing the appropriateness of the image for that word (suggesting that we think in words, not images), the speaker also must know prior to uttering a sentence the meaning to be thrust at in the sentence. To line up atomistic images and read the words (sounds) off these images would require a prior knowledge of what the sentence has to say independent of the selection of the images. But if we know what the sentence must say prior to choosing the meanings (images) whereby to say it, then we didn't need the images in order to have the meaning. The empiricist theory of language and meaning is totally inadequate to the phenomena of meaning found in speaking and hearing.

14. See for instance David Hume's analysis of moral feeling in *An Inquiry Concerning the Principles of Morals*. Hume argues that there is an inexplicable origin of morality in the feelings persons have which can be characterized as "pleasure/pain" feelings. Based on the tendency of an act or attitude to make persons feel good, it attains a value status. It thus becomes possible empirically to ground values in the inner experience of pleasure/pain. Here is a sample of Hume's argument (p. 78):

It must still be allowed, that every quality of the mind, which is *useful* or *agreeable* to the *person himself* or to *others*, communicates a pleasure to the spectator, engages his esteem, and is admitted under the honourable denomination virtue or merit. Are not justice, fidelity, honour, veracity, allegiance, chastity, esteemed solely on account of their tendency to promote the good of society? Is not that tendency inseparable from humanity, benevolence, lenity, generosity, gratitude, moderation, tenderness, friendship, and all the other social virtues? Can it possibly be doubted, that industry, discretion, frugality, secrecy, order, perseverance, forethought, judgment, and this whole class of virtues and accomplishments, of which many pages would not contain the catalogue; can it be doubted, I say, that the tendency of these qualities to promote the interest and happiness of their possessor, is the sole foundation of their merit?

The task of those interested in religious experience is to cultivate those acts and attitudes which produce good feelings. This empirical grounding for religious feeling allows religion to have a utilitarian value, just as morality does.

15. In Christendom "glossolalia" is uncontrollable "speaking in tongues" inspired by the Holy Spirit.

16. Even the legal system can be called on to sanctify the practice of an otherwise illegal use of peyote in Native American religions.

17. Since inner experience is unique, how can one know the feelings of another? The argument for our being able to recognize others' feelings is typically based on analogy—they behave as I would in similar circumstances.

18. Sigmund Freud, *The Future of an Illusion*, tr and ed.: James Strachey (W. W. Norton & Co., 1961, [orig., 1927])

19. *Ib.*, p. 3.

20. It has been argued by a number of people (Freud, Marx, Nietzsche) that religion is an oppressive force. In reality, behavioral patterns are necessitated by the societal requirements for survival. When churches preach moral values—peace, brotherhood, cooperation—claiming the status of divine law for them, the people oppressed by a social system remain victimized. Churches, unwittingly or not, become parties to maintaining a social status quo.

21. See *Future of an Illusion*, p. 2. One experiment well worth watching, Freud suggested, was found in the application of Karl Marx's principles in the Soviet Union. Apparently he was interested in the idea of a planned economy and its effects.

22. The ideas portrayed in the analysis of man as essentially an economic and social being are fostered by Karl Marx. In Marx, religion is a soporific necessitated by an economic system that creates a class structure. Such a system in which wealth is inequitably distributed requires some means of satisfying those who are unable to participate in that wealth. The benefits of religion, with its promises of a happier life to come, remain for those who are unable to enjoy this life. Thus satisfied, such persons accept their fate in this

world in order to achieve the glories of the next. This acceptance enables the
economic structures which exploit them to remain whole; it is only when
persons are dissatisfied with their station in life that revolution becomes
possible. Thus, religion stands in the way of achieving a better world. To quote
Marx from *Critique of Hegel's 'Philosophy of Right,'* (tr. A. Jolin and J.
O'Malley [Cambridge: University Press, 1970], p. 131f.),

> man makes religion; religion does not make man. Religion is, in fact, the
> self-consciousness and self-esteem of man who had either not yet gained
> himself or has lost himself again. But man is no abstract being squatting
> outside the world. Man is the world of man, the state, society. This state,
> this society, produce religion, which is an inverted world-consciousness,
> because they are an inverted world. Religion is the general theory of this
> world, its encyclopedic compendium, its logic in popular form, its
> spiritualistic *point d'honneur*, its enthusiasm, its moral sanction, its
> solemn complement, its universal basis of consolation and justification.
> It is the fantastic realization of the human being because the human being
> has attained no true reality. Thus, the struggle against religion is
> indirectly the struggle against that world of which religion is the spiritual
> aroma.
>
> The wretchedness of religion is at once an expression of and a protest
> against real wretchedness. Religion is the sigh of the oppressed creature,
> the heart of a heartless world and the soul of soulless conditions. It is the
> opium of the people.
>
> The abolition of religion as the illusory happiness of the people is a
> demand for their true happiness. The call to abandon illusions about their
> condition is the call to abandon a condition which requires illusions.
> Thus, the critique of religion is the critique in embryo of the vale of tears
> of which religion is the halo....
>
> The critique of religion disillusions man so that he will think, act, and
> fashion his reality as a man who has lost his illusions and regained his
> reason, so that he will revolve about himself as his own true sun.
> Religion is only the illusory sun about which man revolves so long as he
> does not revolve about himself.

23. See *ib*. p. 89.

24. The use of "moral" in this context is open to the debate of whether
utilitarianism is a genuine moral theory. The criterion of "happiness" (or what
amount to the same thing—"greatest good for the greatest number") certainly
has a practical ring to it, but would fail in any genuine sense as a moral
concept. This is a different, longer, discussion, one that in fact took place in
Immanuel Kant's response to David Hume's utilitarianism, discussed in the
next chapter. For a contemporary discussion of the problems with utilitarianism, see Bernard Williams, *Morality: An Introduction to Ethics* (New York:
Harper & Row, Publishers, 1972), especially the last chapter, "Utilitarianism,"

or his longer discussion in *Ethics and the Limits of Philosophy* (Cambridge: Harvard University Press, 1985), especially Chapters 5 and 6.

25. (New York: Charles Scribner's Sons, 1959), p. 159.

26. *Ib.*, p. 181ff.

27. Edward O. Wilson's *Sociobiology: The New Synthesis* (Cambridge: Harvard University Press, 1975) and *On Human Nature* (Cambridge: Harvard University Press, 1978) offer a biological theory of why there is social structure, including human social structure. One of the effects of his account is to show why moral ideals are really survival instincts built out of the genetic structure of persons. Even were this attempt to make social structure (and its so-called morality) derivative from naturalistic interests successful (and these works have been much discussed as to whether they succeed), the argument that the universe expresses moral purpose wrought by a divine hand would still seem untouched.

# Chapter IV

---

# The Humanization of Religion

What counts as religious concern has followed where philosophical theories of knowledge and reality have led. Rationalism yielded the God of perfection, intrinsic to the universe, infinite and indestructible. Sublime Reason was endowed with omniscience, omnipotence, and omnipresence. As perfection (the ultimately real) was God's spiritual essence, so its human expression was found in purifying a kindred spiritual substance, the soul. Devout people worshipped supreme being and strove to live in accord with divine reality. This rational (divine) element of life, the purified soul, survived life's material side and upon death relocated in the place of divinity, heaven.

In contrast, the requirement of empiricism that something be experiential to be meaningful changed religious understanding. Rationalism's a priori arguments for the intelligibility of religious ideas became moribund. Empiricism and the new science saw to that. The dawning recognition that all we empirically could know was effected by matter in motion on our brains weakened the religious claims of rationalistic speculation. God and the soul could had no obvious empirical grounding. To avoid being given the status of a fairy tale, religion's apologists would discover "religious experience." The objects of religious experience found their correlates in internal sensations. In the absence of directly sensing of a godly being, these internal sensations included feelings cultivated in social, moral, and aesthetic settings. Although religion was not necessary to a person's life, at least it could number itself among several legitimate options for organizing life. Sensation would validate religion's claims. When mere speculation no longer counted as knowledge, religion became philosophically respectable insofar as it became an element of empirical probability. It would become a natural manifestation of the perceptual powers of a human creature, a way to organize life. Religion would compete with other of life's psychological and social factors to provide for human happiness. Religion joined the modern age.

Yet, despite the effort to legitimize religion through the plausibility of religious experience, it still rested on tenuous grounds. Making certain sensations substitute as the signs of an invisible god was a weakness in empirical arguments. The stronger position saw sensations, phenomena seeking explanation, appealing to natural, not speculative, elements in human experience as their explanation. Should sensations interpreted as religious experiences become intelligible under (say) a general psychological theory of sensation, religion becomes a quaint explanation for certain human experiences. For instance, suppose the near-death experience of "the light at the end of the tunnel" were in fact the play of brain-state chemistry under a state of severe stress. Emerging into another realm becomes a romantic explanation for a natural experience, and nothing of eternity becomes plausible because of the experience. Those seeking to validate religion through religious experience remain under the threat that some thoroughgoing scientific account of those same experiences would undo their religious force. An analogy might be what happened to the idea of phlogiston[1] as an explanation for the phenomenon of fire—it became passé upon the development of caloric theory of heat and the further intricacies of the theory of thermodynamics. One no longer needed phlogiston to explain anything. By reducing knowledge to sensation, empiricism made religious claims just one among a set of possible explanations of phenomena. The empirical authentication of knowledge, including religious knowledge, in principle remained tentative, limited by human reason and experience. It was this "*human* reason and *human* experience" which would threaten the viability of the religious life. If all knowledge were dependent on *human* attributes and interests, then religion, too, was symptomatic of human behavior—nothing more. The human desire for ultimate reasons had no essential role in the sphere of explanation.

Immanuel Kant (1724-1804) emerged to address this tension, providing a third major impetus for religious thinking. For Kant, religion made moral life intelligible. Morality compelled an adherence to life's religious elements—God, freedom, and immortality.[2] By "rational faith" these concepts must be believed, were one to take moral life seriously: morality required a religious ideology to sustain it.

## Being Conformed to Thought[3]

As with the other philosophers we have studied, Kant, too, began with the question of what it is possible to know—religious claims and assertions are subject to the same limitations as any other knowledge. For Kant, neither religious experience nor rational speculation provided sufficient grounds to justify religion. His reasons centered on his analysis of the limits of knowledge. As a result of his analysis, Christian religious thinking undertook a new emphasis.[4]

With the empiricists, Kant agreed that sensation provided the material for knowledge but denied that a sensation was capable of bearing its own meaning. He thought that in their raw form, sensations entered the mind as isolated and independent bits of unintelligible data. They must be formed into intelligible patterns, and this formation process was the supplement of the mind's rationality to sensation. Thus, the five discrete, distinguishable, particular sensations each collected their respective sense data—taste, sight, smell, sound, and touch. Consciousness united them into a single known object not given by any one of the five senses. Knowledge of a unified object, argued Kant, must come from the mind's capacity to structure its sensations into objects. It molded sensations to its own form, thereby providing them an intelligibility proper to thought itself. Though experience (sensation) was necessary for knowledge, the objects of experience had meaning imputed to them by the structure and activity of our rational consciousness to provide meaning to sensation. Rather than the mind conforming itself to its sensations, sensations conformed themselves to the requirements of intelligibility as these were given in consciousness. Objects appeared as three-dimensional things in the space provided by human rationality itself. The constructive power and interpretative activity of rational consciousness organized sensations. Being conformed to thought.

Meaning was not something that could be known to be intrinsic to the things themselves; nor was meaning the effect of a supreme rationality in which both the thing and consciousness participated.

Knowledge depended on those organizational principles found in consciousness. There could be no way of knowing whether or not the universe itself was structured by the same laws of rationality and being as were found in the human mind. Kant's philosophical project was to describe the rational structures of thought in the absence of which there could be no knowledge. These rules of thought exhaust, Kant argued, what we mean by rationality. Since what could be known was limited to what human reason permitted being known, the thing-as-it-was-for-me could not be known to be the same as the thing-as-it-was-in-itself. Kant barred the path to philosophical thought which (rationally or empirically) claimed to have the ultimately real within its grasp. This unbridgeable gap in knowledge left thought with only its human side, not a metaphysically transcendent side. Knowledge was singularly human. Kant humanized reason by refusing it any claim beyond that of the logical structure of human thinking; and he rationalized experience by making its meaning depend on this reasoning. On the one hand, rational consciousness necessitated intelligible experience. On the other, experience was necessary for knowledge, although it remained unclear whether the sensations known replicated the meaning of the world external to consciousness. After Kant, neither rationalism nor empiricism could make as convincing a case for the sort of intellectual certainty religion hoped for.

## Religious Knowledge

Metaphysical religious concepts represented no more than the innate capacity of reason to provide structure to reality. Theories of reality were produced out of the logic of rationality; nothing of the divine nature was warranted by these configurations of human thought.[5] Although empiricism permitted the theoretical possibility of religious experience, insofar as the sensual conditions of knowledge were given their meaning in consciousness, "religious knowledge" was an empty concept. Viewed as a demand of moral life, however, religion regained credibility. For Kant, religion was not a choice in speculations or an articulation of certain inner sensations but something that emerged out of thinking regarding the moral demands of life. Religion was not warranted by a theory of reality but was an expression of a life-need. It was life that concerned Kant. The question, "How ought I to live?" framed the substance of morality, and, as Kant stated, "Morality ...

leads ineluctably to religion."[6] What, then, was Kant's vision of the moral life? How does this vision end up with faith in religious tenets?

*Requirements of Morality*

As shown in Kant's *Grounding for the Metaphysics of Morals*, experience could teach us about many of life's practical affairs, but it could not teach morality.

> For the pure thought of duty and of the moral law generally, unmixed with any extraneous addition of empirical inducements, has by the way of reason alone ... an influence on the human heart so much more powerful than all other incentives which may be derived from the empirical field that reason in the consciousness of its dignity despises such incentives and is able gradually to become their master. On the other hand, a mixed moral philosophy, compounded both of incentives drawn from feelings and inclinations and at the same time of rational concepts, must make the mind waver between motive that cannot be brought under any principle and that can only by accident lead to the good but often can also lead to the bad.
>
> It is clear from the foregoing that all moral concepts have their seat and origin completely *a priori* in reason, and indeed in the most ordinary human reason just as much as in the most highly speculative.[7]

Morality which did not have the force of principle behind it, morality which was based on feeling and not reason, was not morality but sentimentality. Morality (and subsequently, religion) depended, then, on the creation of moral principles. How did this happen?

Kant assumed that the human mind was comprised of mental faculties among which were included the faculties of feeling or inclination, will, and reason. Many creatures (including persons) possessed the mental faculties of feeling and will, but reason defined the essential property of *human* existence. Reason was not a cultural happenstance but a property of the human mind. Conceivably other sorts of beings (God, for instance) might possess it. Persons did. Given that we knew we were rational, it became important to seek reason's purpose in life. One essential result of reason was that it could define moral principles.[8] The unique capacity of reason to ascertain logical consistency was a sure source for morality. The other faculty that contended for the right to fix moral principle, feeling, was too fickle to be trustworthy.

If one were to be true to one's essential rational nature, one would have to maintain a moral life. How was reason to establish moral principle? The universalization of any proposed human act revealed whether or not that act was self-consistent. To cite Kant's example, it was immediately evident that one could not will that lying be a universal law of nature without making nature contradict itself. To maintain rational consistency and keep being from dissolving into the chaos of contradiction, "I should never act in such a way that I could not also will that my maxim should be a universal law."[9] Thus, "Do not lie" must become an absolute moral principle, for were lying a universal law, everything would be known to be other than it was, thereby stopping the possibility of rationality altogether.

The universality of the moral law as determined in human rationality placed the will under the obligation to be faithful to reason's command. An obedient faculty of a will, following the moral principles determined by reason, directed behavior. Human beings could be led to act from several motives, but motives which were other than obedience to the command of reason (the only faculty man has for determining right and wrong) could have no moral worth. For instance, when people showed kindness because they expected a reward or might "feel good" by so doing, the act of kindness had no moral worth—considerations extraneous to the will to do the good motivated the act, and "they had their reward." In moral matters, there can be no payoff except the satisfaction which comes from knowing that one acted from duty.

Moral demands are unyielding,[10] even though one may think that certain circumstances should allow for an abridgement of the moral law. For instance, suppose one lied with the hope that the lie would result in some good. What was being tested was not morality but foresight. Stretching the moral law presumed that one had insight into the future consequences of an act. Such a lie indeed might result in good, but also it might produce completely unanticipated, unhappy results or evoke the eventual discrediting of the liar. Only God could have sufficient foresight to lie, and as a rational being, God wouldn't lie. If the universalizing of an act revealed it to be rationally consistent, a person was duty-bound to act rightly.

Rigorous in application, severe in demand, morality bound individuals to their highest calling in all settings, on all occasions. If only people were omniscient—like God—then moral law could be made or broken by fiat; one could lie in the name of the good. Knowing the effects of any given act gave one a transcendent reason to act in behalf of the ultimate good. Falling short of omniscience, being cast in the veil of flesh, no divine-like prerogatives permitted a person to step beyond the limits of reason. Reason spoke to consistency, not consequences. To go beyond reason required more than the intellect could provide. The constraint of human existence, then, compelled people to be true to their natures, obedient to the voice of reason, vigilant in the pursuit of the only good which human beings could know.

In reason's capacity to define what is moral, Kant's ethical position yielded a picture of human existence characterized by the dignity and worth of every individual. Because reason could determine the good, persons possessed a characteristic which is beyond all price. Irrespective of time and place, all individuals were equally capable of determining the consistency of a moral principle through the rational process of universalizing the proposal. Morality became the practical foundation of life for rational being. One's worth was innately given in reason. One's character was measured in terms of its ability to remain true to the moral law. Only by obedience to the moral law did persons demonstrate their inherent dignity. Said Kant,

> morality is the condition which alone a rational being can be an end in itself, because only through it is it possible to be a legislative member in the realm of ends. Thus morality and humanity, as far as it is capable of morality, alone have dignity.[11]

The whole of life was claimed by its moral sense. Any other principle placed something less than that which was essential to man's nature—human rationality capable of fixing moral law—at its core. No immoral act, no expedient lie was available to one who willed the good and that absolutely. Anything less took away the authentic mark of human existence. If persons were to be more than animals, they must witness to the highest of which they were capable. To be authentically human required absolute moral devotion.

## Morality and Religion

Morality transcended pragmatic, hypothetical, or cultural considerations. Though there may be objections to Kant's moral theory,[12] it remained as elegant theoretically as it was sensitive to the nature of morality. Christian morality was a prototype rendering of his moral theory. For instance, when scripture says "love your enemy," or "love your neighbor as you love yourself," Kant read this as a command based on absolute moral law. Love required a sense of disinterested duty and, in the case of Jesus, exacted its moral price in self-sacrifice. Thus, love shown irrespective of the moral worth of its object was a law in which results were set aside in the name of doing what was right, a duty which could have adverse personal effects (e.g., death on the cross). Kant regarded Jesus' faithful adherence to moral law as representative of the highest morality of which all persons were capable. The teaching of Jesus "can be no other than those of pure reason, for such alone carry their own proof...."[13] The moral sayings of Jesus were a veritable catalog of the results of reason's moral determinations. Jesus was able to universalize an act to determine its consistency. Of Christianity Kant said:

> Here then is a complete religion, which can be presented to all men comprehensible and convincingly through their own reason; while the possibility and even the necessity of its being an archetype for us to imitate ... have, be it noted, been made evident by means of an example without either the truth of those teachings nor the authority and the worth of the Teacher requiring any external certification....[14]

Kant pronounced Christian morality "complete." Christianity was natural; it was rational. Jesus was the "Great Example" of moral seriousness. He revealed the moral universe as coextensive with a rationally determinable morality. Morality was at the center of human life and the origin of the religious impulse. Suffice it to say, Kant's self-administered baptism of his moral theory into the Christian faith tied the themes of morality and religion together. Although Kant misunderstood the impetus for the religious life, the moral and religious connection effected by Kant's moral theory overwhelmed Christian thinkers. The teachings of Christianity and Kant's moral theory gave life to each other, revealed one another. Christian life was identified with morality; God was implicit in moral reasoning.

## The Religious Force of Morality

Theologically, Kant's account of the limits of knowledge circumscribed what could be said about divine (metaphysical) matters. Kant demonstrated the impossibility of *knowing* that the soul was immortal or that there was a metaphysical god, a "Supreme Being." Still (he maintained) one must believe in immortality and in God in order to take the moral life seriously. His arguments in defense of immortality and God are important for understanding his humanization of Christianity.

*Immortality*

Kant argued that the concept of immortality was necessitated by moral life. Consider as follows: No one can go beyond the limits of human rationality in discerning the moral law. As reason fixed moral limits, it simultaneously set for itself life's path. There was no other genuine source for determining what was moral. Rationality authenticated human existence, and willing the moral life fulfilled one's nature. However, human nature gave Kant a problem:

> complete fitness of the will to the moral law is holiness, which is a perfection of which no rational being in the world of sense is at any time capable.[15]

To exercise reason and will perfectly would imply that the human faculties of reason and will were themselves perfect, a supposition not warranted by experience. Reason must be continually trained, the will perpetually tamed. Flashes of moral righteousness is not a life. Given human rationality, the demand for moral perfection remained ceaseless, although rationality in fact found itself compromised by the desires of the flesh. Since moral perfection could not be achieved in a finite time—moments in time are discrete, each one inviting moral failure—one must assume an infinite time in which to pursue moral purity. An immortal soul was required in order to fulfill moral duty. Says Kant, "the highest good is practically possible only on the supposition of the immortality of the soul."[16]

Belief in the immortality of the soul was not predicated on a metaphysical idea of a person's inner nature. Kant thought of immortality as a ethico/religious concept in which belief in immortality was a practical consequence of taking the moral life seriously. By encouraging belief in the soul's immortality, not only could persons endure in the moral quest, they also could possess an idea which allowed them to take seriously the perfectibility of the soul in eternity, thereby justifying a ceaseless striving for the betterment of self and others. This alliance with religious doctrine supported moral life. Kant summarized the importance of the soul's immortality, thus:

> The thesis of the moral destiny of our nature, viz., that it is able only in an infinite progress toward complete fitness to the moral law, is of great use.... Without it, either the moral law is completely degraded from its holiness, by being made out as lenient (indulgent) and thus compliant to our convenience, or its call and its demands are strained to an unattain-

able destination, i.e., a hoped-for complete attainment of holiness of will.... In either case, we are only hindered in the unceasing striving toward the precise and persistent obedience to a command of reason which is stern, unindulgent, truly commanding, really and not just ideally possible.

Only endless progress from lower to higher stages of moral perfection is possible to a rational but finite being.[17]

The soul's immortality bolstered the seriousness with which we were to take the moral life, the sublime expression of man's rationality.

### God

The concept of God, too, was necessary to provide an assurance that moral striving could be effected in good conscience. Kant's argument on behalf of God depended on agreeing that morality be seen as one's highest happiness. Kant argued as follows.

Our rational nature required that we be moral, but there was no reason to think that nature was causally arranged to achieve the goal. The moral sympathies of the world external to consciousness were concealed from human knowledge. Though a moral duty to inflict no harm, were the world the sort of place were cruelty arose in the place of one's efforts to do good, it would be better not to act at all. The mandate to be moral must assume that the structure of the natural order of being will sustain moral action. We do not *know* whether a causal structure sympathetic to morality is intrinsic to the natural order; yet we must believe it so to invoke moral initiative. We believe with "rational faith" that the universe is created by a moral agent so that our moral acts have their intended consequences. A "happiness proportional to morality"[18] is possible only if human will and the natural world complemented one another. Kant writes that there must be

a cause of the whole of nature, itself distinct from nature which contains the ground of the exact coincidence of happiness with morality. This supreme cause, however, must contain the ground of the agreement of nature not merely with a law of the will of rational beings but with the idea of this law so far as they make it the supreme ground of determination of the will. Thus it contains the ground of the agreement of nature not merely with actions moral in their form but also with their morality as the motives to such actions, i.e., with their moral intention.[19]

If nature were caused by a rationality which acted not simply "with a

law of the will of rational beings but with the idea of this law,"
nature's causal forces would be imbued with a moral force as well.[20]
One was provided a motive to strive for moral perfection inasmuch as
one's own moral strivings complemented the general moral character
of being. The motivation to be moral would be coextensive with a
"rational faith" in God, the cause of all being.[21]

> Therefore, the supreme cause of nature, in so far as it must be presup-
> posed for the highest good, is a being which is the cause ... of nature
> through understanding and will, i.e., God. As a consequence, the
> postulate of the possibility of a highest derived good (the best world) is
> at the same time the postulate of the reality of a highest original good,
> namely, the existence of God.[22]

The harmonization between man and nature, ends and means, motive
and inclination, all represented by moral perfection, was reason's state
of absolute happiness. Reason's assurance that pursuit of the highest
good could be undertaken in faith required people to "postulate" the
existence of God. Then there could be "the existence of a cause
adequate to this effect" and thus "happiness proportional to that
morality."[23]

## Religion Revised

A new sense of religion was at hand. Moral life was augmented by
religion; religion was necessitated by the moral life. The belief in God
and immortality, regarded as necessary to religion, additionally
provided motivation for moral striving. Such belief met

> our natural need to conceive of some sort of final end for all actions and
> abstentions, taken as a whole, an end which can be justified by reason
> and the absence of which would be a hindrance to moral decision.[24]

But not only did religion underlie morality, its practice reinforced
morality: God could be worshipped and adored as the preserver of
moral law. In brief Kant said that

> the strictest obedience to moral laws is to be considered the cause of the
> ushering in of the highest good (as end), then, since human capacity does
> not suffice for bringing about happiness in the world proportionate to
> worthiness to be happy, an omnipotent moral Being must be postulated
> as ruler of the world, under whose care this [balance] occurs. That is,
> morality leads inevitably to religion.[25]

Religion earned a central place in Kantian philosophy; but it was a modernized religion, one not infatuated with divinity but instead focused on a moral humanity. As this religious outlook took hold, religion no longer need be centered in awe and wonder but in action, action which called both for personal purity and social justice. The humanizing force of Kantian morality where all persons should be treated as ends in themselves and not as means to an end provided additional impetus to nineteenth-century Christianity's activism in the anti-slavery movement.[26]

Moral action presumed the "inherent dignity of man," a dignity due to the fact that only rational beings could be moral, i.e., create value through obedience to the principles of morality. The capacity of persons to be moral gave them an importance "above all price."[27] Stated in Biblical terms, persons were "created a little lower than the angels." They were "the salt of the earth." Nothing could supplant this highest expression of rationality. Thus, the capacity to recognize value pointed to a dignity inherent in persons and in God. With the Kantian binding of morality and religion, the concept "God" was transformed. Though diminished in cosmological importance, God gained in moral significance. Rationality became the source of human dignity and divine sublimity.

The assertion of human dignity did not mean that people were necessarily good. A person became good or evil through choices made.[28] People were the authors of their character. Says Kant,

> Man *himself* must make or have made himself into whatever, in a moral sense, whether good or evil, he is or is to become. Either condition must be an effect of his free choice; for otherwise he could not be held responsible for it and could therefore be *morally* neither good nor evil.[29]

Persons were responsible for their lives. In matters of character, persons possessed the power of gods on earth—the power to create, transform, make right. Religious doctrine was secondary to religious life. Moral choices were to exemplify and enhance the highest of which persons were capable, enhance human "dignity and worth," and become the subject matter of religion. Religion was given a humanistic cast in that rationally produced moral commandments—the contrivance of the human intellect—were covered by religiousness. Put another way, religion possessed no special feature which had a special claim on life. The call to moral values, the exhortation to "live up to the highest one knows" fulfilled the requirements of religion, though the issue of what this "highest" involved might be grounds for concern.[30] Religion was a logical structure, a supplemental motivation for moral seriousness. Religion became "religiosity" whose idea of God and immortality enhanced moral life.[31]

For Kant, moral life was a matter of character rather than acts: "man's moral growth of necessity begins not in the improvement of his practices but rather in the transforming of his cast of mind and in the grounding of a character."[32] The way one thought about moral character was echoed in the religious language of scripture. For instance, the Sermon on the Mount states,

> You have heard that it was said, "You shall not commit adultery. But I say to you that every one who looks at a woman lustfully has already committed adultery with her in his heart" (Mt. 5:27-28).

For Kant, morality achieved the force of "God's law" as scripture gave voice to reason's dictates. Christian exhortations directed persons "to have the mind of Christ." Moral character relentlessly held to purity. The understanding of oneself as a human being was at issue. Through and through, the seriousness of being human—of being a moral individual—oriented life. The Christianity which came under Kant's humanizing influence stressed the development of personal character through moral striving. Christianity was not to engage metaphysical speculation, be it with the elements of rational perfection or religious experience, but to enter the human world as the conceptual (and psychological) support for the development of the moral order. Kantian Christianity found its effort directed to "bringing the Kingdom of God on Earth." One was to follow in Jesus' footsteps. If all persons existed with the vision of moral responsibility laid out in the scripture (or by Kant)—honesty, care, justice, the brotherhood of man, good will—the effect would introduce the Kingdom of God. Even Freud enjoined such vision in his thought that reason and will—the rational capacity of people of good will in the pursuit of enlightened goodness—could create an authentic human happiness.

## Conclusion and Criticism

Religion melds itself to what philosophy shows could be known. In the case of rationalism, God was an object worthy of worship and divine perfection toward which to strive. With empiricism, the intimacy of sensation focused in "religious experience" produced worship and emotive security, the harbinger of a meaningful life. Kant generated a third approach to define the nature of religion. Kant humanized it and gave rise to a different sort of religious sensitivity. Kant rejected the metaphysical and epistemological claims to truth of earlier philosophies. There were no divine objects to be "discovered" and worshipped, no experiences to be cultivated, no searching for God. Whereas previous philosophical visions had persons seeking the transcendent and identifying with it by a spiritual questing, Kant was unable to escape the flesh and bones of human existence. People themselves created the human world of value in which they lived. Limited to the human capacity to detect contradiction and consistency, persons forged the moral universe through human reason and will. Neither transcendent reason nor religious experience directed them. Rather, the idea of morality required the elements of religion as part of the logic of moral striving.

Though it was one's duty to strive for perfection, given the nature of human finitude, achieving it was impossible in the limited time of earthly existence—hence the need for immortality. Motivation to be moral was provided if the world itself would sustain a person's moral initiatives. It must be the creation of a moral God. God alone had it with His power to make moral actions have their desired consequences by structuring nature along causal lines. God and immortality had no other justification than the humanistic desire for a moral life. They could not be proven but only believed by "rational faith," philosophically demanded as part of Kant's moral vision. This faith completed Kant's humanizing of religion.

Two things might be said in criticism of the connection between ethics and religion. First, there are questions about Kant's argument itself. Why evoke religion in the service of morality? We know Kant's reasons—logical completeness and moral motivation inspired him. Essentially, however, religion is unnecessary for morality. Given the workings of a human reason to uncover moral truth, religion's supplement gives no more authority to the moral sphere than was initially provided by moral reasoning. Religion's concepts are derived, logical addenda to motivate moral striving. Religious concepts offer rational cogency to the moral life, but in so doing, turn God and immortality into psychological crutches. Although Kant rejected feeling as being relevant for the determination of morals, doesn't it return in the form of religion motives which contribute hope and faith to the idea of a perfect moral state? Because of God and immortality one can feel good about one's moral strivings. There need be nothing intrinsic to *moral* reasoning which required the ideas of God or immortality.

Suppose one dispensed with the psychological need for religious concepts. Why not think that honest recognition of the tentativeness of life and the practical need for moral choice in themselves were sufficient to serve human interests? Why add immortality and God? If morality were to center life, the religious life could be abandoned. Why introduce God if only human reason is required for morality? As Freud argued, God's moral requirements would be no different from what people would expect if left to their own devices as rational beings. In brief, morality can stand on its own merits, independent of religion.[33]

Second, Kant viewed people as creatures of reason and will. Mankind's glory and eventual salvation depended on the possession of reason and will. Persons were akin to gods. This aspect of Kant's thought extended a philosophical tradition dating back to Plato. Kant's image of man is overly optimistic. Removed from the adulation of this self-serving praise, the same qualities used to romanticize human existence are its condemnation as well. It will suffice to point to the epilogue of Dostoyevsky's *Crime and Punishment* to indicate what this condemnation entails. The point of the book was to display a life predicated on the hypothesis that persons may be creatures of reason and will.

> Raskolnikov was in the hospital during the last weeks of Lent and Easter week. When convalescing, he remembered the dreams he had while running a high temperature and in delirium. He dreamt that the whole world was ravaged by an unknown and terrible plague that had spread across Europe from the depths of Asia. All except a few chosen ones were doomed to perish. New kinds of germs—microscopic creatures which lodged in the bodies of men—made their appearance. But these creatures were spirits endowed with reason and will. People who became infected with them at once became mad and violent. But never had people considered themselves as wise and strong in their pursuit of truth as these plague-ridden people. Never had they thought their decisions, their scientific conclusions, and their moral convictions so unshakable or so incontestably right.[34]

Dostoyevsky characterizes people infected by reason and will as being in the grip of a disease. To seek life on rational terms was to destroy it. Dostoyevsky's critique denied that reason possessed the self-evident qualities attributed to it. Rather than its glory, reason and will were mankind's original sin and its damnation.

The Enlightenment culminated in Kant, a life in transition into the nineteenth century. In the nineteenth century, religion once again became subject to the fortunes of philosophy. The vision put forward by Kant was overtaken by the workings of "world spirit." The new religious cliché of religious understanding lifted up "God working in history" as the center point of religious understanding. George W. F. Hegel's thought became the new mode of the day. If Kant should suffer at the hand of secularism or a romanticized version of human nature, the vision of religion tied to Kant's moral philosophy prepared the way for a new sense of religion. Morality was not simply a human project; the divine hand was involved in all of history. We turn to Hegel.

## Notes

1. In the nineteenth century, phlogiston was thought to be a volatile substance in all combustible things which caused them to burn. If one could distill it, one would have a powerful essence to use for all sorts of purposes.

2. The topic of freedom is omitted in this discussion. However, Kant includes "freedom" with "God and immortality" as conceptual conditions for the possibility of morality. Perhaps the analysis of freedom's necessity for morality is the easiest of the three to grasp. In order to be held morally accountable, one must be free to choose between options. Were persons forced into their choices by environmental conditioning, they could not be held morally responsible for that over which they had no control. But since people are held responsible for what they do, they must be assumed to be free to choose their deeds. However, there is no proof for the notion that the will is free—the evidence and reasoning which supports the notion of human freedom as well can be used in support of determinism. There is one option left: if there is to be morality, freedom must be *assumed* as its logical condition. Reason does enlighten persons as to what duty demands, so presumably the moral life is possible; in view of this possibility, one must posit a free will in order to allow the idea of a morally willed act to be meaningful.

3. In *The Concluding Unscientific Postscript* (Princeton: Princeton University Press, 1941), at the beginning of Chapter II, "The Subjective Truth, Inwardness; Truth is Subjectivity," Soren Kierkegaard distinguishes between epistemologies that see a conformity between thought and being (empiricism) and those that argue on behalf of a conformity between being and thought (idealism). This heading draws on that passage.

4. Immanuel Kant is one of a handful of seminal philosophers who have made major contributions to our understanding of the limits of knowledge. His *magnum opus*, *The Critique of Pure Reason* (1787) is much too involved and demanding to go further than the sketch presented here.

5. A more thorough discussion of Kant's epistemology would detract from the central task of exploring his work's implications for Christianity. Still, something should be said about how consciousness extracts religious meaning when there can be no objects outside consciousness which would become the occasion for meaning. How would Kant address himself to religious knowledge? Kant suggested that the idea of God (and attendant concepts, e.g., immaterial being, universal rationality) enabled reason to find

> completion and satisfaction which it can never hope for in the derivation of appearances from their homogeneous ground; [yet] we can never know these beings of understanding as they are in themselves....

He continued:

> Suppose, I attribute to the Supreme being understanding, for instance. I have no concept of understanding other than my own, one that must receive its intuitions by the senses and which is occupied in bringing them under rules of the unity of consciousness. Then the elements of my concept would always lie in the appearance; I should, however, by the insufficiency of the appearance have to go beyond them to the concept of a being which neither depends upon appearances nor is bound up with them as conditions of its determination. But if I separate understanding from sensibility to obtain a pure understanding, then nothing remains but the mere form of thinking without intuition, by which form alone I can know nothing definite and consequently no object. For that purpose I should finally have to conceive another understanding, such as would intuit its object but of which I have not the least concept, because the human understanding is discursive and can know only by means of general concepts. And the very same difficulties arise if we attribute a will to the Supreme Being, for I have this concept only by drawing it from my inner experience, and therefore from my dependence for satisfaction upon objects whose existence I require; and so the concept rests upon sensibility, which is absolutely incompatible with the pure concept of the Supreme Being (Immanuel Kant, *Prolegomena to Any Future Metaphysics*, translated by Lewis White Beck. Copyright ©1950 by Macmillan College Publishing Company, Inc., p. 103f. [The original text was published in 1783.])

Kant evoked a kind of religious humility in realizing that the conditions for knowledge made knowledge of God impossible. He stated

> these so remarkable Ideas serve merely for marking the bounds of human reason. On the one hand, they give warning not boundlessly to extend knowledge of experience, as if nothing but world remained for us to know, and yet, on the other hand, not to transgress the bounds of experience and to think of judging about things beyond them as things in

themselves (*ib.* p. 105).

What then can be said of God?

> We thereby acknowledge that the Supreme Being is quite inscrutable and
> even unthinkable in any definite way as to what it is in itself. We are
> thereby kept, on the one hand, from making a transcendent use of the
> concepts which we have reason as an efficient cause (by means of the
> will), in order to determine the Divine Nature by properties which are
> only borrowed from human nature, and from losing ourselves in gross
> and extravagant notions; and, on the other hand, from deluging the
> contemplation of the world with hyperphysical modes of explanation
> according to our notions of human reason which we transfer to God, and
> so from losing for this contemplation its proper role, according to which
> it should be a rational study of mere nature and not a presumptuous
> derivation of its appearances from a Supreme Reason. The expression
> suited to our feeble notions is: we conceive the world *as if* it came, in its
> existence and internal plan, from a Supreme Reason. By this, on the one
> hand, we know the constitution which belongs to the world itself without
> pretending to determine the nature of the cause in itself; and, on the
> other hand, we transfer the ground of this constitution (of the form of
> reason in the world) upon the *relation* of the Supreme Cause to the world
> without finding the world sufficiently by itself for that purpose (*ib.*, p.
> 108).

6. Kant, Immanuel, *Religion Within the Limits of Reason Alone*, tr., T. M.
Greene, and H. H. Hudson (New York: Harper and Row, 1960 [1793]), p. 5.

7. *Grounding for the Metaphysics of Morals*, J. W. Ellington, tr. (Indianapolis, Hackett Publishing Co., 1981 [orig. 1785]) p. 22f.

8. Kant offers a naturalistic justification for his appeal to the faculty of
reason as determinative of morality. He states:

> In the natural constitution of an organized being, i.e., one suitably
> adapted to the purpose of life, let there be taken as a principle that in
> such a being no organ is to be found for any end unless it be the most fit
> and the best adapted for that end (*ib.*, p. 8).

> But inasmuch as reason has been imparted to us as a practical faculty,
> i.e., as one which is to have influence on the will, its true function must
> be to produce a will which is not merely good as a means to some
> further end, but is good in itself (*ib.*, p. 9).

> Indeed happiness can ... be reduced to less than nothing, without nature's
> failing thereby in her purpose; for reason recognizes as its highest
> practical function the establishment of a good will, whereby in the
> attainment of this end reason is capable only of its own kind of satisfac-
> tion, viz., that of fulfilling a purpose which is in turn determined only by

reason, even though such fulfillment were often to interfere with the purposes of inclination (*ib.*).

9. *Ib.*, p. 14. Kant calls the rule for universalizing an act to determine its consistency "the categorical imperative." He stated it in several ways. Here is another one: "Act as if the maxim of your action were to become through your will a universal law of nature" (*ib.*, p. 30).

10. Kant's *Lectures on Ethics* (tr. L. Infield, [Indianapolis: Hackett Publishing Co., 1963, orig. 1775-1780]) discusses the specifics of acting morally. Matters are not as rigid (at least in this editing of student notes for that course of Kant's) as other of his discussions might lead us to believe. For instance, the need to lie in desperate situations (e.g., when one's life is threatened by a criminal) is all right. Consider the matter of lying.

> But as men are malicious, it cannot be denied that to be punctiliously truthful is often dangerous. This has given rise to the conception of a white lie, the lie enforced upon us by necessity—a difficult point for moral philosophers (p. 228).

The discussions in this book are varied and fruitful.

11. *Grounding...*, p. 53. Kant's concept of dignity and worth was unlike that of traditional rationalisms. For Kant, the soul had no knowledge of God as the absolute source of all being. He did not appeal to the soul's affinity to the divine to provide sanctification to human life. Rather, the ability of persons to compose moral law, and that universally, was the origin of the idea of human dignity and worth. As the creators of a moral reasoning, as the one creature who could respond dutifully to will morality, human beings became ends in themselves. Herein lay their infinite worth. God transcended man in that God's will and reason were synonymous.

His theme of the dignity and infinite worth of the individual became utilized in Christianity as if it were its own, although one strains to find New Testament support for the notion of inherent dignity and worth. Perhaps the most used passages are in the Sermon on the Mount, respectively, Matthew 5:13 and 6:26: "You are the salt of the earth...," and "Look at the birds of the air: they neither sow nor reap nor gather into barns, and yet your heavenly Father feeds them. Are you not of more value than they?" Neither passage is about dignity and worth, however, but about God's *agape*.

12. Objections take different forms. For instance, Kant placed a premium on reason and will to the exclusion of feeling in his analysis of the foundations of morality. This commitment stems from his belief that the defining quality of human existence is its rationality. The effect was to insist on the logical properties of moral concepts as determinative of a rational person's moral life. Nevertheless, it seems that people's sense for moral existence extends beyond conceptual consistence. Thus one objection might take the form that though it is true that contradiction—universal lying as a law of nature, for in-

stance—would bring thinking to a halt, *this* "halt" is purely logical and not a matter of practical knowledge. Judgments concerning the moral affairs of life are made independent of the knowledge gleaned by Kant's rational test. These are pragmatic, hypothetical, cultural, personally creative, and the like.

Thus, it can be argued that despite the logical contradiction revealed in universalizing an act, one still needs to understand something of the goodness or evil of an action on grounds other than purely rational ones, and that Kant's test was incidental to moral knowledge. Even Kant says that it is acceptable to lie in certain circumstances (see note 10 above). He reasons his way to a pragmatic conclusion contrary to the purity of the moral theory put forward in the *Grounding*; yet we have a sense that this is the right conclusion.

Pure rationality is not a suitable measure for morality, simply because lying is plausible for life in a way a contradiction is not. To appeal to Kant's distinction, whether or not one should lie is not determinable by a categorical imperative (a moral principle having no exceptions because its universalization reveals self-destruction in contradiction) but by the hypothetical imperative ("if ... then" speculations about what is likely to happen under certain circumstances). We can indeed agree with Kant about the irrationality of lying and still assert that one must know more about what is good and bad than simply that asserting "p" in the face of "-p" violates rationality.

Even Kant seems to appeal to the effects of an act as when he rightly points out that once branded a "liar," it is difficult to redeem credibility. The notion of credibility is a practical one, not a rational one. Why should he worry about credibility were the immorality of lying so self-evident? There is something in the practice of life itself that becomes determinative of morality.

13. *Religion Within* ..., p. 147.

14. *Ib.*, p. 150.

15. Immanuel Kant, *Critique of Practical Reason,* translated by Lewis White Beck. Copyright ©1956 by Macmillan College Publishing Company, Inc., p. 126. [The text was originally published in 1788.]

16. *Ib.*, p. 127.

17. *Ib.*

18. *Ib.* p. 129; that is, supreme happiness.

19. *Ib.*, p. 129.

20. Kant argues elsewhere that moral beings are of this sort. They act not only from "the will of rational beings but with the idea of this law."

21. See *ib.* p. 130f. where Kant says "it can be called *faith* and even pure *rational faith,* because pure reason alone (by its theoretical as well as practical employment) is the source from which it springs." This is Kant's harmonization of the faith and reason issue. As we shall see in Chapter V, this notion of "faith" is not a religious one.

22. *Ib.*, p. 130.

23. *Ib.* p. 129. Given Kant's position that the world-as-it-is-in-itself is beyond knowledge, he has another reason to presume that its causal structure is compatible with moral action. Were a person to act for moral purposes in a world with an unpredictable causal structure, the results of moral actions might well be thwarted by a capricious nature. To act morally, one must presume that one's acts and their results are reliable. Thus, a rational universe which is sympathetic to morality as part of its intrinsic structure must be assumed both to make sense of the idea of a highest good and to motivate the will in persevering in moral strivings; and this sort of universe which binds life to morality requires the presumption of a morally constituted and constituting God. "Therefore, it is morally necessary to assume the existence of God" (p. 130).

24. *Religion Within ...*, *op. cit.*, p. 5.

25. *Ib.*, p. 7n.

26. G. W. F. Hegel, in a complex way an intellectual successor to Kant (and the subject of the next chapter) offers a different theoretical justification for social action.

27. *Groundings ...*, p. 40.

28. The Biblical notion of original sin is different from the notion of moral sin. There is nothing one need do to be a sinner in "original sin." But then, the significance of this Biblical notion is a religious one, not an ethical one.

29. *Religion Within ...*, p. 40.

30. Rationality may not be as instructive in moral matters as Kant imagined. For instance, is there a clear test using the categorical imperative which allows one to determine whether homosexuality or abortion is immoral? Should morality insist on the redistribution of wealth in the name of social justice? Is it moral to love your enemies? Are peace, ecology, or population control moral concerns or merely the pragmatic concerns of species survival? If morality is seen from the point of view that it establishes values and a value structure for living, then there is sufficient ambiguity about what direction life ought to take that rational certainty in moral matters falters. If reason is not decisive in moral matters, what then of its vaunted dignity? And wouldn't the need for immortality and God become ambiguous and arguments for human dignity and consequently God and immortality suffer? (We might be pushed to a notion of "original sin.") Moral uncertainty would force an ambiguity with respect to religion's necessity.

31. Since the tie between morality and religion is not limited to western religions, it has been argued that the world's religions more often than not are at heart the same. The same force that prompts moral concern in one cultural context does it in another also. Presumably, then one could retain morality without any specific religious underpinnings. At least in the United States, a morality tied to religion engenders little public incentive for its advocacy for fear of becoming a champion for a particular religion. Instead, secularized

moral training is taught in the form of prudent behavior ("just say no"), basic honesty, value sensitivity, professional ethics, or the general appreciation of all value concerns. None captures the meaning of Kantian moral duty.

There is another observation that disconnects morality and Christian faith. It may be that what looks like moral concerns in Christianity are not that at all. The "teachings of Jesus" are more probably ways of addressing the fundamental meaninglessness of human existence.

32. *Religion Within ...*, p. 43.

33. A secularized morality is expressed in those social institutions which care for the sick, ignorant, and poor. People collectively do good as part of a general human moral responsibility. Medicine and schooling are no longer the burden of the religious establishment. The poor are served by public assistance.

Though perhaps originally imitative of religious ministries to the needful, the non-sectarian efforts and concerns of the larger social order extracts resources to address need. Thus, the inclination of social sciences is to change the conditions which produced need. Improved scientific techniques, economic reform, social engineering, and good psychological therapy in the long run will improve the lot of the needful, so it is argued. The humanizing of life diminishes the need for religion.

34. Tr. D. Magarshack (Baltimore, MD: Penguin Books, 1966 [orig. 1870]), p. 555.

# Chapter V

## Timely Religion

To him who looks at the world rationally, the world looks rationally back.[1]

*Reason in History*
Hegel

Philosophical theorizing affects religion's self-understanding: awe generated in reason's perfection, emotive satisfaction sought in religious experience, religious pragmatics set in motion by morality—each shapes religious thinking. The intensity of each of these individual ideas was caught up in Georg Wilhelm Friedrich Hegel's (1770-1831) subtle and seductive philosophical scheme, the consummate expression of philosophical system-building. It is not unexpected, then, that he would have a decisive effect on religion, bequeathing to Christianity its twentieth-century parameters. Nothing following Hegel has matched his speculative philosophy.[2] In fact, much of what transpired in philosophy following Hegel was either the modification of a basic Hegelian insight or the denial of it. In either case, the direction of philosophy was transformed. Those who thought him to be correct worked toward systematizing and describing reality so that one can act on what one knows. Those thinking him wrong showed that Hegel had stepped outside the limits of what can be said. We begin our discussion with the Hegelian vision of reality.

## Dialectical Reality

Twenty six years separated the publication of Kant's *Critique of Pure Reason* (1781) and Hegel's seminal work, *The Phenomenology of Spirit* (1807). A logical point put Kant to the test and set the Hegelian wheels in motion. Kant showed in the *Critique* that what we perceptually know was shaped by the way the mind's forms of sensibility (space and time) organized sensations. Likewise, knowledge depended on the concepts of understanding and judgments (quantity, quality, relation, and modality) which structured the form our thinking must take. Objects of knowledge were thus the creations of the logical processes of consciousness. The presence of these ideal objects of consciousness implied the existence of a world external to consciousness, but a world which could not be known as it was in itself, because forms and concepts interposed themselves between the world and the known idea. Rather than truth as it was for God, Kant's position resulted in a truth shaped to ideas which were exhausted by a rationality implicit in human consciousness. The ideal distinction between the "thing-for-me" and the "thing-in-itself" allowed scientific conclusions to be true to the demands of thought and reason without ever needing to prove that scientific knowledge was synonymous with the world as it was in itself. Things-in-themselves remained hidden from direct knowledge; the thing-for-me was all that could be known.

For Kant, knowledge was possible because of the ideal structure of human reason.[3] The humanization of knowledge was a powerful attraction to those frustrated by the elusive quality of absolute truth. They need not be possessed by the urge to find transcendent truth. Human rationality limited what could be known to its own structures. This dismantling of the quest for absolute truth drove thinkers to a more protected shelter, however. It began by noticing a logical problem which arose in the premise that there is a "thing-in-itself." The point of vulnerability was this: if knowledge were the function of a structuring consciousness, on what grounds could the reality of "things-in-themselves" be postulated? In other words, if what we knew were only things-for-me, what made it possible even to posit things-in-themselves? That, too, would have to be an idea.

For Kant, the recognition of reality external to consciousness was a necessary postulation, because it accounted for the material of sensation. However, on Kant's own grounds, the postulation of something "out there," "the thing-in-itself," must be a postulation of thought and nothing more. This tension between the reality of an objective world and its postulation as an idea of thought brought about a reevaluation of the nature of thought and the objective world.[4] It is a logical critique but one which must be resolved for the sake of cogency. Peter Singer reiterates Kant's problem in his book, *Hegel*.

> Kant argued that we can never see reality as it is; for we can only comprehend our experiences within the frameworks of space, time and causation. Space, time and causation are not part of reality, but the necessary forms in which we grasp it; therefore we can never know things as they are independently of our knowledge.[5]

Hegel's task became one of demonstrating "the possibility of genuine knowledge, and thus to serve ... philosophy's aim of providing ... 'actual knowledge of what truly is'."[6] Hegel sketched the requirements for regaining absolute knowledge. Accordingly, religious discourse about God, man, and nature changed as well. Hegel's analysis of knowledge and reality, his absolute idealism, was revisionary. In order to understand what transpired, we begin with the motif which organized Hegel's thinking, namely, the place of reason in reality.

Unlike the pre-Kantian rationalists who viewed reason as an extra-natural perfection in which nature participated, Hegel thought reason was "both *substance and infinite power*, in itself the infinite material of all natural and spiritual life as well as the *infinite form*, the actualization of itself as content." He continued

> It [reason] is *substance*, that is to say, that by which and in which all reality has its being and subsistence. It is infinite *power*, for Reason is not so impotent as to bring about only the ideal, the ought, and to remain in existence outside of reality—who knows where—as something peculiar in the heads of a few people. It is the infinite *content* of all essence and truth, for it does not require, as does finite activity, the condition of external materials, of given data from which to draw nourishment and objects of its activity; it supplies its own nourishment and is its own reference. And it is infinite *form*, for only in its image and by its fiat do phenomena arise and begin to live. It is its own exclusive presupposition and absolutely final purpose, and itself works out this purpose from potentiality into actuality, from inward source to outward appearance, not only in the natural but also in the spiritual universe, in world history.[7]

Unlike Kant who saw reason as the forms of thinking and sensation as its content, Hegel asserted that reason was both form and content, merged together in a unity embracing all reality. Hegel's "Reason" was a dialectical process. Thus, whereas Kant saw time as a form of sensible intuition, one of the rational settings whereby sensation received its meaning, for Hegel, time and timelessness were aspects of an eternal sameness incarnated in being. A description of the movement of the eternal in time became "evidence" for the rightness of his dialectical conception of reason. Said Hegel,

> only the study of world history itself can show that it has proceeded rationally, that it represents the rationally necessary course of World Spirit, the Spirit whose nature is indeed always one and the same, but whose one nature unfolds in the course of the world.[8]

Rationality unfolded itself in history, fulfilling its own nature. To repeat: "It is its own exclusive presupposition and absolutely final purpose, and itself works out this purpose from potentiality into actuality, from inward source to outward appearance, not only in the natural but also in the spiritual universe, in world history." Individuals' thoughts unfolded the presence of that reality on which all being depended—a dialectical rationality which "supplies its own nourishment and its own reference."

Hegel posited a dialectical sense of rationality which contrasted with the static, timeless rationality familiar to philosophy. Traditionally, reason took the form of self-evident, axiomatic truths. One axiom was complementary with all others. In a perfect completeness, the entire system was self-sufficient, and, like the truths of Euclid's geometry, expressed eternal laws of being.[9] Beginning with Socrates, logic was at the heart of the rationalistic tradition; contradiction could not exist.

Hegel revised this tradition. According to Hegel, a living reality did not display the uniformity of non-contradictory logical laws in which being participated. Rather, being continually denied itself. If the logical law stated that a thing could not be both itself and not itself, that it must be one thing or another, reality taught that not only was negation necessary for understanding what a thing was (things are understood by what they are not) but integral to things were the conditions which denied their natures. History revealed a perpetual self-alienation which it unfolded in time. Negation, opposition, and contradiction were the stuff of being. If the logical law stated that a thing is what it is, reality revealed a living logic—things in time became other than they were; self-contradiction implied that a thing embraced its opposites in its unevolved nature.[10] The logic identified with the philosophical tradition was mere abstraction.

Hegel provided this illustration of how dialectical reality works. To construct a house one must appeal to the laws of gravity in order to *raise* the building. Yet these same laws sought to *raze* the structure.

[W]hen someone starts building a house, his decision to do so is freely made. But all the elements must help. And yet the house is being built to protect man against the elements. Hence the elements are here used against themselves. But the general law of nature is not disturbed thereby. The building of a house is, in the first instance a subjective aim and design. On the other hand we have, as means, the several substances required for the work—iron, wood, stones. The elements are used in preparing this material: fire to melt the iron, wind to blow the fire, water to set wheels in motion in order to cut the wood, etc. The result is that the wind, which has helped to build the house, is shut out by the house; so also are the violence of rains and floods and the destructive powers of fire, so far as the house is made fire-proof. The stones and beams obey the law of gravity and press downward so that the high walls are held up. Thus the elements are made use of in accordance with their nature and cooperate for a product by which they become constrained. In a similar way the passions of men satisfy themselves; they develop themselves and their purposes in accordance with their natural destination and produce the edifice of human society.[11]

This model of dialectical reasoning became an analogy for understanding all experience. History revealed a general sense of dialectical progress. Through both accomplishment and failure, things, events, and persons proceeded with the tasks at hand, bringing about eventualities which may not even have been anticipated at their outset, moving toward something presumed to be "higher."

Dialectical movement was captured by the words: thesis, antithesis, synthesis. However, these concepts are easily misunderstood if they are seen as independent moments of an on-going process. It would be a mistake to think that something happens (the thesis) which generated opposition (the antithesis) which resolved itself in a new formulation of the situation (the synthesis). The dialectical movement of thought was more complex than its popular, three-part reduction suggests. It was not a collaboration of discrete events and independent wills. Opposition in the form of an antithesis was not created and brought to situations. It was integral with them, the expression of an organic unity unfolding and evolving in time. Thesis, antithesis, and synthesis were not episodic but synchronic.

> The flame consumes the air; it is nourished by wood. The air is the sole
> condition for the growing of trees. In the wood's endeavor to consume
> the air through fire, it fights against itself and against its own source.
> And yet oxygen continues in the air and the trees do not cease to grow
> green.[12]

In the unity of burning wood, we witness simultaneously the elements
of its dissolution. Dialectic found no independent thesis, antithesis, or
synthesis, though analysis broke things apart into a triad. Put another
way, the real world was engulfed by contradiction out of which a
rational harmony was forged. "Reason governs the world."[13]

The consummate power of dialectical Reason was imitated in
religious concerns. Dialectical, rational movement created nature and
lent purpose to human affairs and history. As universal reason or
World Spirit unfolded itself, it moved beyond itself. Reason furthered
its nature in the particulars of experience and created contexts for
overcoming the limits imposed by any particular expression. A self-
conscious direction to rational spirit became concrete in human
existence. Persons made decisions in the face of the hard realities of
ordinary life. The living situation was the stage on which life was
played out. Life was earnest. Human passion and will, dialectically
tempered, searched out satisfying possibilities to enable life's continuation: "the actions of men spring from their needs, their passions, their
interests, their characters, and their talents."[14] From the reality of the
mundane—needs, passions, character, interests, ideas—as well as the
novel, an unstoppable, heightened rationality emerged. Rational spirit
welled up out of joy and suffering, goodness and immorality, wisdom
and ignorance, affinity and antipathy. The negative was something to
be overcome by a reason intrinsic to the realities of life.

> We may, perhaps, see the ideal of Reason actualized in those who adopt
> such aims and in the spheres of their influence; but their number is small
> in proportion to the mass of the human race in their influence accord-
> ingly limited. Passions, private aims, and the satisfaction of selfish
> desires are, on the contrary, tremendous springs of action. Their power
> lies in the fact that they respect none of the limitations which law and
> morality would impose on them; and that these natural impulses are clos-
> er to the core of human nature than the artificial and troublesome disci-
> pline that tends toward order, self-restraint, law, and morality.[15]

The unfolding of Spirit was occasioned by the particular, but the place of the individual, of thought, of truth, was subsumed under a historical/dialectical process. Each was crucial to reality; each was dissipated in its own final insignificance. The picture of reality found Spirit in turmoil as it came to a consciousness of itself as rational.

[W]orld history does not begin with any conscious aim.... But world history begins its *general* aim—to realize the idea of spirit—only in an implicit form, namely, as Nature—as in innermost, unconscious instinct. And the whole business of history ... is to bring it into consciousness.[16]

Reason is immanent in historical existence and reaches its own perfection in and through this existence.[17]

The transition of its [Spirit's] potentiality into actuality is mediated through consciousness and will.... Thus Spirit is at war with itself. It must overcome itself as its own enemy and formidable obstacle.... What Spirit wants is to attain its own concept. But it hides it from itself and is proud and full of enjoyment in this alienation from itself.

Historical development, therefore, is not the harmless and unopposed simple growth of organic life but hard, unwilling labor against itself.... This end we have stated from the beginning: it is Spirit in its essence, the concept of freedom. This is the fundamental object and hence the leading principle of development.[18]

On the one hand, reason was engaged in dialectical disruptiveness; on the other, it was unity struggling to actualize itself. Reality thus came into being in the concrete. Its past became the condition for future development. The moment embodied the past and contained within itself the reality which became the future. In the unity of being, nothing was wasted; everything became an aspect of dialectical movement toward even greater rationality.

The very essence of spirit is *action*. It makes itself what it essentially is; it is its own product, its own work. Thus it becomes object of itself, thus it is presented to itself as an external existence. Likewise the spirit of a people; it is as definite spirit which builds itself to an objective world.[19]

Rationality is not a divinely contrived plan applied from eternity. It became what it was as a dialectical adjustment toward greater and greater rational actuality. Says Hegel,

The result of this process ... is that Spirit in objectifying itself and thinking its own being, on the one hand, destroys this (particular) determination of its own being, and on the other hand, grasps its universality.[20]

Reality was dialectical; dialectical reason was reality. There was no thing-in-itself to be contrasted with consciousness, for there was no consciousness unless it were consciousness of something. Kant's assumption that there were thinking subjects and the things they thought was mistaken. This distinction was an abstraction. Consciousness and things shared in unfolding a unified World Spirit. They yielded their essence as part of the dialectical interplay with a knowing consciousness.[21]

Divine reality received new meaning. What "the new" meant was the exercise of rationality in the heightened development of the human spirit. There was to be progress in history. "Progress" need not be optimistic, however: "development is connected with the degradation, destruction, annihilation of the preceding mode of actuality which the concept of the Spirit had evolved."[22] Nevertheless, a kind of arrogance marks dialectical thinking: changes in value-structures and life-forms supersede those of our forebears and represent progress. Thus, we are more tolerant, patient, and broadminded than those preceding. We understand the deeper causes, the desired goals, the complexity of situations. Our age is more enlightened respecting race, nationalism, sexism. Each generation improved history because of its own struggles.[23] As dialectic overcame life's alienations, the self-conscious capacity of persons to aid in the movement of history provided special challenges to religion. All involvements of living were expressions of World Spirit, so that nothing escaped divinity.

## Dialectic and the Divine

Dialectical thinking is a hermeneutical tool; it can be applied to any area of thought. Its religious application was especially fruitful. There were three effects of Hegelian thought for religion. First, being was transformed into something religious. Second, theological discourse was understood as proto-scientific language. Third, moral objectivity was set aside in favor of "relevance."

### World Spirit and Religion

Everyone and everything may be properly understood as a manifestation of the divine. Were such divinity labeled "God," then God was not something to be worshipped, for God could not be something to be in awe of. Rather, God's life was expressed in human terms as this sought to transform itself into something higher. God was finite, and unlike the problem of evil for the earlier God of perfection, the God bound by dialectical Reason struggled against evil as its part in the synthesizing of being. In metaphorical language, it might be said that man and God were partners, bringing about His kingdom on earth. Activity fulfilled divine spirit. Rational spirit swept up everything in effecting its own nature. Even lethargy contributed to the realization of rational spirit by creating the need for concern. The inescapable force of dialectic defined existence. Life was Spirit-bound. The reason one might think that existence had a religious bearing was clear: the idea of "God," all of life, worked in terms of rational spirit.

World Spirit was active, involved. It struggled in human struggles. Hurt, humiliation, and anger provoked dialectical movement. As a pleasing force, it succeeded and triumphed. The old was set aside; the new burst forth. Life struggled to fulfill rational spirit. If this picture of reality were believed (and try to deny it, for in the passion of denial it became a pole for dialectical motion, an antithesis—Hegel called this "the cunning of Reason"[24]), then life was a participation in Spirit's derivation of its own nature. Life was a reflection of the absolute—the divine. From the perspective of an evolving rationality, World Spirit ascended to ever higher self-actualization. As situations extended themselves into time, they defined themselves both positively and negatively; and in the opposition of forces intrinsic to the situation, something different (third) evolved from the situation. The novel setting in its turn was lived through, defined positively and negatively, transformed in its overcoming adversity, and was thus freed to a new situation; and so on. These expressions of both nature and history were the visible signs of divine activity. Life in its entirety was religious.[25]

## Religious Versus Scientific Discourse

The divine quality of existence suggests the second point: religious discourse portended a more adequate scientific language. In the inception of ancient religions, people struggled to recognize the first inklings of their rational self-consciousness. There were questions of origins and purpose. Religious speculation solved life's mysteries and struggles in an evolution of world views appropriate to the times. These views might be considered proto-scientific languages which articulated a sense for the perplexities of human existence in myth.

As mythical, religious language didn't reflect ignorance but man's inner yearnings. However, when one understood reality in its dialectical workings (an understanding which in its objective content appeared as science), one saw that religious concepts reflected overarching human concerns which underlay all of life. Though speakers of religious language believed themselves to be gripped by reality, a demythologized language unraveled life's perplexities in a manner more nearly in the form of science. Scientific knowledge permitted one to state clearly what religious language veiled.

Consider, then, the doctrines of Christianity, explicable in terms of the dialectical operations of reason. Alienation between earth-bound human life and the divine was represented in Jesus' incarnation. The eternal came into time in a person. Opposites were united, and incarnation showed us symbolically our own natures. As such, religious language was an authentic characterization of human existence, but symbolic.[26] It was a proto-scientific language. Hegel turned religious language into scientific language in three ways. One dealt with thought about God, a second with the emergence of the idea of a person, and the third with the idea of history.

*God.* In philosophical tradition God was invisible. Thus, questions respecting the reality of God took an intellectual turn. For instance, Plato showed that it was reasonable to claim that divine things existed in order to explain being and knowledge. In the hands of Christian thinkers, the ideal of rational perfection became God's character. God was perfect in purpose, nature, and substance. In contrast, the Hebraic anthropomorphic God had plans and directed history, knew right from wrong, and exercised power to change circumstances—social as well as natural. People worshipped the one on whom existence depended.

Hegel resisted attempts to hypostatize perfection into "God." Hypostatized perfection was a mythological depiction of powerful natural and social forces. In reality God did not exist as thing, did not think, plan, or evoke, did not know, devise, or direct. God was not a being—though our conceptualization of him made him appear so. A demythologized image of God would have us realize

> that the actual world is as it ought to be, that the truly good, the universal divine Reason is the power capable of actualizing itself. This good, this Reason, in its most concrete representation, is God. God governs the world. The actual working of His government, the carrying out of His plan is the history of the world.[27]

"God" remained a symbolic representation of dialectical Reason, a representation of what could be stated otherwise through an objective view of existence.[28] The relationship between Spirit and world, including the social setting of human existence, thus took on special significance. From an earlier age where God was the "eye-in-the-sky" whose regulatory powers assured a successful human society, mankind moved forward to modern times where the same goals were accomplished through scientific analysis. From a dialectical viewpoint, religious outlooks were the uncritical products of a Reason which in time would find scientific ways to make clear their essence. The religious goal to create "heaven on earth" was expressed through the hope of social science to create a rational world. Instead of divine action, the new society would be devised by social engineering. Instead of ideologies adopted for survival (for instance, political ideology or "divine" moral law), sociological or psychological techniques would probe the causal factors of human behavior. Religious concern could assume the perspective of science because their goals were the same—to make a meaningful life possible.[29] The goals of social harmony could be achieved without invoking a divine agency. The entire universe was divine purpose, brought forth in the particulars of the dialectical moment.

*Persons.* As with other philosophical positions about the limits of knowledge and the nature of reality, Hegel's views had implications for self-understanding and the moral life. Because dialectic was natural to being, his analysis of personhood likewise assumed a dialectical shape.

Self-consciousness arose dialectically from the background of nature and social forces. Before its dawning, consciousness blindly lurched forward to unveil itself. Primitive peoples were conceived as animal-like creatures driven by greed, lust, and conquest. Passion was fundamental; reason was inarticulate. Spurred by feeling, persons acted to gratify themselves through rapacity, power, cunning, sensuality, and so on. At this primeval stage, exploitation by the powerful served only themselves. However, aggression and conquest set dialectical forces in motion. The aggrieved fought against what was adverse to them. When their passion transformed itself to become consciously articulated, a dialectical synthesis arose in which a spirit of cooperation against the masters also served self-interest. From "Lord/Bondsman" or "Master/Slave" relationships, as Hegel termed it, a broader sense of human freedom emerged to organize human society for its preservation.

Personhood dawned in a revelation of the self as relational.

Society was itself then subjected to the same dialectical forces which created it in the first place. It became a thesis spawning the antithesis latent within it. Stoicism became the stage for articulating the dialectical conflicts inherent in it.

> Stoicism could only appear on the scene in a time of universal fear and bondage, but also a time of universal culture which had raised itself to the level of thought.[30]

Stoic resignation lead to Skepticism.[31] At each step, persons became increasingly self-conscious, at first only because of conflict, but eventually because persons knew themselves as embodied rationality. Rational beings are self-consciously to mediate difficulties and pose solutions. The Enlightenment anticipated that a general, rational ordering of life was a realizable goal.

Religious language became symbolic. It marked out a beginning point for self-consciousness and the eventual cognizance of the workings of World Spirit. Consciousness could become attentive to its alienation from a pure nature and begin to dwell on its own intrinsic freedom and self-worth. The centrality of consciousness previously captured by religious reference to divinity was transformed by a philosophical language in which people enhanced freedom and self-worth by asserting the dignity and worth of all rational creatures.[32] In this way, Hume and Kant ridded themselves of a divine beginning point. Eventually, all persons participated self-consciously in the divine nature. Dialectic saw to this.

Rational spirit broke forth; reason emerged in the moral life. Hegel stated that human beings

> share in the rational purpose itself and for that reason are ends in themselves.... Man is an end in himself only by virtue of the divine in him—that which we designated at the outset as *Reason*, or, insofar as it has activity and power of self-determination, as *Freedom*. And we say ... that religiosity, morality, etc. have their foundation and source in it and are thus essentially exempt from external necessity and chance.... This is the seal of the absolute and sublime destiny of man, that he knows what is good and what is evil, and that his destiny is his very ability to will either good or evil.[33]

Where religion spoke of the acceptability of persons in God's sight, Hegel found "Man is an end in himself only by virtue of the divine in him." Where religion spoke of following God's law, Hegel appealed to "the absolute and sublime destiny of man" who was freely able to act in moral matters. Reason found itself in the human ability to overcome private interest or passion for the social ideals of reason, justice, and liberty. The social context for mankind's true dignity and worth burst forth dialectically. Religious ideas lost their force to philosophical ideas, which themselves moved toward that final clarity, a full, scientific understanding of our universe. Original religion and philosophy were extinguished, religion now to serve dialectical process and philosophical analysis the detailing of the Hegelian system. h sm, self-consciousness, which began with mythic insensitivities, moved to ever higher levels: religion, philosophy, and finally in rational, scientific understanding. Religious language anticipated scientific discourse about the nature and direction of society, both in the idea of human worth and the idea that people are to become what they are in a social setting. The self-understanding couched in religious terms evolved into a program where self-understanding was perceived in terms of a social science: the definition of self-consciousness took place in society. The contrary as well was true. Society emerged out of the trials of becoming self-conscious. The interaction between the individual and society was like the interaction between persons and God. Society, like God, set limits on human actions. Hegel stated the matter this way. "What counts is the common will. In thus being suppressed the individual will retires into itself."[34] He continued,

> his spiritual content then constitutes the essence of the individual as well
> as that of the people. It is the holy bond that ties the men, the spirits
> together. It is one life in all, a grand object, a great purpose and content
> on which depend all individual happiness and all private decisions.... All
> the value man has, all spiritual reality, he has only through the state
> [society].[35]

Religious people were quick to adapt to Hegel's new philosophical insights. Freed from religious mythology to seek a more direct expression of its goals in social action, "liberal" Christianity came forward to join with social science for the creation of what, it said, all along was meant by "the kingdom of God on earth." There was no reason not to utilize the emotional force of religious language to effect human well-being. Christianity would work toward a desirable society which was in accord with God's divine kingdom, a euphemism for the inexorable unfolding of dialectical process. God worked through persons. Mankind's hands were God's hands. The only issue was that of the means to accomplish the goal.[36] Instead of a mythological, divine intervention and sudden transformation of society, science enabled religion to achieve what were its genuine goals all along. "The kingdom of God" became symbolic for the work of people within the social reality of dialectical movement.

James Russell Lowell (1819-1891) gave voice to the Hegelian spirit in Christian thought in the poem "The Present Crisis" (published in the Boston *Courrier*, 1845). Himself a man of letters, his abolitionist sentiments made him indignant at the prospects of admitting pro-slave Texas into the Union. He crystallized his feeling in an eighteen-stanza poem which a later editor abbreviated to become a four-stanza church hymn. It is this version that commands our attention, for it nicely illustrates the new theology inspired by Hegelian philosophy.[37]

> Once to every man and nation
> Comes the moment to decide,
> In the strife of truth with falsehood,
> For the good or evil side;
> Some great cause, God's new Messiah,
> Offering each the bloom or blight,
> And the choice goes by forever
> Twixt that darkness and that light.[38]

The first stanza called people to social responsibility. The thesis (truth, good, and light) struggles with the antithesis (falsehood, evil, and darkness), and through a moment's decision, a synthesis is evoked (the overcoming of evil with good). But a victory does not finish the battle, for dialectic ("the choice") is eternally present ("goes by forever"). History's movement was a matter of causes. The promoter of a cause that created a new world became a savior of the world, a Messiah. Messiahs were created by time and place. They quested for human dignity, for justice and freedom.

> Then to side with truth is noble,
> When we share her wretched crust,
> Ere her cause bring fame and profit,
> And 'tis prosperous to be just;
> Then it is the brave man chooses
> While the coward stands aside,
> Till the multitude make virtue
> Of that faith they had denied.[39]

The second stanza revealed the manner in which truth arose to engulf its foes. A situation (the thesis defined by pragmatic realities—entrenched and exploitive wealth) is confronted by the messianic "brave man." He opposes the injustice of the system and risks personal suffering to confront it. Nevertheless, he persists. Reason is moved toward a greater consciousness of its own harmony. Heros may suffer, but through their selfless and courageous acts, reason dawns as well on the multitude. A concrete individual witnessed to truth. There was movement in history toward the kingdom of God.

> By the light of burning martyrs,
> Christ, thy bleeding feet we track,
> Toiling up new Calvaries ever
> With the cross that turns not back;
> New occasions teach new duties,
> Time makes ancient good uncouth;
> They must upward still and onward,
> Who would keep abreast of truth.[40]

Christ was a martyr for a cause—he overcame exploitation and injustice in his time; and we, too, can be like Christ for our own times. He had his Calvary, we ours. The aim is the same: that of creating a just society. The goal of human existence and society is found in "the brotherhood of man under the fatherhood of God."

Important to note here is that particular values are not eternal: the way in which successive generations might define problems and solutions will be different. Our fathers' values may be inappropriate for us and may even stifle the needs of a modern generation—"New occasions teach new duties, Time makes ancient good uncouth." The truth is unfolded in time, the product of increased rational understanding. The transformation of society into a better world depends on the success to which the oppressive values of a prior age can be overcome. In the particular and concrete present, nothing called a value need really be moral. Circumstances merely become the occasions for "new duties." Religion and morality were unified in a common task of promoting an overarching "brotherhood" of man. Life is drawn to ever greater harmonies.

> Though the cause of evil prosper,
> Yet 'tis truth alone is strong;
> Though her portion be the scaffold,
> And upon the throne be wrong:
> Yet that scaffold sways the future,

And, behind the dim unknown,
Standeth God within the shadow
Keeping watch above his own.[41]

The final stanza of the hymn caps its Hegelian temper. God was not strident. He existed in the shadow of dialectical movement in time, there to disentangle His nature as rationality. Such dialectical movement was irresistible. In time, as rational spirit came to self-consciousness, it erupted in a concrete expression, defined by and defining historical situations.

Individuals brought forth World Spirit in the particularities of life, and in turn these became the contexts which determined a people's history. Reason possessed a life of its own. People served it, to become heros as well as victims in its advance. In the dialectic, "good guys" didn't always win. Herein lay the hunger for rectification of the wrongs of history. Human yearnings—commitment to ideals, a fulfilling way of life, justice—were the spring of action. Without the ideals which motivated individual strivings, life would remain an animal existence. Speaking anthropomorphically, the sort of power God brought to bear in human affairs sought justice and goodness for all persons in all things.

*History.* History eventually must conform to a dialectical will, a divine will. Tuned by the realities of social structure, religion became a historical force through its anthropomorphic God and His demands on people, demands which modernity saw as the dialectical forces of history. People were dependent on the cause-and-effect relationships of historical movement.[42]

In spite of the inertia of institutions, lethargy of will, and apathy in concern, Christian religious duty would transform circumstances and institutions. This modernized Christianity hoped to bring about an ideal, holy state, the kingdom of God on earth. Human hands were to become God's hands. To be sure, the Biblical idea of "the kingdom of God" was explicit in its depiction of *God* bringing in the end of time and populating an eternal kingdom with persons of His choosing. But given the dialectical nature of history and the new concept of divine reality, the image of the "kingdom of God" which was to serve social purposes had ultimately to be collaborative and cooperative. Persons moved by the dialectical spirit were "to preach good news to the poor, release the captives, recover sight to the blind, set at liberty those who are oppressed, to proclaim the acceptable year of the Lord."[43] A social gospel was set loose by the Hegelian dialectic, a social gospel which aimed to transform the entire social order. It was God's will expressed as the dialectic of history which would regulate life. The "God within the shadow" would prevail.

Hegelian theological sentiment that God works in history dominated interpretation of the Bible. It was read in terms of God's salvation for history.[44] Biblical writings lent themselves to this interpretation. Jesus' emphasis on God's Kingdom on earth suggested God's concern with history.[45] Social activism appeared to be the modern equivalent of the ancient religious view. Its idealism was claimed to parallel the Hebrew concern for social fairness or the early Christian concern for a community of loving individuals. Dressed in modern garb, the idealism of the ancient world was transformed to support an up-dated modern idealism. After Karl Marx, economics was an important basis for understanding historical movement. Those sensitive to human need would improve life's direction by abolishing the economic injustices that inured the human spirit. Class structure bred contempt. The self-satisfaction of the economically privileged hid a deeper social malaise: the less fortunate must suffer for the general good. The alienated minority pleaded from the fringe of society for its redemption from oppression. Their cry was heard by the followers of Jesus who worked for human equality and social rectification. On the one hand was the thesis: life given and endured. On the other is the antithesis: the need to free all the members of society from oppression. A higher sense of social consciousness was the synthesis. Rational Spirit, God, evoked the salvation of history. Hegel put its work this way.

> The principle of *development* implies ... that it is based on an inner principle, a presupposed potentiality, which brings itself into existence. The formal determination is essentially the Spirit whose scene, property, the sphere of realization is world history. It does not founder about in the external play of accidents. On the contrary, it is absolutely determined and firm against them. It uses them for its own purposes and dominates them.
>
> ... Spirit is only that into which it makes itself, and it makes itself actually into that which it is in itself (potentially).... The transition of its potentiality into actuality is mediated through consciousness and will.[46]

Socially aware persons work in behalf of God—the rational ordering of being—to bring in His Kingdom.

*Religion and the Moral Life*

To this point we have developed two implications of Hegelian logic for religion. One was that there is no area of life immune from religious concern, for there is no way to avoid being part of the dialectic of divine mind and spirit. The second focused on the language of religion. It is the mythological representation of truths which have their objective correlate in the social, economic, political, and psychological features of human existence. These concerns, when admixed with the human interest to advance universal compassion, became the authentic purpose of religion and morality. In this section we consider the transformation of moral and religious life in view of Hegelian idealism. Given that existence was dialectical, moral life could not begin with absolute moral truth.

After Hegel, religion and moral value were relative to the cultures that produced them. The challenge to the notion of absolute morality began in the nineteenth century. Lowell captured its spirit:

> New occasions teach new duties;
> Time makes ancient good uncouth;
> They must upward still, and onward,
> who would keep abreast of Truth.

"Time" made moral or religious truth relative to culture. Only absolute Truth stood above all particulars, revealing itself dialectically in the stages of human progress. As Hegel said: "for whatever in the world is acclaimed as noble and glorious there is something even higher. The claim of World Spirit rises above all special claims."[47] Moral proclamations were generated by dialectical episodes in an unfolding of World Spirit. Since there were no absolute truths, morality and religion were not universal but rather the result of "circumstances and the times." They did not define a culture; but culture or society, dialectical Reason's effects, defined them. It was not individuals but World Spirit, in its various guises, striving for a dialectically determined "truth" which was of greatest moment.[48]    The truth of one age launched future truths. There was no final truth, only glimpses of humanity.

World Spirit was at work in all religious struggle.[49] Religion's law evolved from the pragmatics of what a reasonable thinker would have required under the circumstances.[50] Thus it was that modern times, too, should transform Biblical Christianity. Christians who came under the influence of Hegelian philosophy were to "go into the world" to create a loving society. Instead of saving individuals through the dogmatics of creedal confession, religious people involved themselves in the struggles to overcome human friction. They sought reconciliation. Out of discord, exploitation, and suffering were to come human dignity, economic justice. From political social action in behalf of equality and civil rights to breaking down intolerance to alternative life styles, religious workers wanted to hasten the dialectical Divine Will that no person be alienated, that all persons benefit equally in the affairs of living. "The brotherhood of man under the fatherhood of God" would prevail.[51] There would be "Peace with Justice."

Where there was evil, the moral corrective required structural changes in society. Evil was not a matter of character or the will to be wicked. In a Hegelian setting, evil had social roots. Persons suffered it involuntarily. The process began in "the prophetic voice," a voice incensed by alienation, intolerance, injustice, the lack of freedom, hunger, pain, all the sufferings of an anxious world. It was this "voice of one crying in the wilderness," a voice which sensitized persons to the need for change, which prodded a lethargic society to a humane posture. The prophetic voice was contextual. It did not cry for eternal truth but for solutions to problems which caused suffering. It was the voice of conscience. A new moral sense with new values arose from the past. Every historical era was a stage for furthering anew developments in peace and justice. Time brought forth new prophets in the service of new causes. Reconstructed by Hegelian thought, a liberal Judeo-Christian religious tradition became intellectually attractive. Its themes of the equality of persons, social justice, human well being, and so on, recognized that religious institutions have the potential to be agents of change. A coalition of progressive thinkers which included both the secular and sacred sides of society could come together to initiate social progress. Freedom, justice and fair-play, peace and many other themes became shared goals.

The pragmatics of action, however, brought about incongruent attitudes. Social action was idealistically pure in the notion that society could be changed for a rationally determinable "better." Its pragmatic side could not be so innocent. Whatever worked to bring about change was good. How does one choose between violence and passive resistance?[52] Violence was not given to harmony but to domination, a condition for alienation. But presume that reality unfolded itself in alienation and eventual conciliation; violence merely became the occasion for future reconciliation. Intrinsically, violence had positive moral significance. Passive resistance worked the same way. It was a matter of strategy and practical experience as to whether passive resistance actually worked more quickly with better results than violence.

Religious moralists who adopted a Hegelian position were non-judgmental with respect to those values from which no oppressive results seemed to flow. Value, both good and evil, was the effect of social forces. Since there was no "original" sin—all "sin" was derived—individual persons remained guiltless in what they did and believed. Given dialectical logic, one must be open to all of life's possibilities. Since religious claims of eternal morality or the divine origins of value were themselves culturally produced, what was left was increasing moral sensitivity and moral progress. Thus, if the Bible condemns homosexuality, armed with claims about the randomness of sexual preference (like being born with tendencies to left or right handedness), the judgments of the past are dismissed by their cultural narrowness. Prejudice against "alternative lifestyles" were unwarranted. Thus, the oppression of homosexuals brings opposing forces to life with their calls for reconciliation. Regarding negative values which generate oppression, the role of church and synagogue was to be the leading edge of social change and conciliation.

Those enamored with Hegelian thought found it difficult in principle to condemn the lives of sincere people. If change were the reality of being, any idea or practice which was antithetical to prevailing custom became a needed dialectical yeast to bring about change and the moral improvement of a future society. The eventual effect of Hegelian philosophy in religious liberalism was that of promoting caring, loving relationships without regard to matters of dogma or moral truth. Sincere commitments were to replace dogma and morality. An enlightened culture was to appreciate social diversity. Values were products of social need. Value structures were responses to historical circumstances. Though contextual, values were the serious instruments of decision-making.[53] Once in place, they could also become the stuff of intellectual analysis, enabling persons to rationalize their activities and fortify their interests. "Rationalize" is the right word here, for human judgments reflected and represented the life necessities of dialectical movement. The particular value structures of any given era were devised to reflect the conditions of life. With this picture of human and social reality, the stance of people toward values was not to defend their absolute truth. Values possessed no absolute truth.

Nothing absolute existed except dialectical movement. If a value adversely affected human beings, knowledge of its social causes could be the first step in changing a society, thus eliminating the negative. If values were transitory, religion's role was not to defend any particular status quo. It was to bring about God's kingdom of peace and justice by using religion as a catalyst for change. The character of Christianity was transformed. Religion had something to do. Religion maintained respectability by becoming dialectically involved in the affairs of life.

## Respectable Religion

The Hegelian theory of dialectical reason gave impetus to social theory and social science. Social transformation could be explained and change effected by understanding and utilizing the force of dialectical reason. Indeed, one ignores scientific canons at one's intellectual peril insofar as science has emerged as the *sine qua non* of intelligent discourse. Religious thinkers who adopted a Hegelian theory saw an opportunity to participate in the broad spirit of the rising science of social reality.

People who embraced Hegelian thought interpreted claims about the divine nature as dialectical rationality at work in time; they were empirical claims. Rather than the naive thought that nature was the spontaneous invention of a divine will, natural and social events were construed as revealing a transcendent dimension through dialectical movement. As they located themselves in the natural world of economics, politics, geography, and social history, people moved toward a heightened sense of rational self-consciousness. The moral life, too, resolved itself as the workings of rational spirit in time. Experience was caught up in the trans-historical design of dialectic which itself had explanatory power, and this design was arguably verifiable in the concrete actuality of historical situations. The religious (spiritual) reality of life could be reaffirmed, and religion's traditional forms appreciated because of their reflection of and contribution to the self-awareness of reason.

Christianity could complement the scientific mind. It need not treat its claims in a literal way. It need not anthropomorphize God or mythologize nature. One ignored science's capacity to authenticate the truth of its conclusions at the risk of losing intellectual viability. In Christianity, those willing to become scientific in their thinking and those who refused to do so created, respectively, liberalism and fundamentalism.[54] Unwilling to suffer intellectual ignominy, liberal Christianity used Hegel's thought to impart philosophical respectability to Christianity. Science posed no threat to the Christian liberal. Dialectically, both science and religion were necessary. Reason emanated from every facet of nature and history. Every idea, thing, or event was an expression of a deeper, underlying reality. Thus, for instance, a comparison of psychology and religion found them sharing the common aim of making a person whole, to "feel at home in the world." Religion spoke of sin, psychology of guilt. Both sought release to a fuller life unhampered by feelings of inadequacy. And what might "the fuller life" involve?—the need to feel accepted and loved. Training in Christianity looked to psychology for support. What could be more intellectually respectable?

## Religious Activities

The principles of social science introduced a way in which liberal Christianity could become an instrument of psychological health or social change. Christianity need no longer be intellectually irrelevant. It had something to do. Not only would social progress be its goal, but personal mental health as well would be augmented through religion's "spiritual" dimension. Religious people worked for humanistic good.[55] The good life was one of service, reconciliation, love, justice. Such "doing" was not done in general; it was specific. One must understand the actual workings of people and society. Scientific methodology would unleash God's power in the world.

The following examples illustrate how contemporary Christian religious discourse took over the Hegelian world view for its own purposes.[56] How would one fight against a general disinterest in the problem of hunger? An article written for clergy advises:

> Only as we work at this problem will we learn and will we earn the right to enter the arena [of fighting the lethargy concerning the problem of hunger]. This is a very proper task for the church in ... this century. The plight of two thirds of a malnourished humanity in a threatened biosphere suggests that this is proper work.[57]

Coming to grips with world hunger is religious work because it addresses human alienation and suffering. Such problems are of equal concern to a "secular" world, since from a Hegelian perspective, a "sacred/secular" distinction is arbitrary. The religiously unconcerned equally may act out of humanitarian concerns. God doesn't choose sides when directing his Will to solving problems. The difficulty for committed clergy was to sensitize church people and those in positions of authority to human need. Those robed in God's spirit saw themselves as stimuli in dialectical movement, irritants attempting to influence public policy respecting food management programs. Thus, in the case at hand, church people should make

> their concerns visible by signing an appeal to Congress that the Right to Food resolution ... be brought to a hearing rather than remaining bottled up in congressional committees. They also suggested numerous [other] ways in which the church might influence U. S. policy.[58]

The range of concern represented by "other ways" was not narrow: related problem areas included

> military spending, food stamps, domestic-foreign land use, land reform, ownership incentives, people versus profits, ecology, appropriate technologies, government attitudes toward changing life styles, energy conservation and utilization, aid for emergencies, reduction of production, unemployment/welfare/food stamps, nutrition, water use, population, world view of survival systems, theology of a new vision of humanity in the world.[59]

The ever-widening circle of study generated as each particular of this list was attacked, too, would need study as part of the food supply problem. Study would prepare the way for concrete action and a dialectically transformed life.

Good nutrition was a problem. But how did this issue become appropriate for religious concern?

> The need is to set at liberty the oppressed. We, as a community of Christian people around the world, must see ourselves as midwives giving birth to new life. We have a choice to try to make it or to cop out. We have to rally the troops. Policy will give us a conceptual framework in a theological and ethical construct within which we can work as midwives in the process of swinging orientation from profit and power to survival.[60]

Note the elements of Hegel, especially the rallying cry of "liberty" sanctified by the allusion to scripture. Oppression and the drive to free the human spirit is of the very stuff of the dialectic at work in history. In the midst of conflict, a promise of the synthesis appears—birth and new life. The Idea would awaken the multitude; reason would dawn into an articulate consciousness. Since a starving humanity can never be what it was meant to be without solving "the hunger problem," and since God "wants" the full actualization of every human personality, eating well becomes a religious calling.

If agrarian realities are suitable for religious discourse, so are political realities. It is God's will that human freedom prevails. Introduce the name, "God," into work against human rights violations and economic injustice, and by that token political issues became religious ones. Social injustice choked God's will—rights violations and economic inequality. Life's religious role was to oppose the offending conditions. Change for good required change in "the system." Corrective acts became religious ones when enacted by persons seized by divine Spirit. They were prophetic, the righteous ones; they possessed a caring conscience.

> God is at work among us, in our little systems.... Systems can be changed by forces.... With God's help, we must seek, find, and work to change the systems for the betterment of ... people.[61]

As situations are lived through, whatever generates rancor in a system will come to light, that to be tempered by its being overcome in a new rational structure. Life does not end here, either—"New occasions teach new duties." Thus, the above writer says,

> The role of the church in poor communities, among people who are suffering deprivation and powerlessness, can be a crucial one in reversing trends toward further disenfranchisement and despair. As community members and church members interact ..., the historic role of the church as redeemer can surge to a new prominence.[62]

The poor in spirit, those who mourn, the meek will never receive their redemption until dialectical confrontation brings about the inauguration of God's kingdom. The method is at hand when one understands the nature of reality in a Hegelian manner. Political activity to correct the violation of human rights by witting or unwitting oppressors and a transformation of economic society in the name of a more equitable distribution of wealth must become the source of hope and comfort for the disenfranchised and oppressed. The Biblical kingdom of God is seen as the symbolic representation of man's activity to bring about social justice and goodness.

The church is called to continue its involvement in the process of enabling the self-development of peoples and the creation of a world at peace.[63]

"Involvement" means engaging in those activities which change political and social systems.

> There will be no peace with justice unless liberation is gained by those who have been manipulated and victimized by interests that have been willing to profit from the continued deprivation of the weak and the powerless. But, the oppressor needs to be liberated as truly as the oppressed. Liberation affects the whole person. It is salvation; it is humanization. It is social, economic, political and spiritual. It calls for the structural implementation of those values announced by our Lord when he said he had come that the "broken victims" of life might "go free" (see Luke 4:18).[64]

Religious sensitivities (molded by the Hegelian spirit) brought God's will into concrete reality by overcoming "oppressing" systems which trammelled human rights. Practical suggestions for achieving God's will in the fight against injustice included seeking elective political office, lobbying legislative bodies and state officials, and infiltrating advisory boards. Suffering dialectically ignites a drive toward freedom. The church is a social redeemer. It encourages the self-development of people and the liberation of the human spirit. Once Hegelian philosophy took root in the Christian mind, social action became the task of the religiously motivated person.

God's full nature only came into being in time, merged into human consciousness. Consciousness embodied itself socially as definite economic, political, attitudinal structures. God's will thus came into being socially through the continual readjustment of social structures to ever greater rational harmony. The political and socio-economic sphere was the sanctuary for worship, at least for those knowledgeable church people possessing the Hegelian view of existence.

## Conclusion

Hegelian thought provided another philosophical matrix for locating religious concerns. Unlike the philosophical theories of rationalism and empiricism which molded religion, unlike the definition of religion as something required to complete a Kantian morality, Hegelian theorizing was naturally religious in its concept. Its far-reaching theory of reality as dialectical Reason evolving in time would spawn equivalent religious affirmations of the reality of God. God was known in human society through dialectical movement in time. It was a reality discoverable in scientific terms, through social science. The human spirit emerged in self-consciousness and was freed to seek self-fulfillment in rational existence. The first struggling effort at self-awareness was articulated through religion's symbols and became refined by a modern psychological and social consciousness. The exposed symbol further freed consciousness. Religion now could take the aura of scientific and social respectability. The facilitator of Reason's dialectical expansion, Christianity would participate in activities aimed at human well-being. The "social gospel" was born; Christianity remained a "timely religion."

The divine and man, good and evil, the present and future were all facets of Hegelian religious/philosophical aspirations. Hegel provided the seduction of speculative answers to questions of reality and human existence. Philosophy gave substance to religion; religion supplemented the truth of philosophy. The question not asked was whether religion has a sense of its own. It is an unthought assumption that without philosophy, religion would be vacuous. It took Soren Kierkegaard's disavowal of the connection between philosophy and religion to see what is philosophical and what is intrinsic to the idea of religion. We turn next to Kierkegaard.

## Notes

1. GWF Hegel, *Reason in History,* translated by Robert S. Hartman. Copyright ©1953 by Macmillan College Publishing Company, Inc., p. 13. [This book was published posthumously and is a compilation of Hegel's lecture notes and extensive class notes by two of Hegel's students. The text first appeared around 1837.]

2. It remains to be seen whether the metaphysical writings of Alfred North Whitehead (1861-1947) will have an enduring effect. Although "process" theologians have traced out implications of Whitehead's philosophy for the religious life, most of the philosophical community is disinterested in Whitehead. Nevertheless, time has not yet rendered its judgment of the lasting value of Whitehead for either philosophy or religion.

3. To call Kant or Hegel idealists revises earlier notions of the nature of ideas. From Plato through the modern rationalists (e.g., Descartes, Spinoza, Leibnitz) "ideal" referred to an objective rational structure existing independently of consciousness. Material things partook of its perfection. With Kant there can be no knowledge of an ideal world external to consciousness. It is consciousness itself which endows knowledge with its own idea structures.

4. Such a critique was formed by Friedrich Heinrich Jacobi (1743-1819).

5. (Oxford and New York: Oxford University Press, 1983), p. 50.

6. *Ib*. p. 52.

7. *Reason in History*, p. 11. This book constitutes his lecture notes (cross-checked with the notes of some students who at the time took his course). Although he writes on religion elsewhere, what religion finds to be decisively influential is contained here.

8. *Ib*. p. 12. Note the groundwork laid for what was to become a pervasive tool of theological hermeneutics: God is revealed in history.

9. Thus, the logical "law of identity" (which asserts that a thing is itself: A←→A), the "law of excluded middle" (a thing is either itself or not itself: A v -A), and the "law of non-contradiction" (a thing cannot be both itself and not itself: -(A & -A), were regarded not merely as logical truths, self-evident in their universality, but indeed as laws of being, ordained by God.

10. In other words, the genuine expression of existence is conceived in terms of contradiction (A & -A) instead of the abstraction of non-contradiction, -(A & -A).

11. *Ib*. p. 34f.

12. *Ib*. p. 34.

13. *Ib*. p. 31.

14. *Ib*. p. 26.

15. *Ib*. p. 26.

16. *Ib*., p. 21.

17. *Ib*.

18. *Ib*., p. 69f.

19. *Ib*., p. 89f.

20. *Ib*., p. 94. Utilizing Hegelian dialectic, Karl Marx likewise offered a general theory of the manner in which historical situations created value in his analysis of capitalism. Marx rejected Hegel's idea of "World Spirit" and instead argued that matter needed no additional explanatory device. It behaved dialectically because of its own nature.

21. Hegel's "Preface" to his *Phenomenology of Spirit*, tr. A. V. Miller (Oxford and New York: Oxford University Press, 1977, orig., 1807), provides an analysis of Kant's problem of the thing-in-itself. I only touch at the solution.

22. *Reason in History*, p. 39.

23. Dialectic feeds the human ego. Are we not indeed a more knowledgeable culture than those which have gone before? Yet, who is this "we"? It applies to the whole, not the individuals which comprise it. There is embarrassment here. Why do "barbarians" remain in our midst? Is societal progress in fact illusory?

24. See *Reason in History*, p. 43f.

25. Karl Marx, whose thought was shaped by the Hegelian dialectic, rejected Hegel's idea of "World Spirit." Matter behaved dialectically because of its own nature and needed no additional explanatory devices by way of World Spirit. I use his analysis of capitalism to illustrate how the material world created value. This analysis is also helpful in seeing how the idea of dialectic works. We begin with his recognition that in capitalism, private wealth is created by profit. It is important to keep in mind what profit is. It is what is left over after *all* the costs of business (including the salary a capitalist might give himself as a manager) are subtracted from income. This surplus money has "no strings attached" to it. Profit does not represent the costs for the production of wealth. All the capitalist had to do to get it was to own something and exploit its capacity to gain more in sales than it cost to produce the item. Profit was the unattached, "free" money, of what was left over after subtracting the costs of doing business.

The owner of this money, the capitalist, could use it for whatever purposes pleased him—addition to his income, reinvestment as capital (to manufacture greater future profits), bonuses, distribution as dividends, contributions to charity, and so on.

Marx thought the capitalist system exploitive. He argued that labor created wealth. Thus, the excess money created by unrewarded labor shortchanged the working person for his/her efforts. The worker none the less would serve a capitalist master rather than starve. Since workers viewed their survival as dependent on capitalist prosperity in the marketplace, they were torn in their loyalties. Willing to allow the suppression of their wages to assure capitalist success—without profit, the capitalist would terminate production—they nevertheless clamored for their own well-being. From the capitalist viewpoint, workers were needed for the production of goods on which profits depend, so the capitalist paid wages great enough to allow the worker to continue to live. However, if workers managed to earn excessive wages, they might invest their discretionary funds, accumulating capital for themselves, thus to compete in business. The prospect of increased competition was not attractive, for competition not only holds down profits but threatens the existence of marginal producers. Wages sufficient for subsistence but not wealth was all the worker could expect. The owners of capital thus enriched themselves off the sweat of labor. Herein an entire realm of values, both negative and positive, is created.

Survival was the worker's motive for resignation to life's unfairness, but as well the capitalist himself had to survive a social situation which was indifferent to his success, so the worker had reason to be pacified by the half loaf. Costs had to be minimized in order for profit to be maximized.

Socially altruistic goals designed into a capitalist system in the final analysis were compromised by the motives for producing them. Public social pressure created the laws mandating clean air, and although perhaps appeased by assurances of short- versus long-run advantages of the ecological future, the risk to the profitability of involved companies was generally not something they would have chosen for themselves.

Since a multifaceted life of exploitation made up the fabric of the economic system, it likewise structured the value system. Although the Marxist account of reality ruled out the Enlightenment "individual" as a real entity, it becomes a social fiction dedicated to serving a capitalist ideology, one which had revolutionary effect in the period of time surrounding the initiation of the nineteenth-century.

In fact, thought Marx, persons were social beings whose behavior was shaped by the surrounding "material conditions of life." Illustrative of this idea is his attitude toward crime. As exploitation was a necessary value in a capitalist society, one could expect to find a parallel expression in crime. Profit was 'something for nothing; so was crime. Inasmuch as criminal behavior threatened the stability of capitalist organizations, the value expressions against crime took a spiritual turn by appealing to the idea of individual self-control. In opposition, Marx argued that the society was itself responsible for the creation of criminals, that the capitalist ideology which saw individuals responsible for their own lives was mistaken.

As is inevitable in the dialectical organization of history, the idea of "the individual" is double edged. The capitalist must be an individual, free to exploit. This individual became divinely endowed with freedom and rights as universal values. These spiritual entitlements for the few enlivened a democratic spirit in the many. Freedom and rights were broadened in their meanings to include the interests of workers, practically expressed in the oppressed worker's to unionize or in laws to control trade, competition, and development. The ideology established to secure capitalism's stability eventually, dialectically, transformed it.

For those who veered from behavioral norms, "freedom and rights" became the absolute value used to justify eccentricity and opposition. Values were not eternal verities. All people were equally deserving of life's advantages, as these were defined by the moment. Feelings of exploitation bred tension, and given the dialectical structure of history, persons sought release from their perceived oppression. To void life of its tension, the economic system had to be modified—communized to rid it of exploitation.

In the new society, what would freedom mean? How would persons view themselves? Freedom could no longer mean the right to exploit, for there would be no advantage to be gained since all equally owned the means of production. Rather, Marx described the transformed idea of freedom as

> socialized mankind, the associated producers, [regulating] their interchange with Nature rationally, [to bring] it under their common control, instead of being ruled by it as by some blind power, and [accomplishing] their task with the least expenditure of energy and under such conditions as are proper and worthy for human beings.

When searching for an example in American experience which might be something like the communism Marx had in mind, one might consider the public school system. It is controlled by a school board which is elected by the public and is responsible to both public and teachers. The teachers' interests are guided by bringing the world of learning in the best possible ways to their charges—the institutionalization of rationality. No one anticipates "getting rich" because of such public service; neither do they suffer.

What was devised to justify capitalism, freedom and rights, became the vehicle for its transformation. Against capitalistic maneuvering, Marx's "blind power," genuine freedom arose in rationally planning for human needs. In order to find ways to retain the benefits of profit-created wealth while overcoming the enslavement of persons, Marx called for a synthesis to overcome alienation: replace capitalist economic structure with an economic system which was collectively owned (commune-ism). Human needs would be satisfied through a planned economy, and there would be an attendant benefit in improvements in social awareness.

A planned economy would represent freedom, a new value in which (instead of individual freedom) rational and collective planning was a collective freedom. The values of individualism ceased. Competition for personal advantage through exploitive relationships would not be part of the idea of a planned economy. The motivations which conditioned crime would cease. Rather than an emphasis on a competitive individualism, a collective concern for the functioning of the total society would produce a humanism of global proportions. Individuality lost its value. Functioning in the collective situation gained its value.

26. Religious language is very often understood symbolically. For instance, what is being claimed when Christian scripture asserts that Jesus Christ is the Son of God? In a contemporary idiom, no literal account will suffice to give sense to these words. Thus, to understand their meaning, one must first understand the context for their use and then translate their use into a contemporary setting. Scripture's depiction of the life of Jesus as God's son became interpreted as the humanization of the divine life portrayed in the categories of human experience. Like Socrates, Jesus was martyred, crucified, in behalf of truth.

Each major concept required interpretation if its sense were to receive credibility in the contemporary ear. Even anti-religious Freud resolved religious language into appropriate, psychological components.

What typically characterizes the attempt to understand religious language is a presumption that it contains a reality to be known, though one which might more adequately be approached in language that overcomes its earlier mythical consciousness. But as correct or insightful as such analyses can be, there is something misleading about them, too. I argue in Chapter VI that religious language is more than symbolic; it is existential.

27. *Reason in History*, p. 47.

28. Both empiricism and rationalism view words as sounds standing for a more fundamental reality—images, ideas, things. This pervasive thought that words represent things makes us want to look for the thing that represents "God." It is a mistaken view that words name. Martin Heidegger (1889-1976), Maurice Merleau-Ponty (1908-1961), and Ludwig Wittgenstein (1889-1951), to name three, offer analyses that challenge the more traditional view of language as something symbolic.

29. In this century, the liberal education of the clergy presumes that psychology and sociology are necessary tools (more practical than the need to understand theology and the scriptures) in "meeting the needs of people." This emphasis, I submit, received its due because of the influences of Hegelian thinking.

30. *Reason in History*, p. 121.

31. In the *Phenomenology of Spirit (op. cit.)* Hegel develops how self-consciousness dialectically reveals itself. The section on "Freedom of Self-Consciousness" is especially instructive. Eventually differing religious outlooks, especially those ideas contained in Christianity (which Hegel interprets as demonstrating the unfolding of dialectical processes, e.g., the Trinity), are included as expressions of the way consciousness unfolds itself. For the particulars of Hegel's assessment of religious life in medieval times, see the part on "the unhappy consciousness" (*op. cit.*, p. 126ff.).

32. Unlike Hume who reveled in the human self-sufficiency of moral awareness, Kant appealed to God, freedom, and immortality to complete moral consciousness. In either case, Hume and Kant complement the general Hegelian thesis of religion's symbolic role in pointing to the divinity of mankind.

The Judeo-Christian tradition conceives persons as inferior to God and completely subject to divine sovereignty. For instance, Job's lament concluded with the verse,

I had heard of thee by the hearing of the ear, but now my eye sees thee; therefore I despise myself and repent in dust and ashes (Job 42:5-6).

Or St. Paul insists that "all have sinned and fall short of the glory of God" (Romans 3:23). Such characterizations lament human nature and conceive of mankind as forever dependent on God. The Judeo-Christian tradition required divine intervention to bring about a state of human redemption. It is my contention that, in contrast to philosophy which makes persons divine, views which begin with human dependence are authentically religious.

33. *Reason in History*, p. 44f.

34. *Ib.*, p. 50f.

35. *Ib.*, p. 52.

36. John H. Yoder's *The Politics of Jesus* (Grand Rapids: William Eerdmans Publishing Co., 1972) advocates the passive resistance techniques of Martin Luther King, for instance, saying that this was Jesus' innovative contribution to the methodology of change.

37. This hymn is found in *The Book of Hymns*, copyright ©1964, 1966 by Board of Publication of the Methodist Church, Inc. Used by permission.

38. From stanza 5, omitting verse 4.

39. From Stanza 11, omitting verse 4.

40. The first four lines are from stanza 13, omitting verses 3-5. The second four lines are from stanza 18, omitting verses 3-5.

41. The first two lines are from stanza 6, verse 3; the remainder is from stanza 8, verses 3-5 with verse 3 modified.

42. The revision of self-understanding laid down by Hegel is influential in the work of the early twentieth-century sociologist, Émile Durkheim. In *The Elementary Forms of Religious Life* (London: George Allen & Unwin, Ltd., 1915) he argues that religion is a reflection of social reality which can be scientifically described in terms of dialectical movement. Scientific understanding will free the mind to achieve its highest potential, not religion. One task of clear thinking, then, is to free oneself of myth. Reveal the mythological attraction of religion, and render it obsolete.

43. Is. 61:1-2; quoted by Jesus in Lk. 4:18-19. Liberal Christianity saw this charge as its essential task. Liberation theology, motivated by the Marxist analysis of history spun from Hegel, centers on these ideas as well.

44. For one group of Biblical scholars (notable among whom in recent times is Oscar Cullmann—see especially his *Christ and Time*, tr. F. Filston [Philadelphia, Westminster Press, 1964]), the notion of *Heilsgeschichte* or God's redemption of his holiness in history is an important hermeneutical tool. In general such scholars believe that the events of Biblical importance demonstrate God's saving work in ancient history. This notion is extended to claim that there is every reason to suppose that even contemporary events are used to effect God's work. Though scripture may lend itself to such an interpretation, I'm not so sure that it is a helpful view of scripture or the religious life. An alternative, non-philosophical context for viewing scripture is proposed in the concluding chapters of this work.

45. I believe that this hermeneutical approach, though attractive, distorts (what I take to be) the religious thrust of the Bible. One who thinks in terms of *Heilsgeschichte* has a much too philosophical view of the religious underpinnings of Judeo-Christian thinking. In the face of the grander theme of salvation history, the existential theme of *agape* in the New Testament diminishes in significance. Where *agape* is used as the hermeneutical feature of the New Testament, however, one can make sense of the points of tension with the surrounding Jewish culture which would indicate that it abides in that same existential hermeneutic.

46. *Reason in History*, p. 69.

47. *Ib.*, p. 48.

48. The dialectical movement of reality forbad the superiority of any particular religion or morality, inasmuch as value is a function of circumstances. An implication of this position is that there can be no moral sin. Rather than "sin," persons commit indiscretions, suffer error, are negligent or are thoughtless, and so on. The positive side finds sincerity as a prime value. Sincerity becomes an overriding value in moral strivings since there isn't something ultimate which needs to be taken seriously.

49. Hegel believed Christianity to have moved further down the path. For instance, the Jewish God of anthropomorphic proportions was too parochial. Christianity moved to a God of global proportions where Jesus is spoken of in terms of "spirit" as well as flesh. The incarnation resolved spirit and matter into the person of Jesus, overcoming the dialectical tension between the two facets of creation. Hegel regarded this as progress over those religions which held to an absolute gulf between mankind and the divine.

50. This commonplace line of reasoning concerning the "moral law" was developed by turn-of-the-century thinkers such as Émile Durkheim (sociology), William Graham Sumner (anthropology), and Sigmund Freud (psychology).

51. Anti-sexist concerns likewise illustrate the point. In the phrase "the brotherhood of man" (and it is completed with the words, "under the fatherhood of God"—in toto, a popular religious cliche of the mid-twentieth century) women might become alienated from the general sense of divine goodness by the masculine grammar of the phrase. To subdue the alienation created in such apparent insensitivity toward women, language needed revision. It's not that the generic sense of "man" could not be understood. But lurking beneath the masculine text is the subconscious perpetuation of female subservience, a form of alienation which requires the reformation of language, if not into a gender neutral form ("a mutual respect of all persons for each other") at least into something inclusive ("the brotherhood and sisterhood of persons").

52. Such a debate occurs within liberation theology. How aggressive does the Christian faith permit one to be in the causes of social change?

53. When there can be no absolute moral standards, the ethical "expert" emerges as a logical consequence of the Hegelian position. Ethical experts arise when one must think through the diversity of values that erupt as responses to diverse situations and cultures. People become trained as "experts" to think through value questions. Among other things they aim to diminish the risk of bias or parochialism in moral thinking. It is assumed that the ordinary person's moral intuitions may be inadequate or flawed because such a person is not trained to see the whole picture. Ethical "think tanks" arise to focus on value questions in society (spun by medical technology for example); professional "ethicists" give advice (to business leadership for instance) about whether position "a" or "b" is more ethical. The persons receiving the services of such

"ethicists" have the assurance that since their choice has been "scientifically" appraised, they possess the advantage of diminished responsibility for choices made.

54. Christianity persisted in claims about a triune divine nature, made assertions about the supernatural intervention in natural events, portrayed human existence in terms of sin/salvation, and offered declarations about supernatural rewards and punishments. These and the like purported to inform us about the divine order of being. But how could the truth of such statements be checked? Such thinking was a remanent of pre-scientific thought which in its simple-mindedness had seduced uncritical people.

As the successes in understanding the physical world multiplied, and we saw natural cause at work in the social and mental facets of life, the possibility of understanding life through a religious outlook was diminished to little and then to nothing. The natural world was the limit of thought and certainty. Verifiability in experience and pragmatic workability were the measures of truth. Were fundamentalism to attempt to adopt some measure of scientific analysis (perhaps as was found in its claims regarding creationism) such science inevitably invoked an exercise of Ockham's Razor. There were more suitable explanations and postulates to be supplied in natural models. Religious theorizing became superfluous, inadequate, unnecessary, or simply wrong with respect to natural and human experience.

55. Numerous Christian hymns bear witness to the Christian theme of "work." In modern times a confluence of factors could be cited apropos of the urge to work. The theme persists, however. I cite the first lines of some verses: "Lead on, O King Eternal, The day of march has come," "Onward, Christian soldiers!" "Hark, the voice of Jesus calling, 'Who will go and work today?'" "Go, labor on! spend and be spent; Thy joy to do the Father's will," "Work, for the night is coming," "We thank Thee, Lord, Thy paths of service lead to blazoned heights and down the slopes of need," and many others.

56. These quotations are taken from an ecclesiastical journal, *The Interpreter*, a program journal for The United Methodist Church. American liberal protestantism will be typified by the sorts of statements found in this journal. Equivalent statements could be found in the pronouncements of other liberal churches.

57. "Solve the Hunger Problem," *The Interpreter*, 20:7 (July, August, 1976), p. 7.

58. *Ib.* p. 8.

59. *Ib.*

60. *Ib.*

61. "New Hope for Appalachia," *The Interpreter*, 21:2 (February, 1977) p. 34.

62. "Expressing Christian Concern," *The Interpreter*, 20:10 (November, December, 1976), p. 16.

63. "Equal Rights and Justice for All," *The Interpreter*, 20:8 (September, 1976), p. 6.

64. *Ib*. This remark comes from the 1972 General Conference of the United Methodist Church as contained in the "Bishops' Call for Peace and the Self-Development of Peoples."

# Part II: The Existing Individual and Religion

## Chapter VI

---

# The Logic of Being a Subject[1]

> [P]hilosophy teaches that the way is to become objective, while Christianity teaches that the way is to become subjective, i.e. to become a subject in truth.[2]
>
> *Concluding Unscientific Postscript*
> Kierkegaard

## Uncertainty and Objectivity

Philosophical concepts and distinctions influenced religious thinking with regard to what made sense and what made no sense: about divinity, the soul and immortality, good and evil, religious knowledge and experience, faith and reason, God in time, personal meaning, history's purpose, to begin a list.[3] As each philosophy imposed its own test for intelligibility, it yielded a corresponding religious impulse which sought a philosophical imprimatur. Christian thought became the sycophant of philosophy. It justified itself in terms specified by philosophy.[4]

Open to advances in philosophical reasoning, religious apologetics enhanced their own credibility concerning ideas of "God" by virtue of philosophical theories of knowledge and reality.[5] A "God" that bolstered ancient metaphysical concerns about first causes and global rationality was worthy of being a Christian god.[6] When ancient philosophy developed the relationships of reasons and causes, the stuff of an objective, intellectual world, early Christian thinkers found the truth of Christianity in these same positions. After all, philosophy's prerogative was to determine the legitimacy or acceptability of all truth, and even Christians possess a natural urge to want to be right.

As the conceptual vehicles of religious life became antiquated in view of advancing philosophical requirements for "relevance," new theological viewpoints were demanded[7] in order to remain on the purported "cutting-edge" of thinking. By the mid-eighteenth century, religious thought was pulled in several directions. Initially, the grip of the ancient notion of rational perfection which regulated medieval religious speculations went limp under Newton's Laws of Motion, the Cartesian starting point of a thinking individual, and the appeal to knowledge by experience alone. Metaphysical speculations were displaced by the new rationalism and modern empiricism. Humanity's faith in its own power to discover objective truths, truths by which its possessors could judge, cajole, evaluate, and live, came to dominate religion's claims and practices.

Thus, as empiricist beliefs reshaped what "truth" meant, the empirical religious thinker rejected metaphysical speculation, conveniently finding elements in inner experience that pointed to the existence of God, if in no more than the experiences of wonder and awe. Kant tied an objectively definable morality to religion, arguing that the moral life required religion's concepts for its completion. Hegel's "truth" unfolded itself as dialectical rationality which legitimized the social activism of Christian thinkers. Human hands became divine, helping to bring about God's kingdom on earth.[8] Religious philosophers and theologians found innovative ways to reflect the demands of any philosophy. Christian thinkers could pick up the threads of philosophical order and, keeping with the times, "stay abreast of truth."

Touched by theories of reality, religious people cherished the hope for objective truth and leapt to join them. Ideas breathed life into people, and philosophy assured them that commitment to objective truth would save them from mere existence. Ideas—scientific and logical ones as well as those bearing on the religious, ethical, political, and aesthetic—became the abode for living. Ideas, anchored and sustained by cultural familiarity, would give people reference points for their activities and reflections. Shaped by philosophical reasoning and its requirements for objective truth, religious thinking remained malleable, amendable by novel intellectual theories. Christianity gave itself up to objectivity. But an irony emerged: religion itself became problematic.

An overarching philosophical urge for objectivity made religion its prey: make the sense of life include follow-feelings, an adequately comfortable existence, artistic joy, political stability and justice, individual respect, and the like, and the motivation for religion merges with humanizing urges of all mankind. The religious quest was seen merely as one more expression of a parade of ideas, all of which sought truth.[9] It, too, was a piece of social history explained by the commitments and goals, knitting and unraveling of an intellect itself captured by "whys" and "hows" of a particular age. There was nothing intrinsic to religion which could not be requisitioned elsewhere from the wealth of social existence. There could be heroes, doctrines, offices, rituals, and mental health in non-religious settings. Social programs established on humanitarian grounds could effect the same goals as a Christian concern for the well-being of persons. Religious perspectives became one of many ways of imputing meaning to human existence. The conclusion is inevitable. Religious life becomes an incidental depreciated commodity, a matter of personal taste, psychological need, or social convenience—all this the inevitable consequence of devotion to philosophical objectivity.

As the seductive call for objective truth lured those with religious aspirations to accede to truth's demands, the possibility that religion inhabited a region different from philosophy was overlooked. Thus when Soren Kierkegaard probed what is involved in religious concern, he had also to show the inappropriateness of philosophy to religious outlooks. Instead of developing new theories of knowledge and reality, Kierkegaard analyzed what was involved in creating any philosophical theory. The effect was to deflate the significance of philosophical theorizing for Christianity.[10] We look at three facets of Kierkegaard's analysis. First is the particularity of philosophy, second is the impossibility of an existing individual 'thinking God's thoughts after Him,' and third is the role of thought in life.

## The Individual Philosophizing

Human thought was a particular address at a particular time to particular issues, events, problems, or activities, which particular individuals devised, participated in, confronted, and encouraged.

Systems emerged from questions that confounded some particular human being. The thinker stood at the center of theorizing as that presence which created in thought an intellectual world to the measure of the thinker.

Kierkegaard's point can be seen if we turn the statement "There is a reason for everything" (a common presumption at all levels of sophistication) on itself. That rare and skeptic rejoinder: "And what is the reason, then, for there being a reason for everything?" won't be satisfied by a clever responder who might provide a reason. The question is not stayed. If there is a reason for everything, "What's the reason for that?" can always be asked one more time.

> How do I put an end to the reflection which was set up in order to reach the beginning here in question? Reflection has the remarkable property of being infinite. But to say that it is infinite is equivalent, in any case, to saying that it cannot be stopped by itself; because in attempting to stop itself it must use itself, and is thus stopped in the same way that a disease is cured when it is allowed to choose its own treatment, which is to say that it waxes and thrives.[11]

There is no way of justifying the proposition that there is a reason for everything, because the reasoning meant to be the context for getting at reality invites of itself a perpetual questioning. Philosophy can have no rational ending point. What Kierkegaard saw was that thought begins with an individual's doing it, not with a participation in Thought. It is a human activity.

However, if thought is human, then Kierkegaard must show why it is a confusion to think that a philosophical theory can provide a meaning for the existence out of which it came. Philosophical theories are conceptual or organizational ways of looking at things that enable people to make sense of the world lived. We devise methods and concepts that satisfy our interests and curiosities, or render a critique of our understandings in light of new insights. The task of evolving meaning reflects what is involved in being human. Collectively, persons bring worlds into their grasp, devise ways of understanding, and reflect on the implications of and conditions for their understanding. When our intellectualizing about the facets of our existence goes further and we argue that some particular way of making sense holds a privileged position in reality, we transcend our humanity and fly thither with the gods. At the point we seek an objective sanction for the sense made, we move away from formulating and evaluating the lived-world to privileging this sort of intellectual world of sense above all others. Kierkegaard objects not to philosophy but to the thought that there is a greater justification of our intellectual activity than the mere fact that we do it.

To place one's faith in philosophical theories which presume to reveal the order of knowledge and reality, one should have certainty regarding the theory's finality. However, finality is checked by the merest *possibility* of refinement, new discoveries, or novelty in thought. The conceivability that a system could be perspectival or modifiable is sufficient to deny that the system is absolute. Kierkegaard spoke to this difficulty in the following way.

> System and finality are pretty much one and the same, so much so that if the system is not finished, there is no system.... [A] system which is not quite finished is an hypothesis; ... to speak of a half-finished system is nonsense.[12]

Kierkegaard's perspective sees hypotheses *used* without the further claim of their being absolute. The implication of being "used" is that human interests are fulfilled; and although one tentatively adheres to the demands of an objective way of understanding existence, the intent of the hypothesis remains pragmatic. In order for a system of reality to be "finished," one must know that the system could not be modified by new data or perspectives. God rightly could claim objective finality for a theory; but by what measure of certainty could one assert that the system whereby one understands experience is universal, "Existing as he does in his thought"?[13] The appeal of objective truth made a person forget that people were the creators and sustainers of meanings and that the concept of "objective" was intrinsic to a system, not external to it. That something is thought provides context for the multiplication of meanings, all of which are human artifacts reflecting a dialectical grappling with life. Persons fortify their thoughts, only on another occasion to return to destroy them. Nevertheless, persons will posit an objective system[14] and forgetfully thrust themselves into its defining web, claiming that this thinking is representative of and intrinsic to the structure of being.[15] People defined themselves by the efficacy of a philosophical system. They imagined themselves reporters in the service of the system. Asks Kierkegaard,

> 'Who is to write or complete such a system?' Surely a human being ..., an existing individual.[16]

> It is therefore an existing spirit who is now conceived as raising the
> question of truth, presumably in order that he may exist in it; but in
> any case the question is raised by someone who is conscious of being
> a particular existing human being.[17]
>
> ... [I]t is an existing spirit who asks the question, a wholly individual
> human being.[18]

If persons define the issues, pose questions relevant to these issues, and
answer the questions they pose, then the entire conceptual world is a
creature of their own devising. Persons remain at the core of the
defined world. They can never place themselves in the position of
breaking out of what they do conceptually. Thus when they argue for
the objective truth of a philosophical theory, they make the conceptual
world something it is not: a world independent of people's sense
making; and they make of persons something they are not: the authors
of absolute certainty. It is this contrast that Kierkegaard has in mind in
juxtaposing the thinker with what is thought.

> I hold some person responsible for refusing to end the reflective pro-
> cess. And this means, does it not, that I require him to do something?
> ... And what is it that I require of him? I ask him for resolve. And in
> so doing I do well, for in no other way can the process of reflection be
> halted.... But if a resolution of the will is required to end the pre-
> liminary process of reflection, the presuppositionless character of the
> System is renounced. Only when reflection comes to a halt can a begin-
> ning be made, and reflection can be halted only by something quite dif-
> ferent from the logical, being a resolution of the will.[19]

Philosophical thought originates in the "resolution of the will."

Kierkegaard succinctly stated the relationship between what we
know and our existence in the remark "All understanding comes after
the fact."[20] The "fact" in this context is that of human existence. In
other words, out of the grapplings of human existence, questions arise.
There is no Reason of the Hegelian sort seeking to unfold itself.
Rather, caught up in life in such a way that various matters become
perplexities for the person, an existing individual calls forth explanations. Explanation is appropriated in terms deemed applicable to human
interests. What we mean by understanding something, then, depends on
the manner in which we exist as persons.

If "all understanding comes after the fact of human existence," then
the recognition that the sense we forge is our deed makes the existing
individual the source of the meanings and reasonings which comprise

the intellectual enterprise. At the point of creating sense, there is no philosophy; there is only the practical task of forging these meanings which became the conceptual world we live. Like God whose Word creates, an individual creates out of his word. Meaning is wrestled from chaos. This capacity to raise and answer questions singles out the human species. Ideas define us as we bring them into being through our authorship. Yet we stand outside our creation, for even the edifices of explanation which we erect are subject to erosion by criticism. The ideas in whose terms we live and which wrap our lives into their sense point only to the creative power of human beings and not beyond.[21] The "whys" and "hows" of explanation perpetually pull meaning into ever new and cogent unities, leaving the question of a final objective truth in suspension.

In contrast to that objectivity which uncovers the structure of reality and man's place in it, Kierkegaard sought ways to confront the ungrounded life of a question-asker.[22] He began with the involvements of raising a question—it is not the objective world of philosophical measures which is to be held in question, but rather man as a question-asker is himself held in question. The old propensities toward universal design and consistency, objectification through experience, or the integrations of disparate elements into a unified whole are merely ways of willing an intellectual existence. Creative proposals for understanding one's existence can be dissipated in amended thought as intellectual attainments crumble before the tectonic forces of re-evaluation, criticism, and revision. The variegations of thought become the receding horizon of philosophy. Though the power and dignity of ideas gain in plausibility in their capacity to fend off criticism, new ideas vie with old, hoping to supplant them. There is much about which to be serious, but there is no way of gaining the final objectivity which such seriousness requires. Nevertheless, the thinker who accepts the provisional quality of ideas is still bound to finitude, and there is nothing in this existence which can become the object of understanding without falling victim to its tentativeness. Thinking is not the fulfillment of the demands of abstract reason, sensation, or dialectic. It is a life-task. Persons engage in the practical affair of making sense; they form conceptual worlds. If their conceptual commitments are designed to satisfy manipulating the natural world, and if whatever ends the person finds interesting are being achieved in view of some understanding of what is involved in being successful, then nothing more need be required in terms of the practical affairs of living. The world one lives is satisfied.[23] Systems are occasioned by questions which have no systematic origin but are formulated—created—in the presence of lived concerns. In looking at the fact of our sense making, we construe systems which are finally "a resolution of the will."[24] That is, the intellectual worlds in which we live are themselves grounded in our interest to make worlds of some sort appear. In this vein, Kierkegaard comments:

> If the System is presumed to come after [human] existence, ... then the system is of course *ex post facto* [formulated or enacted], and so does not begin immediately with the immediacy with which existence began.... The beginning which begins with the immediate is thus itself reached by means of a process of reflection.[25]

Thus, there can be no reason for everything if the necessity of rationality itself cannot be displayed; nor can there be a sensation to inform us of the truth of the claim that all knowledge depends on experience. The essential feature of such humanity is that, despite a passion for absolute truth, one eternally fails to know that one knows it. Ideas have a place and importance in human existence as part of the striving after truth, but there can be no confidence that *human* significance is established in the objectivity of its conclusions, be they in science, politics, sociology, psychology, ethics, or philosophy.

## Left and Right Handedness

Hegel's proclamation of the absolute Truth of dialectic has a kind of validity. The idea of dialectic cannot be refuted, for to do so would demonstrate its necessity: the thesis would have produced an antithesis demonstrating that dialectical reason itself produced its antithesis by dialectical reason. It is a human dream to possess absolute truth. Hegelian idealism swept across the nineteenth-century intellectual world into the twentieth century. Kierkegaard protested.

A human being claiming to know an absolute *philosophical* truth stepped beyond what persons were capable of knowing. In the *Postscript* he cited a passage from Lessing who imagined that God approached someone with the offer to transcend finitude and possess absolute truth.

> If God held closed in his right hand all truth, and in his left hand a persistent, ceaseless, active passion for truth, although with the proviso of

one's continual and eternal erring, and he spoke to me, saying: "Choose!" I would fall before his left hand in humility and say: "Father, let me have that! Pure truth is only for you alone."[26]

Possession of ultimate and objectively certain truth is proper to divine being. It is the perfection of rationalistic metaphysics; such knowledge could not be faulted. Lessing's character rejected the right hand and thus suspended or bracketed objective truth. Rather than be like God, persons remain human—ultimately uncertain. Fallible human knowledge framed a contrast with perfect knowledge. Instead, human ideas exist as the result of "persistent striving." Persistent striving reminds one of one's humanity. To forget this and imagine oneself to possess the right hand reveals an unfortunate confusion. It allows a person to play God. The notion of possessing objective, absolute truth became a human vanity.

Kierkegaard developed a piquant image which mocks the idea in the Hegelian "System" that objective truth is at hand. He writes that

> I shall be as willing as the next man to fall down in worship before the System, if only I can manage to set eyes on it. Hitherto I have had no success; and though I have young legs, I am almost weary from running back and forth between Herod and Pilate. Once or twice I have been on the verge of bending the knee. But at the last moment, when I already had my handkerchief spread on the ground, to avoid soiling my trousers, and I made a trusting appeal to one of the initiated who stood by: "Tell me now sincerely, is it entirely finished; for if so I will kneel down before it, even at the risk of ruining a pair of trousers (for on account of the heavy traffic to and fro, the road had become quite muddy),"—I always received the same answer: "No, it is not yet quite finished." And so there was another postponement—of the System, and of my homage.[27]

The issue is whether an intellectual system imparts its objectively valid meaning to human existence. The philosophical tradition thought surely it would. Rationalism defined persons as rational animals, and religious people looked for the rational image of divinity in their souls. The empirical person, a sensate creature, thought he felt the presence of the divine in religious experience. The Kantian person, a volitional animal under the moral constraint of reason, would reach perfection through a perpetual moral striving. The Hegelian divine spirit unloosed a rising self-consciousness in its dialectical force wrought in human acts. History emerged to serve Reason's valiant (though perhaps mysterious)

purposes. Each philosophical theory exacted a view of what was involved in being human and promised a sense for human existence in its
terms. No wonder a religious man might risk a pair of pants to possess
truth. Answer the question "How do I truly know what ultimately is
real?" and one's own existence becomes intelligible. At least this was
the philosophical promise which allowed it easily to seduce religion.

Kierkegaard forced us to linger on the existential uncertainties
regarding the objective truth of a philosophical outlook left dubious in
its capacity to commute sense to human existence. When "the initiated"
could not answer to the completeness of "the System," the alternative
answer, "almost sure," was no assurance at all for the person who has
a life to live.

### The Subject and Objectivity

The person who seeks truth expresses humility in the act of seeking,
for one who seeks does not possess and even with respect to the ideas
on possesses, one maintains a sense of reserve. They are held with
human finitude in view. In a passage characterized by its grasp of the
tension latent in the human capacity for theory building, Kierkegaard
says,

> As soon as it is remembered that philosophizing does not consist in ad-
> dressing fantastic beings in fantastic language, but that those to whom
> the philosopher addresses himself are human beings; ... that the
> question is what existing human beings, in so far as they are existing
> beings, musts needs be content with: then it will be evident that the
> ideal of a persistent striving is the only view of life that does not carry
> with it an inevitable disillusionment.[28]

When we live our lives in terms of ideas, we are persuaded that they
are the defining elements of human existence and that they are crucial
to our being. Yet the very tentativeness of ideas forces us to recognize
that intellectual activity is incapable of providing a final sense to human
existence. Hallowed values and life-determining speculations are
decommissioned, not because any such thought is known to be false but
because of thought's inexhaustible capacity to produce ingenious and
creative ideas—all justified from some standpoint, even though such
ideas may be at cross purposes with each other. There is no finality to
thought. Rather, values and speculations serve the immediacy of human
interests. Thought is thus subject to reassessment and reconsideration.

As such, successful ideological proposals for the redemption of human existence from meaninglessness lie perpetually over the horizon.

"Persistent striving" embraces the human origins of ideas—there is no disillusionment. No claims about "the ultimate nature of things" are made. Finitude bestows on the intellectual world a perpetual expectation of razing the thought which supported the sense of human existence. The decisive feature of this existence is the fact of its meaning-creating activity which when turned inward to provide for its own nature never is powerful enough to trust beyond question. Kierkegaard continually exhorts us to remember that we are "existing human beings." He remarks that

> If the logical thinker is at the same time human enough not to forget that he is an existing individual, even if he completes the system, all the fantasticalness and charlatanry will gradually disappear.[29]

Thus, if systems are human vehicles for creating sense and not reports on that known to be absolute truth, nothing follows of ultimate significance for human existence from within the logic of a system. To think that something did would be "fantastical" and to persist in the thought in the face of the reality of human existence would be "charlatanry." One remains within the confines of existence—thus Kierkegaard's remark: "Truth is subjectivity." One holds fast to being what one is: an existing human being; and objective truth provides no authenticating mark justifying one's life.

Persons themselves remain in the midst of ideas—defiant, yet helpless; powerful, yet meaningless; the creator of reasons, yet unjustified. When the most important ideas can be emptied in the seriousness of reflection about them, the unadorned person is neither affirmed nor denied by ideas. A person is the source of an idea, its progenitor. The person lies beyond its defining power. Thus, any ultimate sacredness or dignity of ideas and values conceived as definitive of human existence must be held in abeyance. The effect of such indeterminacy sustains the intrinsic senselessness of human existence. One brackets philosophy to confront oneself. The focus of traditional philosophy was objectively to ascertain the limits of knowledge and the scope of reality. Following Kierkegaard, many thinkers began to reject philosophical tradition. They redirected the tasks of philosophy along lines laid out by Kierkegaard and inquired into "the logic of being a subject"—into subjectivity.

Kierkegaard saw religion beginning and ending in a reflection on one's existence as a human being—religious language was itself the language of subjectivity. With a broad stroke, Kierkegaard defined two senses for life. There was a sense for objectivity and one for subjectivity. When life became understood in terms of notions of objective truth, penetration of an authentically human existence became distorted, and the religious life with it. The exposition of subjectivity[30] and its implications for understanding religion (particularly Christianity) became the burden of the *Concluding Unscientific Postscript*. Religion was a matter of inwardness or subjectivity; but if this be so, objective, philosophical truth became inappropriate for understanding the religious life—religious concerns were indifferent to philosophical claims.[31]

Kierkegaard was not at all charitable to a view of religion that injected philosophical or cultural concerns into the religious life. If religion were construed (inappropriately) as a cultural response to social needs or seen (mistakenly) as a solution to intellectual problems, one could make no sense of religion.[32] The salutary effects of solving philosophical puzzles or perpetuating a culture were quite a different matter from religion's becoming a "life necessity."[33] The perspective that a religion was a world view, an activity involving the humanization of mankind, a response to psychological need, made of religion merely one more "philosophy of life" clamoring for attention. Adopting views which included divine objects and purposes, sacred acts, or pious stands toward goodness had roots in philosophical pursuits and not religious ones. Approached in terms of the pragmatics of human existence, the person missed what it was that gave rise to religious ideas in the first place. The Kierkegaardian analysis retrieved the uniqueness of religion and removed it from involvements with philosophy. As Kierkegaard showed, it was the state of being human, the sense we have for the finitude of our own existences, that was religiously significant. Religious life gave form to the involvements of subjectivity. Existing individuals remained outside their intellectualizing.

## Subjectivity: On Being Human

Uncertainty concerning the truth of theories of reality or what one thinks about life's meaning left life ungrounded. Nevertheless, the tasks of living continued. In this context Kierkegaard spoke of "faith."

Whenever a beginning is *made* [in the quest for knowledge]...,
unless through being unaware of this the procedure stamps itself

as arbitrary, such a beginning is not the consequence of an immanent movement of thought, but is effected through a resolution of the will, essentially in the strength of faith.[34]

Kierkegaard reoriented "faith." Characteristically, faith was an epistemological faculty used to sustain beliefs left over from the pragmatics and promise of reason and experience. Kierkegaard reversed the relationship. He made the urge to make sense itself the ungrounded project of living in "the left hand" of "a persistent, ceaseless, active passion for truth, although with the proviso of one's continual and eternal erring." One could not provide an ultimate justification for positing reason and experience as foundations of knowledge. Yet one willed an existence shaped by the metaphysics of reason and experience. An unexaminable human existence was philosophy's starting point. Socrates's claim that "the unexamined life is not worth living" presumed standards by which it could be examined; Kierkegaard had no such starting point. There was no a priori appeal to meaningful structures by which human existence and knowledge were to be understood. One was unable to lay a sure foundation for claims to an intrinsic meaning for human existence. Instead of "having faith" in epistemological results, one was condemned to exist as faith. Human existence itself remained outside the systems and ideas devised to explain it. Meaning was the creation of a human willing it.

People saturate the world with meaning; but they cannot fill their own existences with meaning without falsifying their subjectivity in its objectification.

> Objectively, we consider only the matter at issue, subjectively have regard to the subject and his subjectivity; and behold, precisely this subjectivity is the matter at issue. This must constantly be borne in mind, namely, that the subjective problem is not something about an objective issue, but is the subjectivity itself.[35]

Traditionally, philosophy purported to explain why (after all) human existence was meaningful, even though matters were never quite settled by such speculation, because the best of theoretical and speculative resourcefulness was subject to the woes of finitude. Persons foundered on what was important and what was incidental, not being able to distinguish between the two. Asks Kierkegaard,

> If an existing individual were really able to transcend himself, the truth would be for him something final and complete; but where is the point

at which he is outside himself?[36]

Kierkegaard's rumination on this question occurs elsewhere. He says.

> It is commonly assumed that no art or skill is required in order to be subjective. To be sure, every human being is a bit of a subject, in a sense. But now to strive to become what one already is: who would take the pains to waste his time on such a task.... But for this very reason alone it is a very difficult task, the most difficult of all tasks in fact, precisely because every human being has a strong natural bent and passion to become something more and different. ... To think about the simple things of life ... is extremely forbidding; for the differential distinction attainable even through the utmost possible exertion is by no means obvious to the sensual man. No indeed, thinking about the high-falutin is very much more attractive and glorious.

> [P]hilosophy teaches that the way is to become objective, while Christianity teaches that the way is to become subjective, i. e. to become a subject in truth.[37]

For Kierkegaard, theories that in principle promised a meaningful life qualified as "philosophical teachings." In the twentieth-century the social sciences joined philosophy to establish life's meaning. As sciences, psychology, sociology, anthropology, geography, and their allies were to be taken seriously when it came to pronouncements concerning life's meaning. Psychology and sociology teach us how to minimize stress and live together. Economics figures out whether the equitable distribution of wealth is possible, ultimately in order to increase human happiness. Political science looks for ways of political accommodation. With Voltaire's Candide we should stay free of pollyannish philosophy and religion and, "cultivating our garden" through the practical agronomy of the social sciences, pay attention to objective truth.[38] Insofar as they ignore objective social science (so it is said), philosophy and religion at best are intellectual entertainment. Their sort of stabilization of life in terms of divinely sanctioned value stupefies the tasks of satisfying real human need. At least, such is the claim of Marx and Freud, who viewed Christians as praying for peace and awaiting God's Kingdom, expecting miracles and anticipating heavenly reward, instead of producing the scientific work needed to induce social harmony. Religion negated life—it didn't create it.[39] Freud's argument for the impracticality of religion held that everything religion promised, science could deliver. Objective systems would elevate human existence to a sublime point of value. The parameters of "objective" thought were clear enough. As persons evanesced—into natures, roles, society—scientific objectivity would give them existential significance or relevance. It masked human subjectivity. How, then, should we speak of human existence? Kierkegaard draws a contrast between two types of thought.

> While objective thought is indifferent to the thinking subject and his existence, the subjective thinker is as an existing individual essentially interested in his own thinking, existing as he does in his thought. His thinking has therefore a different type of reflection, namely the reflection of inwardness, or possession, by virtue of which it belongs to the thinking subject and to no one else. While objective thought translates everything into results, and helps all mankind to cheat, by copying these off and reciting them by rote, subjective thought puts everything in process and omits the result; ...as an existing individual he is constantly in the process of coming to be, which holds true of every human being who has not permitted himself to be deceived into becoming objective, inhumanly identifying himself with speculative philosophy in the abstract.[40]

It was the notion of "subjective" thought that was bothersome. "Subjective thought puts everything in process and omits the result." A way of getting at subjective thinking is demonstrable through the idea of "humility."[41] One cannot objectively explain "humility" without misleading the hearer as to what it involves. Suppose one sought an answer to the question: what must I do to become humble? Instructions in humility are given: be unpretentious, modest in bearing, deferential, meek. When walking stoop a bit to punctuate the effort at humility. Always submit. Choose the lowly to associate with, strip yourself of wealth, become plain and simple, shun affectations. Submissive to others, servile in self-presentation, one designs one's humility. Objectively, one knows its marks. At what proud moment, then, can the person say "I have achieved the goal; I am a humble person"? At that moment, everything is lost.

The tension between being humble and objectively knowing what it takes to be humble is the tension between subjectivity (being a person) and objectivity ("copying off the results and reciting them by rote"). We could learn humility and not be so. The depiction of humility catches us up in its objective mode. What is revealed directs our attention away from being to knowing. Being humble is quite a different matter. It could not be taught but comes into being with the dawning consciousness of our finite existence. One is set awash in humility as one focuses on the left hand. Humility is of the essence of one's living. Though its presence is the occasion for its objective delineation, humility is not conceived and sought but leaps out of what is involved in being a person. One lives as a subject, present to oneself as finite. No pretense of objectivity shields one's finite existence and the world it creates.

## A Digression: Being a Subject and Indirect Communication

By marking the distinction between subjectivity and objectivity, Kierkegaard breaks the hold of the idea that objective discourse alone determines what is ultimately meaningful. He denied the common assumption that "no art or skill is required in order to be subjective." To become aware of one's subjectivity was a "very difficult task, the most difficult of all tasks." Its difficulty was not like that of learning calculus or remembering irregular German verbs. It was that of breaking through objectivity's hold on our thinking. One has to find a way into subjectivity without becoming objective. No more than one can be taught to think, or be moral, or be Christian, can one be taught subjectivity. So "how" one moves to self-understanding has no directly communicable content. Subjective discourse draws speaker and hearer to address a sense of existence that remains untouchable through objective discourse. Kierkegaard calls it an "indirect communication." An indirect communication brings persons to confront themselves. Here are some instances of indirect communication.

Certain poetry suitably expresses a sense of life, the expression of which could only appear in its poetic utterance. From Elizabeth Barrett Browning's *Sonnets from the Portuguese*—

How do I love thee? Let me count the ways.
I love thee to the depth and breadth and height
My soul can reach, when feeling out of sight
For the ends of Being and ideal Grace.
I love thee to the level of everyday's
Most quiet need, by sun and candle-light.
I love thee freely, as men strive for Right;
I love thee purely, as they turn from Praise.
I love thee with the passion put to use
In my old griefs, and with my childhood's faith.
I love thee with a love I seemed to lose

With my lost saints,—I love thee with the breath,
Smiles, tears, of all my life!—and, if God choose,
I shall but love thee better after death.[42]

The words of the poem express commitment, abandonment, a volitional
sustaining of relationship. The love is an expression of Elizabeth,
especially in view of the details of her life (sketched in the endnote).
The difficulty of expressing love is well noted. If transformed into an
objective soliloquy, a psychological analysis, objectivity would call for
quantification. The enumeration of appealing qualities of the other
person would be appropriate, along with some measurement of love's
intensity. Instead of love, perhaps a personality index which matched
the lovers' psychological profiles (compatibilities in backgrounds and
values) should be praised as an assurance of the validity of their
pending engagement. As valid as the objective analysis for a sociologi-
cally sound marriage might be, in becoming married, something quite
different comes into focus. Relationship is established in the subjectivity
of commitment, not in statistical studies. As one approaches the fated
wedding day, no analysis suffices for the question, "am I doing the
right thing?" Love is sustained in its continued presentation. Elizabeth
Barrett Browning confessed love. "How do I love thee?" is not an
invitation to enumerate the ways. It is an indirect communication of
love made definitive in its poetic expression.

For Kierkegaard the sense of human existence, subjectivity, is
grasped in an indirect communication. It is conceivable that Socrates
had such a contrast between subjectivity and objectivity in mind in the
*Lysis.* In the warmth of a Mediterranean afternoon Socrates and two
young friends became curious about how exactly "being a friend"
should be defined. They analyzed various possibilities as their
arguments coursed through the afternoon. Interrupted by dusk, their
philosophically hopeful conversation remained unresolved, and
unhappily they had to part.

> However, just as they were leaving, I managed to call out, Well, Lysis
> and Menexenus, we have made ourselves rather ridiculous today, I, an
> old man, and you children. For our hearers here will carry away the
> report that though we conceive ourselves to be friends with each
> other—you see I class myself with you—we have not as yet been able
> to discover what we mean by a friend.[43]

In this ironic closing passage of the book, Socrates indicted their
conversation as "ridiculous." They sought objectivity, definition as to

the nature of friendship. The reality of friendship took place in the sphere of subjectivity: "we conceive ourselves to be friends with each other ... [and] we have not as yet been able to discover what we mean by a friend." The ironic remark became an indirect communication. Friendship was not a thing objectively defined but was lived.

How easy it is to imagine an equivalent scene in a Palestinian setting, the warm afternoon, a group of men concerned about life's meaning, a discussion to settle such matters.

> "What shall I do to inherit eternal life?"
> "You shall love the Lord your God, and your neighbor as yourself."
> "And who is my neighbor?"

Often Biblical literature utilizes an indirect communication to enable its readers/hearers to reflect on their own existences. The Good Samaritan (Luke 10:29-37) is striking in its portrayal of direct and indirect communication.

> But he, desiring to justify himself, said to Jesus, "And who is my neighbor?"

"Who is my neighbor?" is a question very much like Socrates's question in the *Lysis*, what is a friend? It invites objective definition, testing with cases, as the logical parameters of the idea of friendship are developed. Like with the participants in a Socratic dialogue, the question invites these men to establish the essence of neighborliness. The story was told of the Samaritan's good will to the man who "fell among thieves." A concluding question was then asked. "Which of these three, do you think, proved neighbor to the man who fell among the robbers?" The objective first question fell before the second question of subjectivity. The former was direct, requiring an objective answer; the latter was an indirect communication.

Telling the story of the Good Samaritan made the objective issue of definition irrelevant. The initial question was revised to become a question of subjectivity: "Am I the neighbor?" Inwardness, subjectivity, creation of life, being human—these become the focus of attention when such a question is asked. Instead of calling the world into question (deciding what counts as a neighbor) one is oneself called into question. It is a matter of subjectivity. The objective task places one outside the sphere of existence. Were dusk to interrupt the discussion, little would be lost. But when one is oneself held in question, the dusk interposes itself as a threat to one's own being. Only one's being a neighbor brings neighborliness to pass, not speculations about its meaning. Like Socrates who recognized the distinction between knowing and being, Jesus, too, engaged in an indirect communication on being human.

Another illustrative story from Christianity is entitled "The Rich Young Man" (Mark 10:17-31). The young man came to Jesus and asked "Good Teacher, what must I do to inherit eternal life?" The question was a serious one, for he wanted to know the conditions which would create his life as meaningful. He was interested in the redemption of his life from a kind of emptiness. Jesus reminded him of the objective conditions of Jewish living. An authentic Jewish life would fill the God-given requirements for life. He was to be obedient in the prescribed manner. The young man protested: he was obedient to God and fulfilled the law. Objectively, nothing more could be required. The iteration of a value structure would not answer the young man's question. What could be added or changed from what God had given to authenticate the sense of life? "You lack one thing; go, sell what you have, and give to the poor, and you will have treasure in heaven; and come, follow me."[44] The objective concerns of the young man were transformed by those of subjectivity. Emptied of worth, devoid of anything that would hide him from himself, he confronted his essential nature—dependent, meaningless, helpless. The injunction became an indirect communication directed against the objectivity wherewith the young man understood his life—a case of the difficulty in becoming subjective. His being as human was held in question; he was confronted by his own subjectivity (and confounded by it, he went away sorrowful). Objectively he understood what it meant to be Jewish. Unhappily, he was troubled by subjectivity.

The realm of subjectivity has 'being human' as its concern, and within human concern are issues like the manner of living (the ethical, the political), the matter of living (the technological, the aesthetic), and finally the point of any of it. Where there is a point, "philosophy" erupts to show it. In contrast, dwelling in the senselessness of life brings forth religion.[45] Kierkegaard provides a framework for these distinctions in some remarks about Christianity.

> Christianity is not a doctrine but an existential communication expressing an existential contradiction. If Christianity were a doctrine it would *eo ipso* not be an opposite to speculative thought, but rather a phase within it. Christianity has to do with existence, with the act of existing; but existence and existing constitute precisely the opposite of

speculation. The Eleatic doctrine, for example, is not relevant to existing but to speculation, and it is therefore proper to assign to it a
place within speculative thought. Precisely because Christianity is not
a doctrine it exhibits the principle ... that there is a tremendous difference between knowing what Christianity is and being a Christian. In
connection with a doctrine such a distinction is unthinkable, because a
doctrine is not relevant to existing. It is not my fault that the age in
which we live has reversed the relationship, and transformed Christianity into a philosophical doctrine that asks to be understood, and
turned *being* a Christian into a triviality. To assume that this denial that
Christianity is a doctrine should imply that Christianity is contentless,
is merely a *chicane*. When the believer exists in his faith his existence
acquires tremendous content, but not in the sense of paragraph-
material.[46]

Kierkegaard restructured the philosophical task by reminding us that
"reality itself is a system—for God; but it cannot be a system for any
existing spirit."[47] The traditional pursuit of objective certainty may
remain, but Kierkegaard showed how a retraction of philosophy's
traditional claim of universality opened the way for religion. No longer
need religion concern itself with definitions of persons as experiential
or rational animals capable of touching ultimate reality. Religion's
sense was directed to that human being who is the ground for whatever
is meant by "world." Religion addressed the senselessness of being
human as this is uncovered in one's subjectivity; religious language
becomes what one speaks to confront one's being.

# Conclusion: A Sense for Religion

The traditional search for objective finality in knowledge directed
attention away from the subject. Kierkegaard broke tradition by
dwelling on being a subject. Kierkegaard pointed at human existence as
the source of every meaning except its own. A similar theme is
developed in the work of Maurice Merleau-Ponty (1908-1961), who
likewise rejected the notion of pure objectivity longed for by philosophy. He wrote,

All my knowledge of the world, even my scientific knowledge, is
gained from my own particular point of view, or from some experience
of the world without which the symbols of science would be meaningless. [Thus] ... I am, not a 'living creature' nor even a 'man', nor
again even 'a consciousness' endowed with all the characteristics which

zoology, social anatomy or inductive psychology recognize in these various products of the natural or historical process—I am the absolute source, my existence does not stem from my antecedents, from my physical and social environment; instead it moves out towards them and sustains them, for I alone bring for myself (and therefore into being in the only sense that the word can have for me) the tradition which I elect to carry on....[48]

Merleau-Ponty abandoned the search for an all-embracing objectivity and saw the world lived as a function of human concern. In our concluding remarks, then, we want to sketch two ideas to be developed from this thought. First, we are forced to the idea that life's significance cannot be humanly established. Second, the incapacity to give sense to human existence allows an authentic sense to religion, freed from philosophy.

## Stuck in Uncertainty

Kierkegaard separated objectivity and being human. The products of objective thought—society, history, literature, chemistry, economics, and so on—were dependent on existing individuals.

That the knowing spirit is an existing individual spirit, and that every human being is such an entity existing for himself, is a truth I cannot too often repeat; for the fantastic neglect of this is responsible for much confusion.[49]

Any description of human existence, any category used to make life intelligible, never captured the person who provided the distinction. From Plato through Hegel, the philosophical themes we have studied each derived a specific understanding of human existence. Platonic Reason bespoke a divine nature where all were created in the image of God. It gave sense to existence and dignity and worth to life. Alternatively, sensate beings whose knowledge was restricted to experience would find meaningfulness established through their power to manipulate the material reality which defined them and in which they participated. In any case, mankind's power to discern causal structures gave it the potential for control; through their manipulative power person's became "demi-gods" in their own right. There was nothing greater than human being. Kant argued for God and immortality as adjuncts to a rational moral life. Persons partook of divine spirit by perfecting the sublime self. An intrinsic value was accorded people and gave them the right to heaven. Like Kant, Hegel echoed the notion of human partnership with "God" as Reason lived itself out through life and nature. The whole of creation with humankind as the highest natural expression of Reason's power implied an intrinsic worth. Gods to themselves, intrinsically worthy in their capacity to fathom nature and experience, morality would be determined by pleasure and pain; the quality of the aesthetic, political, social, or religious life would be found in the capacity of ideas to satisfy human needs. Human nature defined by reason and will still accorded to persons a supreme place. No measure of humility need be added to human existence. Mankind would itself have to be sufficient for the meaning of its being. There would be problems of self-interpretation: are we individual natures or aspects of a more general structure of society and society's products? However, establish a science of existence, and one might live. Meanwhile, what shall we do as we await the sufficiency of an answer?

The self-adulation which raised human existence to divine heights now returns to earth. Philosophy would not provide an avenue of escape from finitude. Kierkegaard's insistence on finitude as central to human existence is echoed in a suggestive myth created by Jean-Paul Sartre. Sartre imagined that individuals were cast into existence and defined that existence. It is empty of meaning until a person created the world of meaning to a human measure.

> What is meant here by saying the existence precedes essence? It means that, first of all, man exists, turns up, appears on the scene, and, only afterwards, defines himself.[50]

This characterization of existence denied that things possessed intrinsic natures and meanings. Sense-making was a human activity. Human living precedes theory, or in Sartre's words "existence precedes essence."[51] The contrast between existence and essence, subjectivity and objectivity in Kierkegaard's terms, shelves any view of what authentic human existence entails. Philosophical proposals that search for natures came after the fact of living.

What, then, are we to understand by "being human"? "Human nature," too, is an intellectual creation, not a given. There are no hidden "natures" to uncover. One creates meaning in order to conduct life. It is precisely this state of affairs that increases a state of being which Kierkegaard called "dread." Life cannot be filled out with humanizing values because the redeeming truth of any value remains undetermined. Sartre's advice for authentic living ended in a hollow challenge to be responsible for one's choices, choices which in the next moment might be undone.

Wilhelm Friedrich Nietzsche (1844-1900) sees that authenticity is found in the strength of will which effects its resolution. At one point in *The Genealogy of Morals* Nietzsche writes:

> This fully emancipated man, master of his will, who dares make promises—how should he not be aware of his superiority over those who are unable to stand security for themselves? Think how much trust, fear, reverence he inspires (all three fully *deserved*), and how, having that sovereign rule over himself, he has mastery too over all weaker-willed and less reliable creatures! Being truly free and possessor of a long-range, pertinacious will, he also possesses a scale of values. Viewing others from the center of his own being, he either honors or disdains them.[52]

A bit further he continues,

> To speak of right and wrong *per se* makes no sense at all. No act of violence, rape, exploitation, destruction, is intrinsically "unjust," since life itself is violent, rapacious, exploitative, and destructive and cannot be conceived otherwise. Even more disturbingly, we have to admit that from the biological point of view legal conditions are necessarily exceptional conditions, since they limit the radical life-will bent on power and must finally subserve, as means, life's collective purpose, which is to create greater power constellations. To accept any legal system as sovereign and universal ... is an anti-vital principle which can only bring about man's utter demoralization and, indirectly, a reign of nothingness.[53]

No hesitance concerning the bludgeoning effect of asserting value daunts Nietzsche. Rather Nietzsche asserts that value only gains force in its assertion. "The radical life-will bent on power" is that "vital principle" of human existence, the frustration of which brings about man's "nothingness." The genuineness of the assertion needs only the person who speaks to fall back on. Therein lies the strength of the "fully emancipated man, master of his will, who dares make promises—how should he not be aware of his superiority over those who are unable to stand security for themselves?" Nietzsche asserts the *Übermensch*, that person who announces the world of value.

Yet in unhappy irony, as finitude magnifies the meaninglessness of existence, the assertion of meaning in "the will to power" likewise turns out illegitimately to warrant life. If in the implicit knowledge that our living is stifled by death, we nevertheless assert ourselves in order to annihilate emptiness and boredom through the creation of meaning, the meaning produced in turn elicits a boring theological/metaphysical busyness. The fading excitement of a new idea is revealed in calls for renewal which arise because of weariness and apathy. Optimism and pessimism alike become pollyannish. The conclusion follows: human existence is empty of intrinsic meaning, so that whatever fills one's time in an ordinary sense suffices for meaning—play, study, work, the routines of life ranging from dressing for the day to listening to the bedtime news. The striving against meaninglessness which ignited a philosophical hope to discover meaning was quenched by life's persistence in the ordinary. Striving for something called "a meaningful human existence" foundered on the realities of human existence. The reflective moment found the struggle pointless. It is this state of being which initiates religious life.

## Authentic Religion

Religion requires no philosophical musings for its vindication and authenticity, for unlike philosophy, religion addresses life's perpetual meaninglessness.[54] The aim of religious practices in classical Hinduism is release from life's continuum through acts of spiritual discipline. If this life is illusory as to its values, there is reality that a person can become at one with, thereby escaping life's meaninglessness as lived. In overcoming life by the immersion of one's self into the totality of being, care for the mundane is obliterated and meaninglessness is overcome by the purification of consciousness from concern. The aim of such thought is to put consciousness at rest. Ordinary human distinctions—matter, life, mind, logical form—destroy the possibility of freeing the soul. Freedom comes by an immediate, intuitive grasp of being and the abandonment of self in the embrace of this unity. Rather than to overcome the emptiness, human existence is affirmed by its denial, and release from its bondage requires the extinction of that self-consciousness which holds human tensions in its grip. Zen Buddhism takes as its task the obliteration of human efforts at establishing a meaningful existence, as well. The training associated with answering the paradoxical Zen puzzles (e.g., the proverbial 'what is the sound of one hand clapping?') is meant to cultivate an abandonment of thought as the source of life's meaning. Rather than appeal to metaphysical speculations to provide meaning, illumination through a kind of spiritual discipline marks entry into Zen. In Zen life becomes a oneness with one's situation. Repose in existence frees one to live.

In contrast to religions that obliterate a consciousness of self-in-opposition-to-world stand religions that affirm life in frames of mind and ethical living. Some forms can be found in Buddhist thought, others in Judaism—and certain elements in philosophy have religious significance. In order to fill out the meaning of life which otherwise would be void of sense, Buddhism found moral and spiritual knowledge in the teachings of the enlightened Buddha. Judaism appealed to the laws for life revealed in the word of God. In both cases people had no capacity in their own right to make life meaningful. The point of the moral and spiritual life in each case was to overcome an otherwise senseless existence. The philosophical views of Plato and Aristotle (aspects of which medieval Christianity found attractive[55]) aimed at overcoming the senselessness of human existence in the rational design and spiritual purity of the human soul. What gave philosophy a religious bent was its concern with bringing human existence into the sphere of ultimate meaningfulness.[56]

The struggle to bring meaning to that which is empty of meaning defined religion and made its beliefs, concepts, and rituals conspire to fasten meaning in life. An individual's confrontation of his/her own nothingness remained a perpetual prospect, not a developmental task; but only as an individual confessed an ultimate emptiness did an authentic religious language provide cogency to efforts to think about their state of being. This is why religion in some form pervades the world's cultures. The existential condition of meaninglessness knows no cultural boundaries. It is "the human condition." Nevertheless it is easily ignored. Kierkegaard says that

> Just as Christianity did not come into the world during the childhood of mankind but in the fullness of time, so, too, in its decisive form it is not equally appropriate to every age in a man's life. There are periods in a man's life which require something which Christianity wants, as it were, to leave out altogether, something which at a certain age seems to be the absolute, although the same man at a later period of life sees the vanity of it.[57]

No formula suffices to derive "the vanity of it." Nevertheless, life's tentativeness remains a source of wonder.

On a cosmic scale, our lives are designed accidents. Given the probable origins of solar systems, there are countless occasions in which a planetary glob of correct proportional mass and distance from a star could retain the necessary gasses for life and be bathed in sufficient solar warmth to maintain life. From the random collection of gasses in a vast space, life appeared as a chemical concatenation of elements, the appearance of which provided a novel force to be reckoned with in the natural environment. This same environment modified life in an evolving and mutating form, each successive step creating an ever-mushrooming natural complexity, for a time, an ecologically unbounded environment. Our planet's time is catastrophically finite. In its aging process, the sun's fusion reactions cause it to grow in such proportion that the inner planets, including the earth, will become incinerated. The sun then collapses in on itself, its energy dissipated: from dust to dust. The self-conscious beings which we are arise in the midst of this time.

Within the microcosm of our own lives, we have no choice as to the circumstances of our birth; yet this birth becomes the condition for all future resolve. Not asking to be born, we live, only to die. Death becomes an intrusion into the sense we attempt for ourselves. Life's seriousness is threatened by its being no more than an amusement. On the one hand is the confession of being human; on the other is the glimpse of context and meaning. Religion addresses the meaninglessness of human existence.

Kierkegaard provided a framework for understanding religion which did not begin with speculation about knowledge and reality but with an explication of human existence. Unlike an objective proposition, the truth of which is always liable to demonstration and debate, the religious sense of life begins with nothing that is logically necessary or empirically demonstrable. Persons come to themselves in inward reflection. When human existence is held in question, the religious impulse is inescapable. There is nothing capable of establishing human meaning in a direct manner: religion confronts life. Its satisfactions are to be lived through, not as one becomes satisfied by knowing the shortest route, but as a venturing forth, the upshot of which is indeterminate.

# Notes

1. Parts of this chapter rework some ideas in my article titled "Religion Without Truth" in *Man and World*, Vol. 20:121-146 (1987).

2. Kierkegaard, Soren, *Concluding Unscientific Postscript*, trs, Swenson and Lowrie. Copyright ©1941 by Princeton: Princeton University Press, p. 116f. This and all subsequent quotations from the *Postscript* are reprinted by permission of Princeton University Press. The original text was published in 1846.

3. Time testifies to changing insights regarding the tests for "what makes sense." Philosophical genius shows that what one took to be the conditions for intelligibility at one time were in fact wrong. Thus, empiricists offered a severe critique of the rationalists, but themselves come under fire in the twentieth century by the well-taken analyses of ordinary language philosophers or existential phenomenologists. As tenacious as philosophical viewpoints are, they still suffer from their own kind of finitude.

4. For instance, philosophy delineates what counts as having produced a cause or explanation. Theological explanations that fall outside these requirements become pseudo-explanations. To avoid such a turn of events, theology accedes to the requirements of good sense. Thus, when classical philosophy assumed that "man is an animal," pleasure/pain became properly used in explaining the motives of human behavior. Correspondingly, the attractiveness of religion would be explained in direct proportion to its capacity to produce pleasure or to benefit the adherent. Or when philosophy decreed that something's usefulness to human purposes determined its value, religion rushed to show its own utility. What passes for religious sentiment characteristically was born in philosophical passion.

5. Some believers claim to shun philosophy by adopting a dogmatic approach to religion. Characteristically, their denial of philosophy is based on a scriptural verse which states

> See to it that no one makes a prey of you by philosophy and empty
> deceit, according to human tradition, according to the elemental spirits
> of the universe, and not according to Christ (Col. 2:8).

Biblical literalism forces such people to avoid the study of philosophy for fear of becoming its prey, but the dogmatic are not thereby relieved of their philosophical commitments. The religious dogmatist characteristically holds to philosophical viewpoints developed by empiricism or rationalism (without being circumspect about the consistency between the two). A usual manifestation of their dogmatism is in the philosophical notion that words stand for objective meanings. Language is referential or representational. The notion of the literal interpretation of the Bible requires this philosophical position. However, this picture of language concedes all the metaphysical ties necessary to philosophy.

6. Examples of other religious concepts of interest to philosophy might include the ideas of faith versus reason, immortality, the warrant of morality, miracles, and so on.

7. For example, think of liberation theology or black or feminist theology which are outgrowths of a Marxist analysis of alienation.

8. Of course, there are admirable and adequate substitutes for religion in the world of ideas. For instance, the cause of peace and justice need not have a religious setting. Where social tasks can be accomplished without religion's conceptual baggage, why bother with religion in the first place?

Still, in the Hegelian mind, the cause as defined in the dialectical scheme is a religious presence, even were there no believers in a religion. Likewise, the emergence of Whiteheadian process theology (the theological works of John Cobb advocate this position) is a contemporary attempt to insert a religious spirit into this twentieth-century philosophical speculation.

9. Arthur Schopenhauer makes a similar observation in Chapter XVII of *Supplements to the First Book of the World as Will and Idea* (Dolphin Books, Doubleday, 1961).

10. Kierkegaard might be considered a prototype "anti-foundationalist," or "deconstructionist," one who regards philosophical foundations (such as Hegel's) as being human creations.

11. *Postscript*, p. 102.

12. *Ib.*, p. 98.

13. *Ib*, p. 67.

14. Though Kierkegaard had the Hegelian system in mind, it makes no difference what particular metaphysics or epistemology one would appeal to. The varieties of both rationalism and empiricism would qualify equally well for the sort of critique which Kierkegaard makes of Hegel. The problem of "ultimate reality" can't arise if metaphysical questions reflect *human* interests, the inventions of a *person* who wants to understand being. The idea of "religion validated by objective signs of the divine" may be philosophically interesting, but it is religiously impotent. The religious life has nothing to do with "objective signs of divinity."

15. The concluding remarks in Freud's *The Future of an Illusion* (*op. cit.*, p. 55f.) suggest that scientific objectivity itself produced our ideas. In an evolutionary way, the brain in fact acquired a capacity to make decipher the external world's structure in an objective manner. To question the nature of reality and knowledge "is an empty abstraction, devoid of practical interest."

16. *Postscript.*, p. 109.

17. *Ib.*, p. 170.

18. *Ib.*, p. 172.

19. *Ib.*, p. 103.

20. *Ib.*, p. 108.

21. Georges Gusdorf's little book, *Speaking* (tr. P. T. Brockelman [Evanston: Northwestern University Press, 1965; orig., 1953]), is especially suggestive of the theme here outlined.

22. In the idea "God" is placed all the conditions of objectivity. God transcends the uncertainties of perspective and represents absolute knowledge and Truth. As absolute, God possesses the final word, not man.

However, it is precisely this feature of talk about God which simultaneously directs attention to human nature. "God is absolute" is not a claim about the nature and reality of God but about the nature and reality of mankind. An underlying uncertainty infects the intellectual enterprise.

23. William James makes a remark which, it seems to me, parallels Kierkegaard's understanding of the place of systems in human affairs.

New truth ... marries old opinion to new fact so as ever to show a minimum of jolt, a maximum of continuity. We hold a theory true just in proportion to its success in solving this 'problem of maxima and minima.' But success in solving this problem is eminently a matter of approximation. We say this theory solves it on the whole more satisfactorily than that theory; but that means more satisfactorily to ourselves, and individuals will emphasize their points of satisfaction differently. To a certain degree, therefore, everything is plastic. (William James, "What Pragmatism Means," in *Pragmatism*, R. B. Perry, ed., [New York: Meridian Books, 1955 {orig. 1907}] p. 51.).

24. *Postscript*, p. 103.

25. *Ib.*, p. 101f.

26. *Ib.*, p. 97. Kierkegaard provides this German text.

Wenn Gott in seiner Rechten alle Wahrheit, und in seiner Linken den einzigen immer regen Trieb nach Wahrheit, obschon mit dem Zusatze mich immer and ewig zu irren, verschlossen hielte, und sprache zu mir: wähle! Ich fiele ihm mit Demuth in seine Linke und sagte: Vater, gieb! die reine Wahrheit ist ja doch nur für dich allein!

Gotthold Ephraim Lessing (1729-1781) was a dramatist and critic of some note. He is accorded some intellectual fame for his reflections on the difficulty of Enlightenment rationalism to account for history's capriciousness. Although a participant in the rationalism of the Enlightenment (he held that the brotherhood of man and a basic moral code were of the essence of Christianity), Lessing prepared the way for the subsequent romantic reaction against the Enlightenment in the view that the exigencies of life and rational truth did not imply each other. The tidiness of reason and its impersonal demands belonged in a different category from the concreteness of history and the personal engagements it reflects.

Here, Kierkegaard's notion of truth as absolute is less important than the character expressed by a person's striving after it. The subsequent pages of the *Postscript* are a commentary on the difference between the left and right hand in Lessing's fantasy.

27. *Ib.*, p. 97f. Several remarks are appropriate to understanding this passage. Hegelians were persuaded that "the System" was the self-authenticating way in which all reality could be understood. Hegelian logic was universally applicable. As with a scientific analysis, details remained to be placed into "the System."

Kierkegaard amplifies this point: suppose the unaccounted-for "detail" opens the way to novel and unanticipated discoveries, some of which may become the undoing of previously accepted truths. An early twentieth century exposition of Hegel by W. T. Stace, *The Philosophy of Hegel: A Systematic Exposition* (New York: Dover Publications, 1955 [orig., 1924]), provides a foldout "Diagram of the Hegelian System" on its back cover for the edification of the reader. After outlining the tripartite divisions and subdivisions, each one providing more dialectical detail than the last, at the very margin, on the far right hand side, is the disarming "Further Subdivisions" with only questions as its content. This innocent promise of completion of the system was ridiculed by Kierkegaard in the passage at hand.

In the face of incompleteness and novelty, how much weight should be placed on the truth of "the System"? It suits Kierkegaard's purposes to answer, none! The Hegelian, however, lived in a polyannish optimism that the end surely was at hand.

The passage has another feature. Kierkegaard alludes to the concern scholars have with gaining objective insight into the life and times of Jesus, including the place of Christianity in the dialectical scheme of world history. Hegel sanctioned Christianity as objectively valid: a Christian understanding of life fulfilled the dialectical requirements of World Spirit. Christianity could be believed.

Yet Biblical criticism continually raises questions about how exactly to understand the texts and times of Jesus. In this passage, such scholarship is touched by referring to the period between Herod and Pilate, the life of Jesus. Such knowledge gleaned from a historical probe into Jesus' life might be supposed to have a bearing on one's religious life. However, Kierkegaard's irony (the soiled trousers) points to the idea that even if one knew the objective truth about Jesus and his place in world history, a sense of the religious life remains something different from historical knowledge. One way of putting the difficulty is to ask: does belief in the objective dogmas of Christianity make one a Christian? For instance, couldn't one believe the elements of the Apostles' Creed and not be Christian? In part, the *Postscript* was directed against understanding Christianity in view of the demands of objective thought.

28. *Ib.*, p. 110.

29. *Ib.*, p. 107.

30. "Subjectivity" is a term used by Kierkegaard to indicate "the logic of human existence," that is, the implications of human finitude for what one knows and does. Were there an English word, "subjectology" (as there is soci-

ology or psychology), it might have been chosen as a suitable translation for what Kierkegaard seems to be after. Thus when Kierkegaard says that "truth is subjectivity" [i.e., the logic of being human], he recognizes truth's human context, with all the difficulties of finitude *that* suggests. "Subjectivity" should *not* be understood as the advocacy of feeling against logic and fact.

31. To deny the appropriateness of philosophical speculation for religious insight, Kierkegaard must isolate religious concern from philosophical speculation. Kierkegaard runs into a problem in the delineation of the two. He doesn't want to violate the religious sense of being by speaking of it as if it were another fact to be received from the objective point of view. In the struggle to make clear how religion is to be understood and religious language to be heard, Kierkegaard draws a distinction between direct and indirect communication, the first suitable for philosophy, the second for religion. Direct communication belongs in the realm of objectivity. Its effectiveness comes at the point of making clear the terms under discussion. Its power is that it can be replicated immediately by its hearer and discussion furthered in the quest for clarity. Indirect communication brings the hearer to hold his own life in question. Thus, its effectiveness comes at the point of a self-awareness and self-transformation. Its power lies in there being no further need for discussion. An illustration of this contrast is provided in the *Postscript* (p. 70):

> Suppose this, that it happened to be the view of life of a religiously existing subject, that no man ought to have any disciple, that having disciples is an act of treason to God and man; suppose he also happened to be a little stupid, ... and asserted this principle directly, with pathos and unction: what would happen? Why then he would be understood; and he would soon have applications from at least ten candidates, offering to preach this doctrine, in return for merely a free shave once a week. That is to say, he would in further confirmation of his doctrine have experienced the peculiar good fortune of obtaining disciples to accept and disseminate this doctrine of not having any disciples.

Luke 10:25ff. has an objective question introducing the Parable of the Good Samaritan—"who is my neighbor?" and a question of subjectivity concluding it—"Which of these three, do you think, proved neighbor to the man who fell among the robbers?" He said, "The one who showed mercy on him." And Jesus said to him, "Go and do likewise." "Am I the neighbor?" is a question which forces one inward.

32. One might capitulate to cultural forces that condition an acceptance of some particular religion and become an advocate for that position. Would not such an advocacy be purely accidental? What could it mean to say that that person was a devotee of that religion?

Or suppose a person saw that belief in the existence of God was necessary for a cogent explanation of natural order, that the evidence pointed to the existence of God. Is this what it takes to be a religious person? Does one become a religious person by believing in the existence of God? Or, suppose that one thought there was no convincing evidence that God existed. Is one thereby excluded from being a religious person? Is Christian agnosticism impossible?

33. *Postscript*, p. 179n. In part the footnote from which these words are taken reads:

> the postulate [of the existence of God] is so far from being arbitrary that it is precisely a life necessity. It is then not so much that God is a postulate, as that the existing individual's postulation of God is a necessity.

The difference between subjectivity and objectivity lurks in the background of this passage in that it is an objective question as to whether God exists but in the life of a person, given that the objectivity of the issue cannot be established, there is something else that demands attention for which only the concept God is appropriate. This "something else" bears on the nature of one's existence.

34. *Ib.*, p. 169.

35. *Ib.*, p. 115.

36. *Ib.*, p. 176.

37. *Ib.*, p. 116f.

38. The concluding paragraphs of *Candide* reads:

> As to Pangloss, he evidently had a lurking consciousness that his theory required unceasing exertions, and all his ingenuity, to sustain it. Yet he stuck to it to the last; his thinking and talking faculties could hardly be diverted from it for a moment. He seized every occasion to say to Candide, "All the events in this best of possible worlds are admirably connected. If a single link in the great chain were omitted, the harmony of the entire universe would be destroyed. If you had not been expelled from that beautiful castle, with those cruel kicks, for your love to Miss Cunegonde; if you had not been imprisoned by the inquisition; if you had not travelled over great portions of America on foot; if you had not plunged your sword through the baron; if you had not lost all the sheep you brought from that fine country, Eldorado, together with the riches with which they were laden, you would not be here to-day, eating preserved citrons, and pistachio nuts.
>
> "That's very well said, and may all be true," said Candide; "but let's cultivate our garden" (in *The Best Known Works of Voltaire* [New York: Literary Classics, Inc., n.d.]). *Candide* originally was published in 1759.

39. Unlike Freud (or Karl Marx), many psychologists argue for the pragmatics of religious views. Examples would include William James's *The Varieties of Religion Experience: A Study in Human Nature* (1902), Karl Jung's *Psychology and Religion* (1938), or Eric Fromm's *The Art of Loving* (1956). These are samples of influential psychological works that purport to give scientific legitimacy to religion. Of course, the defenders of objective religion are delighted by such legitimation.

40. *Postscript*, p. 67f. When sociologists see social reality in terms of the idea of a "role," they are disinterested in the individuals who populate those roles. The role creates the person. Kierkegaard dwells on the subjective individual, not the objective role. As an existing individual, I live as the creator of life and once lived, give the sociologist something to study—roles. Kierkegaard hints in this passage that in reflecting on my creation of life, there is no guidepost to give me bearing as to my life's authentic direction. Thought directed to this insight is the thought of subjectivity, i.e., the logic of being a subject.

41. It is in such contexts as this that one might understand certain remarks by Heidegger about Being. Consider this passage from the "Letter on Humanism" (in Martin Heidegger, *Basic Writings*, ed. D. F. Krell [New York: Harper and Row, Publishers, 1977]), p. 228.

> To think against "values" is not to maintain that everything interpreted as "a value"—"culture," "art," "science," "human dignity," "world," and "God"— is valueless. Rather, it is important finally to realize that precisely through the characterization of something as "a value" what is so valued is robbed of its worth. That is to say, by the assessment of something as a value what is valued is admitted only as an object for man's estimation. But what a thing is in its Being is not exhausted by its being an object, particularly when objectivity takes the form of value. Every valuating, even where it values positively, is a subjectivizing. It does not let beings: be. Rather, valuing lets beings: be valid—solely as the objects of its doing. The bizarre effort to prove the objectivity of values does not know what it is doing.

I take it that like that actor who thanks his audience for recognizing the wonderful actor he really is, the person who assigns value because of the wonderful objectifier he really is does not understand what it means to value. The complement to letting "beings: be" is the censure of human being. That is, though the being of the world is the effect of human presence, no validation of being in "valuating" is redemptive of being. These are and remain the projects of persons condemned to their finitude. Thus,

> When one proclaims "God" the altogether "highest value," this is a degradation of God's essence. Here as elsewhere thinking in values is the greatest blasphemy imaginable against Being. To think against

values therefore does not mean to beat the drum for the valuelessness and nullity of beings. It means rather to bring the lighting of the truth of Being before thinking, as against subjectivizing beings into mere objects.

*This* "subjectivizing" takes place in the realm of Cartesian certainty where the ego stands at the center of knowledge. It is not Kierkegaardian "subjectivity" which receives in humility the left hand of God with its perpetual recognition that one is forever and a day doomed to stray. To think of a pure truth left to God alone is here echoed by Heidegger and seems to me to fall into the region of Kierkegaardian subjectivity.

42. Sonnet XLIII, *The Complete Works of Elizabeth Barrett Browning*, Vol III, eds.: C. Porter, H. A. Clarke (New York: Thomas Y. Crowell & Co., 1900 [Reprinted by AMS Press, Inc., New York, 1973]), p. 248. In *The Literature of England* (Vol. 2, Woods, Watt, and Anderson, eds. [Chicago: Scott, Foreman and Co., 1948] p. 709), the editors contribute to our understanding and appreciation of her poetry by providing some details of her life. Called "the Portuguese" by her husband because she was dark-complexioned, Elizabeth Barrett Browning lived to be fifty-five years old. The familiar love poems in this collection of sonnets were addressed to her husband, whom she married at the age of forty-one. The prefatory notes of the editors include the following remarks:

> The supreme date in the life of Elizabeth Barrett was September 12, 1846. On that day, by a clandestine marriage, she became Mrs. Robert Browning, and a week later she left her dark and unhappy home at 50 Wimpole Street, London, where she had been dominated by an ogre-like father....
>
> Elizabeth Barrett's tragic life up to her forty-first year has become familiar.... An injury to her spine when she was fifteen, the shock of her brother Edward's death by drowning in July, 1840, and the insane insistence of an unbalanced father that none of his daughters should marry, made her life dark indeed. Elizabeth was confined in her gloomy home by her invalidism and even more by the treatment of it. But she read and wrote...; for Robert Browning read the poems, loved them, loved her, and came to her rescue like Prince Charming in the fairy story.

43. Plato, *Lysis*, tr. J. Wright, in *The Collected Dialogues of Plato*, ed. E. Hamilton and H. Cairns (New Jersey: Princeton University Press, 1961), p. 168.

44. The injunction "come follow me" was not a further requirement. Jesus's stature in first-century Jewish culture was like that of a rabbi, a teacher of Judaism. At this early stage, the person of Jesus had none of the mystical qualities like those to be shortly attributed to him by religious writers near the

end of the first century, so the request to "follow me" would be nothing more than a call for a master-disciple relationship prefatory to a religious life.

45. The expansion of the theme that the religious life is rooted in the senselessness of human being is developed in Chapter VI.

46. *Postscript*, p. 339f. The Eleatic School of philosophy (mentioned in the quotation) flourished during the transition to the fifth century B.C. and is represented by thinkers such as Xenophanes (c. 530 B.C.), Parmenides (c. 495 B.C.), and Zeno (c. 465 B.C.). Their thinking is shaped by a metaphysical notion of the unity of being.)

47. *Postscript*, p. 107.

48. *Phenomenology of Perception*, tr., C. Smith (London: Routledge Kegan Paul; New York: Humanities Press, 1962 [orig. 1945]), p. viiif. The redirection of philosophy begun by Kierkegaard requires an extended conversation. Merleau-Ponty is part of a twentieth-century movement broadly called "continental philosophy" and included figures such as Edmund Husserl, Martin Heidegger, Jean Paul Sartre, Hans Gadamer, the later work of Ludwig Wittgenstein, or the philosophy of deconstruction represented by thinkers such as Jacques Derrida, and a host of others. Continental philosophy successfully broke the hold of metaphysical objectivity on thought.

49. *Postscript*, p. 169.

50. This argument appears in one form in *Existentialism and Human Emotions* (New York: Philosophical Library, 1957), p. 15. Sartre's essay, "Existentialism as a Humanism," is presented in many anthologies on existentialism.

51. Sartre's myth errs at the point of a bifurcation between man and nature. It is a misunderstanding to view the starting point of knowledge as the attempt to unite knowing with the knowable, for there is no isolable consciousness which is simply there to be related to the world. To be sure, I can intellectually isolate objects in a world of objects, even creating myself as an object. In order to be conscious at all, one must be conscious of something. The idea that consciousness appears in the presence of things opposes the notion that consciousness is something in itself, an idea explored by Edmund Husserl. Husserl says

> Every perceiving consciousness has this peculiarity, that it is the consciousness of *the embodied (leibhaftigen) self-presence of an individual object* which on its own side and in a pure logical sense of the term is an individual or some logico-categorical modification of the same (*Ideas*, tr. W. R. B. Gibson [New York, Collier Books, 1962 {orig. 1913}] p. 114).

The idea of a consciousness that is integral with the sense of being is not original with Husserl, however. G. W. F. Hegel in the *Phenomenology of Spirit* says

For consciousness is, on the one hand, consciousness of the object, and
on the other, consciousness of itself; consciousness of what for it is the
True, and consciousness of its knowledge of the truth (tr. A. V. Miller
[New York: Oxford University Press, 1977 {orig. 1807}], p. 54].

But if consciousness is consciousness of something, the idea of a mind
seeking a relationship with the world is an abstraction. It is existentially false
to distinguish between world and consciousness. Persons do not find their egos
juxtaposed to their experiences. Rather, the contrast between self and experience is theoretically contrived.

One finishes the evening newspaper, sets it aside, and gets up from the
chair to turn on the six o'clock news, and one is not a subject to oneself, with
the chair and television an object. The world is lived, not something known in
the manner depicted in philosophical theories of knowledge. One does not
transact commerce between it and oneself. Rather, as occasions and vehicles
for the conduct of life, objects, conventions and habits, anticipations, and so
on appear and disappear as they are lived. One does not relate to situations but
is the focal point in terms of which situations become what they are. But it is
not as if one were autonomous in these matters. Our lives are an inheritance
of the intersecting lives of others. Thus our action in life is both reaction and
participation.

52. Friedrich Nietzsche, *The Birth of Tragedy and The Genealogy of
Morals*, tr. F. Golffing (Garden City, NY: Doubleday and Co., 1956 [The
Genealogy of Morals first published in 1887]), p. 191, "Second Essay,"
Section II.

53. *Ib.*, p. 208, Section XI.

54. One hesitates to summarize religious matters because of the shallowness
that is inevitable in a summary and the exceptions which could be noted. Obviously, were one curious about some particular religion, encyclopedias (including *The Encyclopedia of Philosophy* [New York: Macmillan Publishing Co.,
Inc., & The Free Press]) are a beginning point.

55. I distinguished between Christianity's philosophical forms and its
Biblical sense. It may be a thorny distinction to maintain in any thorough way.
Nevertheless, something like this distinction is reasonable. What I want the
distinction to do is focus what I regard as the critical aspect of Christianity:
specifically, the idea of *agape*. It seems to me that the concept of *agape*
pervades New Testament thinking, so much so that it is *the* hermeneutical tool
for prying into that writing. The topic is given attention in Chapter VII.

56. Philosophical theories that are conceptually incapable of having a bearing on the meaning of existence are religiously sterile. Logical positivism
comes to mind, for in reducing all meaning to knowledge of what is required
in the process of verifying or falsifying a proposition, it becomes nonsense to
attempt to imagine what could count as "the meaning of life."

57. *Postscript*, p. 523.

# Chapter VII

# Religious Language

One etymology of the word "religion" tells us that it comes from *re-*, back, + *ligare*, to bind, fasten; and indeed, it is not too far fetched to think that in an originary way, religion is the binding back of one to one's being. Characteristically, the relationship between God and mankind is such a binding—hence, religion. But religion is not alone in its concern to delineate man's relationship to being. Philosophy often seeks the objective grounds for understanding existence. With inexhaustible enthusiasm, historical philosophy related man to some sort of unity of being, not always one which needed God. Yet religion's confrontation with philosophy found ways to retain "supreme being," if not God. The divine is not easily made to disappear. Malleable and transformable, the concept, "God," fits most intellectual contingencies, so much so that it even survives in those philosophical theories supposedly inimical to it. Any line of thinking about the nature of reality and its meaning for life evoked a complementary notion of what objectivity required *vis a vis* sublime things—characteristically, God. Instead of a fundamental human experience irrupting into something called "religion," religion was enticed by philosophy's demands for a ground common to all thinking.

Christendom joined philosophy by clothing philosophical ideas in religious garb. The effect of this long tradition is a source of what could be called "religious superstition." "Superstition," according to *The Oxford English Dictionary*, etymologically comes from "*super*,

above, + *sistere*, the causal of *stare*, to stand." This way of looking
at its roots suggests that something, an idea or a practice, triumphs
over, stands above, a primary phenomenon. It is in this sense that
philosophy mesmerized Christian tradition.[1] The religious concern with
the meaninglessness of human existence was abandoned in favor of
philosophical promises of intrinsic meaning in a unified being.
Saturated by a philosophical commitment to "truth," religion allowed
philosophy to "triumph over" it, so much so that in religious mattes
persons have difficulty attributing *conceptual* uniqueness to religion.
Christian thinkers persisted in making religion dependent on philosophy.[2] Instead of participating in "truth," however, they unwittingly
reformulated Christianity as an intellectually respectable superstition.[3]

Sigmund Freud's attack on religion was instructive. He accepted it
into the competition for objective truth and took seriously its claim that
persons should stand in awe or fear of an ultimately unknown and
mysterious being, God. He then showed that science required no
bowing to the unknown, that to do so was superstitious. Freud's notion
fits the definition of superstition: unreasoning awe or fear of something
unknown, mysterious, or imaginary, especially as this is founded upon
fear or ignorance, including irrational religious belief or practice. The
key to superstition was the lack of "reason"; and in this, Freud thought
religion qualified—even though religion sought blessing in reason's
highest court: philosophy.[4]

> Religious ideas are teachings and assertions about facts and conditions of
> external (or internal) reality which tell one something one has not
> discovered for oneself and which lay claim to one's belief.[5]

Freud points to religion's pretentiousness in addressing matters of fact
and reality. The derisive "lay claim to one's *belief*" is the key to his
interpretation of religious statements: they had no grounding either in
fact or reality. They were grounded in illusion. Freud remained
sanguine about the long-run capacity of scientific method to regulate
human existence. Science would sustain its claims about "internal and
external reality," not religion.

For Freud, the origin of causality located the arena of proper
scientific discourse; and the capacity of a word to refer to some
experientially determinable object framed the limits of reality and
thought. Freud was right in thinking that religion could not stand
inspection when it thought of itself in terms of describing causal
antecedents and providing for the referentiality of its terms. Objective-

ly, religion which with thoughtless persistence held pseudo answers to scientific questions eventually would be squeezed from consideration when the more adequate scientific explanation was given. Where religion entertains a literalistic concern with natural law, it becomes superstition. For Freud the origin of religion was a quite natural psychological desire for security in an otherwise unstable universe.

Modern defenders of Christianity recognized the danger Freudian-type analysis posed to faith. When this or that aspect of belief might indeed be superstitious, enlightened Christianity purged it from the general body of beliefs, thereby meeting the criteria of cause and reference demanded by philosophy.[6] Freed from ordinary superstitions and demythologized, a purified Christianity could enjoy the privileges of intellectual approval. Philosophy "triumphed over" Christianity insofar as Christianity (and for that matter, any religion) did not understand its grounding in the logic of meaninglessness. When religion engages in an objective quest for a kind of knowledge, it cannot compete with the scientific procedures and outlooks. Confused about its purposes, it takes philosophical objectivity as its hermeneutic, an interpretive outlook to which religion should be indifferent. It is this sense of "religion" that Freud rightly accused of "superstition." Genuine or authentic religious language makes no claims for which causality and referentiality need be appropriate; it is not the language of objectivity. It is an originary language, used to unfold the ultimate senselessness of human existence.[7] Philosophical strivings for meaning, the hope of which was to "bind back" human existence to ultimate value, remained unsatiated because of finitude. There was no solace for one's striving.

## Superstitious Religion

Kierkegaard's effort to break the hold of philosophy on religion remains uncompleted. Contemporary religious theoreticians who persist in the older traditions of tying meaning (characteristically in the form of "value") and religion together still abound. Understand religion to be a search for value and meaning, and one perpetuates a kind of religious superstition, but not an uninformed sort of superstition. Rather, it is the sort of superstition that assumes an intellectual superiority to philosophy which is supposed to have a redemptive effect on religion itself. A case in point is found in Professor John A.

Hutchison's *Paths of Faith*.[8] The book begins by noting that though
there is no agreed upon definition of religion, still, there is some
general notion of what should count as "religion": "*religious experience*
is definable as experience of *ultimate valuation.*"

> The structure of interests, concerns, or values which constitutes a human
> self shows many levels or strata. The idea of ultimate concern or ultimate
> value implies that if we dig deep enough we will come upon an underly-
> ing value or interest which constitutes the final ground of validation or
> justification for a person's whole life, giving meaning and orientation to
> all other interests, providing a functioning answer to the question: "Why
> am I living?" Of experiences of this kind, religions are made.[9]

Matters of "ultimate valuation" are reflected in the "sacred symbol
system": in religious ritual and symbolic language. Hutchison assumes
(1) ultimate things (the things of religion) which are to be approached
through (2) the aegis of "value" which receives special religious status.
Values are then to be symbolized in religious language, in ritual.
"Hence a religion may appropriately be defined as a holy or sacred
symbol system."[10]

Hutchison's view of religious life is determined by his philosophical
commitments. Though well intended, these philosophical commitments
sabotage religious understanding and render it sterile. We investigate
the ideas of religious "value" and "symbol" to see why.

(1) "Value" is uncritically assumed to be "foundational" and a
proper interpretative tool in religious matters. To be sure, there are
aspects of "value" which imitate certain properties of religious life, but
used as religion's interpretative tool, the category "value" distorts one's
understanding of a religion and gives it a superstitious frame. In other
words, though central to the rational concerns of philosophy, "value"
does not occupy the definitive place for *religious* experience.

"Value" is a concept which engages and participates in the canons
of rationality—those ideas which we assume in order to be able to
make sense of anything at all. The questions Hutchison poses which he
claims spawn religious ideas—"'Who am I?' 'Why am I alive?'
'Whence?' 'Whither?'"—each invite an explanation which appeals to
an ordered, causal structure for one's existence. The order of reality
imparts meaning to life—*value* for Hutchison. Value is a discovery, the
result of digging "deep enough." It is a "final ground of validation or
justification." It "gives meaning and orientation to all other interests."
It answers questions about the "why" of living. Hutchison maintains

philosophical tradition by thinking of religion in "value" terms. According to Hutchison, "religion will be interpreted as the functioning answer which people give to these and similar questions."[11]

This philosophical approach to religious thinking creates religious superstition. The philosophical assumption is that we exist in the presence of meanings which we struggle to discover and unfold. "Value" makes religion appear as an adjunct to a general quest for meaning, and religions appear as an addition from the general intellectual culture. A philosophical outlook controls the religious position, and religion is transformed into something it is not—a quest for value. "Value" becomes the token of ontological commitments that shape religious understanding. In this sense, a new turn is given to the meaning of "religious superstition." Its genesis in "standing above" or "triumphing over" marks the effect of a philosophical commitment that stands above or triumphs over religious experience. Religion then shows itself as superstition in being defined by the entire conceptual commitment of which "value" is a part.

That persons use "value" as the fundamental starting point for understanding human experience (including religious experience) is not surprising. Following Plato, values were early entrenched in thought as the organizing principles of meaning and life. Subsequently, the Western intellectual tradition ordered itself in terms of the objectivity of value distinctions. Given Platonic metaphysics, it seemed natural to do so. Philosophy's power was so pervasive that second-century Christian thinkers conceded the importance of "value" despite the earlier New Testament indifference to it.[12] Gnosticism and Stoicism, religious offsprings of Platonism, were the initial philosophical contexts with which Christianity first came to terms. The religious position of Christian gnosticism advanced the idea that Jesus found the way to purify life from its material concerns and its Stoic manifestation looked to the furtherance of the ideal of brotherhood. In attempting to oppose the turning of Christian concern into such discussions of value, early church thinkers did not know how effectively to oppose metaphysical notions of value.

In the case of Gnosticism,[13] the early church's struggle against the "value" language of its gnostic antagonists found its discussions actually defined by its gnostic revisionists.[14] Gnosticism sought to enter the spiritual realm through the possession of a special knowledge which freed the human spirit from the bondage of flesh to return to its heavenly home. In protest, the early church adopted the idea of incarnation to deny Gnosticism's spirit/matter dualism.[15] Christianity pictured life's redemption from meaninglessness by an incarnate *agape* and not by a special knowledge. Christianity had no essential use for metaphysics; its originative concern was with *agape*.[16] So it fought induction into Gnostic metaphysics by the assertion of a metaphysical paradox. The ancient formulation of the nature of Jesus as "wholly God and wholly man" attempted to counter rationalistic philosophy with an irrational quandary—how could Jesus be two contradictory substances, both at once? The formula of the Incarnation could not be warranted by reasoning and normal knowing processes. Since one couldn't deduce this belief from metaphysical givens, a different realm of thought, one that challenged the demands of philosophy, was to counter the philosophical beliefs of Gnosticism. Yet, in so doing, they had to utilize the presumptions they were fighting. The metaphysical stuff of human existence—form and flesh, body and soul—became the underlying context for church discussions about the relationships between God, Jesus, and the Holy Spirit. "Faith" instead of reason or experience was to be the mental disposition required to hold a belief that was otherwise counter-intuitive. (The weighing of 'faith and reason' became a classic topic in theology and the philosophy of religion.) This anti-rationalistic attempt to counter the demands of philosophy in religious matters continued the epistemological concern of philosophy to make sense of the idea of God's revelation in Jesus.

Hegel's dictum that "to him who looks at the world rationally the world looks rationally back"[17] comes to life as the nemesis of religious concern. A heightened sense of value was claimed for Christianity and made it appear to fit a rational understanding of things to which it was in fact indifferent, if not hostile. Instead of Christianity fitting into the broad concerns of value and meaning, it advanced the language of meaninglessness, this theme to be argued later in this chapter. Meaninglessness exacts its own demands from human existence, and the responses to meaninglessness mark the variety and uniqueness of the world's religions.

(2) There is a second assumption which philosophy's long tradition has left unexamined until recent times. Insistence that words refer to meanings which stand beyond the word is another source of religious superstition. Here is the way Hutchinson puts it:

> religious experience takes place in a context of powerful symbolic objects and words. These objects elicit the participants' religious responses. How

natural, then, for them to assume that the holy or sacred actually dwells in these symbolic objects, for it is these objects which mediate their experience of the holy. Conversely, it is the function of eliciting ultimate concern which constitutes these objects as symbols.[18]

The claim here made by Hutchinson is no more than a reiteration of the traditional philosophical claim that words are place markers for the meanings which stand behind them. There are two things, then: words (sounds) and their meanings (the realities). A "referential" theory of meaning, where words refer to something (this "something" itself the object of much philosophical debate) standing behind it, is found in Hutchison's claim that religions can be understood as a "holy or sacred symbol system." Referentiality generates religious superstition by imposing its demands for meanings lying behind religious language on religion. One assumes that religious language refers to shielded or hidden being. Religion searches out those realities which objectively could satisfy its terms. This is the stuff of theological speculation—and religious superstition.

Referentiality requires a warrant for understanding what we hear, the meaning for which the word stands, the word's reality, its cause, something which stands behind it. Although it is common to understand experience and language in terms of the interpretative requirements of causality and referentiality, as ways to proceed in delineating what is religiously intelligible, the hermeneutical tools of causality and referentiality "triumph over" what is religious in religious language. Caught by the hermeneutical requirements of causality and referentiality, liberal and conservative religious believers as well as anti-religious people argue about whether the canons of causality and referentiality are fulfilled. Hermeneutical concerns irrelevant to religion (but quite proper to philosophy) take place. People focus on whether God formulates plans and causes them to happen, whether he answers prayer, sends messengers to reveal his thoughts, rewards the righteous, whether history dialectically forges God's reign of justice, and the like. Commitment to a hermeneutic of causality and referentiality dominates religious phenomenon. By this philosophical sorcery, religion changes its character and function. Attention becomes focused on the objective strength of the religious utterances. Concern with design, evidence, proof and reasonableness are deeded to us in the idea of causality. Philosophy's concern with what makes sense overwhelms religion. Faith and belief are made to accord with the standards of intelligibility fixed by causality. The devout invented explanatory myths to make sense of the formulae of religious language. Religion was metamorphosed. It became a speculative supplement to objective truth instead of the address to human meaninglessness. By introducing causality and referentiality into religious thinking, religion recreated itself as superstition. In contrast, authentic religious life held metaphysical commitments in abeyance. "Reality," "cause," the "referent," had no special religious force. In the following remarks about causality, referentiality, and religious language, I shall claim that causal relationships and theories of referentiality confuse religious discourse by displacing religious concerns with non-religious ones. Finally, I propose that the logic of human finitude is revealed in religious language.

## Causality and Superstition

"Causality" transforms religion into superstition. In order to see this transformation, consider Freud's *The Future of an Illusion*. Freud characterizes religion as "teachings and assertions about reality." This formulation is likely to be agreeable to many proponents of religion. Remarks about the being and nature of God, His creative activity, His will for our lives, begin a list which falls under the rubric of religious teachings and assertions. This concurrence on items appropriate to religious discourse puts religious advocates and Freud on even ground. They can debate whether or not the purported information satisfies the kind of rationality which causality creates. For instance, consider the idea that God answers prayer. No empirical test can be devised to test the causal interaction between prayer and God's answer. Where prayer appears to be answered, the skeptical questioner asks whether it was prayer that got the job done or natural happenstance. Events take a natural course irrespective of the desires of the petitioner, and no logical preference can be given to God's will over chance in such cases, so it is argued. None the less, a kind of piety remains for those caught by causality—"not my will but thine be done." The proviso that God's answer to prayer is not necessarily the one sought by the petitioner saves prayer from being pointless. As with the self-sealing beliefs of the Hopi rain dancers—if the participants have pleased the gods, it rains; if they haven't pleased them, it doesn't rain—everything that happens is God's answer to prayer. Since it either rains or doesn't rain, one can always be assured of the divine presence.[19] The remark "not my will but thine," if seen as a test of divine activity, leads to superstition in its incapacity to delineate between God's causal presence and His absence. It becomes a religious remark only when uttered in the context of human finitude where it reminds one of one's ultimate dependence.

When causal relationships are agreed upon as the source of genuine knowledge, Freud holds the advantage in his debates with a religious person. He argued that the increase of scientific knowledge will drive religion into oblivion. On his side lies the naturalistic realism of scientific investigation. The principle of parsimony prevails, and God is deleted from the list of causal factors as superfluous to causal explanation. Freud is led to ask what causes our ideas of God and offers accounts for the invention of the "God" idea—citing efforts to overcome various human fears (natural disaster, illness, death) or to remedy psychological neuroses. Freud believed that a primitive culture needed an authoritative, moral father figure for purposes of social control. He concluded that religious teachings "are not precipitates of experience or end-results of thinking: they are illusions, fulfillments of the oldest, strongest and most urgent wishes of mankind."[20]

Though they mimic ideas with objective status, religious ideas were borne of wishful thinking and could not abide in a rigorous notion of cause. Religious thinkers looked for signs of God's existence in political and moral design of the world, in evolution or creation, or in so-called religious phenomena such as glossolalia, stigmata, parapsychic phenomena, and so on. Such data were imagined to constitute evidence for divine activity. Religious people relied on causal explanations for warranting the idea of God and created the illusion of results. They appealed to ideas and forces which need not or could not be tested by reason and scientific experience and overstepped their capacity to produce valid results.

Freud's hard-minded irreligiousness is the effect of taking causality's demands seriously. Only science, according to Freud, could succeed in the resolution of disputes about causes. Freud dismissed religion and directed "reason and experience" against religious superstition.[21] "Reason" included the canons of logic and scientific method which bore on what causes what. "Experience" involved whatever can be referenced in the world of tangible things.[22] The truths of existence discovered through reason and experience were to be found in a naturalistic delineation of cause which satisfied all that is required by way of an explanation. No supernatural cause need apply. When religious thinkers willingly submitted to the ontological requirements of causality, the search for objective signs of divine causality eventually would upend religion. Religion would suffer the fate Freud predicted for ideas incapable of sustaining causal rigor. But religion only suffers the fate of irrelevance if one seeks its sense in causality. Were causal demands superfluous to religious interests, were religion without metaphysical assurances, then by setting aside its grounding in causality, religion finds itself "out upon the deep,"[23] and a different starting point for religion must be found.

### Referentiality and Superstition

In its concern with the "what" to which the words refer, referentiality likewise creates superstition. In general "referentiality" embraces the idea that a word is the sign of a reality which lies beyond it. It is usual to think of language in referential terms, to think of a word's meaning lying in the thing or relationship to which it points. Words are thought to be signs of things and their relationships, an intellectual mirror of the objective state of affairs. We imagine words to stand for the elements of transcendental logic and immanent experience.

Because of this unthinking commitment to referentiality, divine invisibility in some measure frustrates religious people. Surely there is some mode of knowing—reason, revelation, experience, mystic intuition—which allows one to see behind the word "God" to the divine presence. "God" becomes a word in search of a referent. Where religious people want to find a referent for "God" in order to establish God's existence, all have a notion of what it is that God must be prior to initiating their search for God[24]—no one thinks, for instance, that God is like two raw eggs thrown in a fan. The motive is clear: if the words of religious language can be made to refer to something objective, they can be taken seriously. These assumptions have nothing to do with discovery. They are tied to prior intellectual commitments and the dogma that words are the signs of meanings.

Thus, it is no wonder that each rational proof of St. Thomas's five proofs for the existence of God (in the *Summa Theologica*[25]) ends with a referring remark: 'this being everyone understands to be, everyone gives the name of, all men speak of as, we call: God.' Although St. Thomas (mis)directs our attention to arguments grounded in the concept of causation and its intellectual or psychological structures, what he seeks is a referent for the word "god," a power standing behind observable causal relationships, thus lending credibility to religious language which uses the word "god." Though religious people seek creditable reasons to think that God(s) exists (proofs for God's existence have a logical charm to them, in part evoked by the notion of cause), they fall short in their capacity to produce God.

If the notion that "words refer" leads people sympathetic to religion to look for God, the same spirit brings about God's dismissal. No possible candidate for divinity is self-evident; so the word "god" could refer to sublime natural processes as easily as divine being. Freud dismisses as neurotic and infantile the idea that the word "god" might have a referent.[26] To explain "god," he looks to "internal" reality, the psychological phenomena of longing for a protective father figure, and he finds a psychological referent for the word which is damaging to religion. In their wish to remain children, people project "God," an imaginary solice for their fear. Please God and one will be safe.[27] Freud and his religious antagonists will agree that the word "god" must refer to something. Things are empirical matters; and if the connection between "god" and an independent and objective meaning cannot be shown, Freud is justified in concluding that it is an illusion to think in terms of objective referents for religious statements which use the word "god." Unlike the things you point at, "god" is seen as a pre-scientific, psychological attempt at description and control. As is appropriate to *scientific* abstraction, Freud looks for a reference for the word "god" and finds it in the psychological world of human neuroses. Freud's argument is a psychological/sociological one. He supposed the concept "god" to be an adjunct to social stability. Submission to the idea that 'words refer' leads one to look for some sort of ostensive meaning.[28] Hence, Freud dismisses the idea of God as the referent for something ultimately real and finds its meaning in psychological reality, and then chides people for maintaining religion in a scientific age. Freud's virtue in attempting to explain the existence of religious language is that he places it in a natural context. Had something else evoked social stability, that too would be revered. If the ideas of causality and referentiality apply to religion (and Freud assumes they do), religion becomes the expression of a non-natural realm of untenable pseudo-causes and of explanations of things "made to order." The elements of religion (including the idea of God) become the natural phenomena of social interaction.

Freud rejects metaphysical speculation, purported evidence from natural events, the requirements of moral or aesthetic being. Psycho-

logical yearnings for stability, however, do make sense. Invoked as a
way to generate stability, religion is incidental to broader social goals.
Stability seems a natural urge, desired for its own sake, and it is
unessential that it erupt in religious expression. The dismissal of a
specifically religious expression of social concern seems reasonable.
Religious language became charged with concerns which were not
religious ones. The philosophical culture transformed religious language
into a language of causes and metaphysical entities.[29]

We should be able to uncover an authentic context for religious life
by removing religion from an ontological grounding in causality and
referentiality and showing religion to be indifferent to issues which
invite speculation about the nature of reality. As historically correct as
it is to say that religion has been subsumed under the intellectual
outlooks of a culture, its concerns still stand independent of a culture's
intellectual requirements. To think otherwise creates religious superstition. However, the authentic religious life must forego philosophical
concerns. This means, among other things, that the ideas of causality
and referentiality are inappropriate to religious concerns. The religious
use of the word "god," for instance, need not require a referent.
Striving after divine value is a religious misappropriation of a philosophical life. To define the parameters of the religious life, I return to
an unlikely beginning point, Freud, who writes:

> Critics persist in describing as 'deeply religious' anyone who admits to
> a sense of man's insignificance or impotence in the face of the universe,
> although what constitutes the essence of the religious attitude is not this
> feeling but only the next step after it, the reaction to it which seeks a
> remedy for it. The man who goes no further, but humbly acquiesces in
> the small part which human beings play in the great world—such a man
> is, on the contrary, irreligious in the truest sense of the word.[30]

Freud is right in saying that essential to religion is the idea of human
finitude. Freud himself didn't follow through on the implications of this
intuition; moreover, he is wrong in thinking that religion failed in
this—primarily because he didn't understand religious language.

## Religious Language

Freud's faith in scientific procedures didn't allow him to give voice
to human "insignificance," although he did have a sense for proper
modesty in the presence of scientific method. In a eulogy to the

humble, acquiescent person—the scientist—who is "irreligious in the truest sense of the word," Freud sees a person whose life is directed by the modest god of "logos"[31] in the search for truth. Though science is imperfect, it is able to correct itself when it gets things wrong, unlike religion. Science allows one to achieve whatever goals are accessible to human beings.[32] Though Freud sympathizes with the person who recognizes "a sense of man's insignificance or impotence in the face of the universe," only scientifically minded people who think the truth, not religious ones who think illusions, are the ones who will lead us through our feelings of insignificance. Feelings of "insignificance" are pieces of data, for Freud, an invitation for therapy. He can claim that religion naively misidentifies the objective state of affairs and projects illusory psychological entities to address the neurosis of insignificance. We can achieve happiness by utilizing procedures, events, and things which have an empirically demonstrable negative or positive effect on the realities of living and the world. If techniques create happiness, these can be scientifically explored and offered in non-religious settings. Religious adaptation to psychological successes simply reinforces Freud's claim that religion is itself impotent in the face of science. Freud's hope was that religion would fade into oblivion with the emergence of a science that would bring about ease in human existence.[33]

Freud's commitments to cause and reference direct him to scientific meaning and structure when he should be probing the idea of meaninglessness itself. Freud's intuition that finitude is a problem for human existence is correct; but he doesn't take his remark seriously, and his solution is impossible. He can't take it seriously because for Freud, there is a denial of finitude, not in the sense that we might rid ourselves of vulnerability, but rather in the sense that we overcome it through scientifically determinable strategies. In part, Freud sees this; but he doesn't see that the language in which this finitude comes to be known is not the language of causality and referentiality. It is a language which stands outside the demands of causality and referentiality. It is religious language.

Freud goes astray in thinking that the objective reference of terms and the causal nature of being have a bearing on religious concerns. Were religious language a matter of "information and teachings," as Freud thinks, a person might well be taught religion and be falsely persuaded by its claims. But if religion is disinterested in information, if it is rather the concern with human finitude, then the language to capture the sense of human existence is not the language of objectivity, but rather it is religious language.

## Saying "God"

Metaphysical statements sometimes have the appearance of religious statements, and to be sure, they are motivated at least in part by the concern to establish causal relationships and realities by which one can fix meaning in human existence. In this regard, one can understand why religious language could mistakenly be understood as a metaphysical theorizing about being.[34] Freud thought of religion in metaphysical terms, and his appeal to scientific reasoning founded in causality and referentiality supported the rejection of this view. No god need appear in the world of human reality. The metaphysical and psychological uses of "god"—circumstances in which objective truth appears to be at stake—allow Freud to focus on the illusion of religion. However, Freud cannot touch human existence in its finitude. His metaphysical commitment to causality and referentiality kept him focused on objective solutions to "man's insignificance or impotence in the face of the universe." Scientific (psychological) solutions were to be found for the problems of insecurity and human fallibility. Patronizing human finitude, he needed no god to address it.

Religious language is misconstrued as an attempt to identify or relate to the realities of being. Rather, religious language begins in an expression (or uncovering) of the consummate *senselessness* of one's being, the disclosure of which forces into the open those few ways (the unique motifs which mark the world's religions) which can be used to address this human condition. The person captured by religious concern sets aside objective explanations of the nature of reality which entail the concept "god." They are religiously irrelevant. Nor is the *religious* use of "god" an aesthetic look for divine things in order that they can be held in awe and worshipped. Such metaphysical urges destroy religious context, although they are integral with philosophical concerns about the nature of reality and a person's relationship to it. It follows that effort expended on identifying "god" is misdirected; constructing proofs of God's existence is a religiously unenlightening task. Nothing so abstract is broached in using the word religiously.

In one way or another, religions promise the creation of a new being, one infused either with meaning or with the release from concern with meaning. Religious language reveals the intricacies of human finitude. The expression and delineation of finitude doesn't exist in the mouth of an indefinite "one." It is a language that is spoken only when an individual confronts his or her own meaninglessness. To be sure, in the absence of religious concern, religious language can be taught and learned; but it could never be spoken. Religious language, the language of human meaninglessness, is the speaking by which human finitude takes its form.[35] Here, the notions of causality and referentiality are disarmed and set aside. They are not decisive in determining the intelligibility of religious statements. A Psalm recalls the desperation of an existence from which nothing can be done to escape.

> But I am a worm, and no man; scorned by men, and despised by the people.
> All who see me mock at me, they make mouths at me, they wag their heads;
> "He committed his cause to the Lord; let him deliver him, let him rescue him, for he delights in him!"
> Yet thou art he who took me from the womb; thou didst keep me safe upon my mother's breasts.
> Upon thee was I cast from my birth, and since my mother bore me thou has been my God.
> Be not far from me, for trouble is near and there is none to help.[36]

The person speaking confesses meaninglessness. Questions of divine objectivity are irrelevant to what is sought in such a religious utterance. Religious language focuses the reality of living. It illuminates a consummate human dependence. The utterance of "God" frames one's finitude. It is a confessional language, one indifferent to objective truth about the nature of reality. When religious language sounds as if it were involved in an objective description of the way *things* are, it in fact distills how *persons* are, therein creating a sense of "world" in which only religious language will suffice in its expression. Human existence receives definition through the prism of religious language.

Hans-Georg Gadamer's analysis of language directs us in how to think about the power of speaking. I quote a passage at length from *Truth and Method.*

> Language and thinking about objects are so bound together that it is an abstraction to conceive of the system of truths as a pre-given system of possibilities of being, with which the signs at the disposal of the signifying subject are associated. A word is not a sign for which one

reaches, nor is it a sign that one makes or gives to another, it is not an existent thing which one takes up and to which one accords the ideality of meaning in order to make something else visible through it. This is a mistake on both counts. Rather, the ideality of the meaning lies in the word itself. It is meaningful already. But that does not imply, on the other hand, that the word precedes all experience and simply joins up with an experience in an external way, by subjecting itself to it. The experience is not wordless to begin with and then an object of reflection by being named, by being subsumed under the universality of the word. Rather, it is part of experience itself that it seeks and finds words that express it. We seek for the right word, ie the word that really belongs to the object, so that in it the object comes into language. Even if we hold to the view that this does not imply any simple copying, the word is still part of the object in that it is not simply allotted to the object as a sign.[37]

Gadamer argues that "language and thinking about objects" are not composed of signs which reference the "possibilities of being." Such a proposal divides thought and things, making the word secondary, a sound, the "sign" of reality, a mark, a meaning residing elsewhere.[38] Gadamer discredits the theory of referentiality where people distinguished between the sign and that of which it is a sign. It is as if one had the capability to think in a wordless language in order to think that a word needed to be contrived in order to mark the thing, the essence of which one knew independently of its being marked by a word. But how could distinctions be contrived in a non-existent language? The distinction marked and the language by which it is marked are synonymous. It is this thinking/language, both "bound together" as our conceptualizing, which (as Gadamer describes it) comprises our existence.

It follows that religious language and religious intuitions are "bound together," an innocuous remark—unless religious people thought religious concepts referred to things which transcended the human world rather than emerged as one's religious being. Gadamer's remark is that experience becomes what it is when one "seeks and finds words that express it." The language of thinking doesn't simply represent things but calls forth and establishes the involvements of living. Our language is the world we live. To repeat Gadamer's remark:

A word is not a sign for which one reaches, nor is it a sign that one makes or gives to another, it is not an existent thing which one takes up and to which one accords the ideality of meaning in order to make something else visible through it.... Rather, it is part of experience itself that it seeks and finds words that express it.

To make religious sense of religious language, one must leave causality and referentiality aside and probe the living context which is given expression in religious language.

Religious language brings the full impact of meaninglessness (called "inwardness" by Kierkegaard) into being.[39] The inevitability of death, an unyielding eventuality, trivializes life's strivings. We endure, filling the time, not comforted by the words: "you've got to die sometime." We regard our own lives as important, when in fact, nothing much hangs on whether any particular individual is dead or alive.[40] This existential confession of meaninglessness is not something overcome in metaphysical assurances. It is here that Kierkegaard reminds us that "the moment of death" brings about religious language,[41] not to be learned as a truth about the world, but as the confession of one's utter incapacity to sustain one's life in meaning. The expression of inwardness finds religious language leaping from the tongue.[42] In this regard, Freud's unthought remark about "a sense of man's insignificance or impotence in the face of the universe" might have become a platform for understanding religious language—except, his ontological and hermeneutical commitments ruled out the possibility.

Gadamer's work enables us to understand religious language. Instead of focusing on objective questions of factual content, one articulates one's being as a subject in a language suitable to the phenomenon. In making religious language serve the concerns of human finitude, traditional commitments of philosophy are set aside. Religious language serves its own ends. It is easy for confusion to emerge here: the superstitious believer (who assents to the framework of ontological and hermeneutical concerns which Freud assumes) and the person who gives expression to the sense of being an "existing individual" (addressed by Kierkegaard)[43] might *say* the same things. However, the one presumes the conceptual requirements of causality and referentiality and never hears what is being said; the other has an existential (ontological) concern inherent in a confession of the ultimate senselessness of human existence. One is religiously superstitious; the other is religious.[44]

## *Agape* and the Unmaking of God

Jesus, it seems, carried meaninglessness to an uncompromised conclusion. Instead of the usual religious/philosophical program to deny ultimate meaninglessness, scriptural Christianity seems best understood if meaninglessness becomes its interpretive tool. One reminder of its realistic attitude toward human existence is found in the primitive church's mythical notion that God would bring about His kingdom on earth in an immediate future, "in the twinkling of an eye," where death no longer would bring living to naught. The coming Kingdom of God where general meaningfulness would prevail stood as a perpetual judgment on any extant meaningful state of existence.

Not possessed by rationalistic assumptions of causality and referentiality, New Testament mythology concerning last things is an existential statement, one which builds from a realism respecting human finitude. The mythologized language of primitive Christianity reflected the project of describing a hollow human existence and its redemption.[45] It is a metaphorical language which utilized the imagery of God incarnate. What was spatially distanced became immediate: "God was in Christ reconciling the world to himself" (2 Cor. 5:19). This religious language attempts to give voice to the reality of human finitude. It is not that God traversed distance to make himself visible in a person. The expression rather gets at the immediacy of an *agape* which steps outside the commitment of philosophy to causality and referentiality. It aims at the implications of finitude.

Failure to understand the context for the use of religious language (and this failure will be shaped by philosophical commitments to causality and referentiality) will change what was religious language into the superstitious language of philosophy when it strains to overcome finitude. The hermeneutics of causality and referentiality invite a curative positivism. However, as we have seen, metaphysical assurances of the meaningfulness of being, constructed with great intellectual effort, profound in their bearing, become de-constructed by equally clever people.[46] "The sum of all this," Kierkegaard says, "is an objective uncertainty"; and one remains "out upon the deep, over seventy thousand fathoms of water."[47] Unlike those philosophically inspired efforts to discover eternal value in order to incorporate it into one's life, early Christian writings despaired of succeeding in such a goal, betrayed by human finitude.

There is no *metaphysical* 'remedy' to insignificance simply because persons, the inventors of theories, stand beyond the theories they invent to explain themselves. Maurice Merleau-Ponty speaks to this point. As "absolute sources" of meaning,[48] persons make the world what it is by their engagement with it—one establishes the meaning of things; one values one's world. Though "value" marks the fact of something's being appreciated, in the world of personal existence, valuing persons is not the same thing as existing in relationship with them. The incestuous appreciation of the other person in terms of his/her value misses what authenticates and confirms relationship. The objective world becomes meaningful in the presence of persons; like God who creates out of his word, people bring about a world. An arrogance is permitted the creators of meaning. But arrogance is entirely out of place in the relationship between persons. It falsifies relationships. So rather than deeding meaning to others, an acceptance (recognition) of the other as an equal participant in the fragility of life itself becomes the authentication of the human world, the world of subjectivity.

Perhaps the model for this openness to others was provided by Jesus's "step-father," Joseph, who on all accounts was not the father of the lad he raised as his son.[49] In a culture where birth legitimated a person, the suspicious circumstances of Jesus's birth surely affected his life. Joseph's acceptance of Jesus as his son created meaning. In his turn Jesus followed Joseph's example, offering fellowship to others where there was no reason to do so, creating meaning where there was none—in the lives of persons who were regarded as without meaning, sinners. Early church writing captured this attitude by the word, *agape*. Both *agape* and *eros* address meaning in human existence. But comparing the two frameworks for understanding human existence, one cannot help but be struck by the contrast between a metaphysically contrived *eros* which sees existence as intrinsically meaningful (thus, it is worth the effort to discover the truth of being and actualize what is already a part of the nature of reality) and *agape*'s dismay and discouragement over meaning in existence. Finding no reason to think of human existence as intrinsically meaningful, *agape* attempts to create meaning where there was none. This is a project of faith, not reason. Here "faith" is ontological, not epistemological. God's establishment of a new being would redeem that which languished in the meaningless-ness of death. Earthly values passed away in favor of divine *agape*. Its features are sketched by Anders Nygren in *Agape and Eros*.[50]

| | |
|---|---|
| Eros is acquisitive desire and longing. | Agape is sacrificial giving. |
| Eros is an upward movement. | Agape comes down. |
| Eros is man's way to God. | Agape is God's way to man. |
| Eros is man's effort: it assumes | Agape is God's grace: salvation is |

| | |
|---|---|
| that man's salvation is his own work. | the work of Divine love. |
| Eros is egocentric love, a form of self-assertion of the highest, noblest, sublimest kind. | Agape is unselfish love, it "seeketh not its own", it gives itself away. |
| Eros seeks to gain its life, a life divine, immortalised. | Agape lives the life of God, therefore dares to "lose it." |
| Eros is the will to get and possess which depends on want and need. | Agape is freedom in giving, which depends on wealth and plenty. |
| Eros is primarily *man's* love; God is the *object* of Eros. Even when it is attributed to God, Eros is patterned on human love. | Agape is primarily *God's* love; "God *is* Agape." Even when it is attributed to man, Agape is patterned on Divine love. |
| Eros *recognises value* in its object —and loves it | Agape loves—and *creates value in its* object. |

Life articulated in the recognition of meaninglessness—do not be angry with your brother, turn the other cheek, love your enemy—radically alters relationship. The axiological perspective of philosophy allows one justifiably to be angry, defend honor, and judge the enemy. The truth of "value" puts one in possession of the just cause. Established truth obligates one to be judgmental—it is no accident that an enemy is such. Where rectitude is presumed, judgment must prevail. Such calculation requires truth in order to judge; relationship must pivot around the equality or worthiness of being in "the truth." A rational universe by which truth is to be discerned requires justice and attendant judgment. There can be no forgiveness.[51] Human relationships are mediated—by propriety, correctness.

In contrast to the portent of divine rectitude which gives one the right to judge, finitude turns this right aside. In the emptiness of human finitude, where the absolute eludes a person, judgment represents a barrier to relationship with another persons. One must forgive, refuse to judge, accept others (which in the New Testament context also turned out to be those who themselves were all too aware of their own meaninglessness, the "sinners"). Notions of intrinsic meaning were to be set aside.

> Judge not, that you be not judged. For with the judgment you pronounce you will be judged, and the measure you give will be the measure you get. Why do you see the speck that is in your brother's eye, but do not

notice the log that is in your own eye? (Matt. 7:1-3).

*Agape* suffers rather than inflicts suffering, constrains itself rather than abides in its freedom, humbles itself rather than insists on its way. Such qualities reflect *agape's* grounding in the ontology of meaninglessness.

There are other implications. A familiar Pauline theme proposed that righteousness was irrelevant to one's salvation, that even adherence to religious commandments which promised life will not overcome a meaningless existence—"For I do not do the good I want, but the evil I do not want is what I do" (Rom. 7:19). The Sermon on the Mount (Matt. 5-7) reflected on that existence which characterized a person in the state of meaninglessness. The Beatitudes, for instance, promised that in the midst of this despair, God created meaning in what otherwise was hopeless. There was no suggestion of an axiology which sought truth in value. A promise, a hope, an assurance has no metaphysically guaranteed warrant. The underpinning of finitude, of uncertainty, remained.

The mythological context for developing this underlying sense of finitude appealed to the coming kingdom of God, but were one to focus on the result—an affair of causality and referentiality rather than a hope which was a matter of inwardness—the point of the myth to hold the emptiness of human existence before one disappears into metaphysical schemes (whereby one might even be driven to participate in the dialectic of change). The language of myth was the vehicle for the New Testament idea of *agape* and pulls forth its meaning. Nygren's summary account of the contrast between *agape* and *eros*, when stripped of the format of mythological language denies the rigors of a universe regulated by rational cause and effect: *agape* is "sacrificial, unselfish, losing itself, spontaneous, overflowing, unmotivated, creative of value." The beginning point for understanding *agape* is its grounding in finitude. The uncertainties of finitude makes judgment a divine prerogative. To meet the other at the point where one lives as a finite being leaves forgiveness as the basis for relationship—"Then those who were at table with him began to say among themselves, 'Who is this, who even forgives sins?'" (Lk. 7:49).

# Conclusion

Causality and referentiality transform religion into an intellectual endeavor to hear religious statements as facts and information. This hermeneutical milieu shrouds religion in superstition—religion becomes understood in a way which is not true to it. Meaninglessness characterizes religious interests and concerns; meaning forms the arena for philosophy. It is no wonder then that these related concerns might be blurred and even be dominated by a philosophical arrogance and its sundry claims to truth. Philosophy's traditional guarantees wrought from causality and referentiality seduce the religious. The pragmatics of a theory of reality and a set of values raise a humanistic hope that work toward their accomplishment will redeem life. When the perversity of life refuses this concession, where value becomes a human conceit and not a vital accomplishment, where existential realism confirms a meaningless human existence, then (in the mythological language of the first century) the *agape* of God addresses that state of being.

Religious language is to be spoken so that, as Gadamer says, "it is part of experience itself that it seeks and finds words that express it." Meaning is created. As such, religious language is not Freud's "teachings and information" about the meaning of being and the final efficacy of value. These metaphysical quests are the domain of philosophical ventures. Freud recognized "man's insignificance or impotence" but thought that a concern with fallibility was a neurosis in search of a remedy. Untutored psychological need drove people to the illusory solution of religion where they could arrest and overcome fallibility by invoking reason's "higher" powers.

Freud faced reality—not to rid ourselves of vulnerability but scientifically to achieve a state in which mankind could be happy. Human meaninglessness had no other implications. Freud thus explained religion away by putting it forward as the feeling of powerlessness in the face of an inexorable nature and the attempt to control life by "stroking" the gods, cajoling them to act in our behalf. Religion thus arose in pre-scientific attempts to dominate and explain: things, guilt, society. The commitment to causality and referentiality, the sources of Freud's hermeneutic, allowed the thinker to dismiss religious explanations. They failed to produce verifiable results. Freud avowed humility in the face of scientific endeavor—a kind of philosophical uneasiness, psychologically contrived to accommodate an ultimate uncertainty regarding scientific claims. Something might change in the scientific assessment of things. Nevertheless, barring any evidence to the contrary, the sciences as well as a misguided superstitious religion rest in the conceit that they "got it right." They recognize the need to hold statements of absolute truth in abeyance—expressed in terms of "faith in the results." Such prudent epistemological humility is not the religious one of reflecting on one's being as human. What is uncertain must still be believed for cogency's sake. It belongs to epistemic faith. To the scientific person (and the religiously superstitious) the finitude of an existing individual is unessential.

Freud's naturalistic stance sees moral entreaties or social action as inaugurating a meaningful existence. The religious "liberal," agreeing with Freud's naturalistic analysis of human experience, additionally wants to bolster the social and ethical life with assurances of the divine approval of these otherwise natural events. Freud notes this. Indeed, he claims that religious people seek the same humanistic values that he does. But religious additions are psychologically driven, not empirically needed. In the dawning of human rationality, such psychological diversions will not be needed. With its consent and cooperation, Freud brought his charges against religion in the context of hearing a metaphysical language. Religious ideas cease being religious when seen as a cosmology, the physics of first things, or a social science. They become superstitious in their pseudo-scientific urge to offer remedy and explanation. Insofar as both metaphysics and religion are thought to deal with the meaning of existence, metaphysical concerns generated by causality and referentiality successfully usurp religious language in talk of God, value and judgment, potentiality and actuality, a divine plan of being and the life of meaning.

The metaphysically uttered word becomes a teaching aiming at facts and reality. One evokes the power of explanation—causes are understood, realities are named. Christian thinkers allowed metaphysical concepts to become elements of religion; and it seemed, in Robert Browning's words, that "God's in his heaven. All's right with the world." The grandeur of metaphysics, its wonder and awe, inspires an aesthetic assemblage of feelings which were ingenuously and piously thought to participate in religious effects, invoking magical words of explanation and manipulation, injecting a hocus-pocus of ritual, prayer, and sacrament.[52] As in the myths of primitive peoples where the name of the God(s) is given extraordinary power, so with the philosophical concepts of causality and referentiality: one names a metaphysical God.

The real source of illusion, however, is to think that moral, social, scientific, or aesthetic matters address a persistent finitude. Authentically religious people remain bound to the reality of their finitude. Against Freud, I submit that individuals who give expression to their own finitude and its implications find themselves speaking "religious language."[53] Thus, religious concern has its origins in a different order of being than Freud thought. Religious language arises to express and reflect on the awful truth that in death we are emptied of all intrinsic meaning. To this end, people in Christendom speak of God, sin, forgiveness, redemption, humility, and see their lives redeemed from meaninglessness in *agape.*

The sense for meaninglessness is a natural one, though as Kierkegaard says, its speaking "is not equally appropriate to every age in a man's life."[54] Its language frames a common experience of living.[55] The authentic rendering of religious language is thus indifferent to the concern with causality and referentiality, and instead, the words which bring forth one's being create religious context and meaning. In general, insofar as religions disabuse the efforts of persons to usurp divine prerogatives, they share a common starting point in the expression of human meaninglessness. Whereas the presence of value orients ethical and metaphysical concerns, its underlying absence is addressed by religion.

## Notes

1. By making an alien form of understanding become the reality which is to represent an original understanding, much more may be superstitious than one first imagines. For instance, I expect I would find statements in sociobiology that would meet this criterion, although they are passed for scientific statements. In this regard see Michael Malone's "From Up Here They Look Like Ants," in *Inquiry*, 1987, pp. 407-22.

2. To be sure, worship and sacrament allowed religious life psychologically to inhabit a special spot in human affairs. Worship and sacrament can become shibboleths to religiosity, behavioral supplements to ideas derivative from philosophy. Religion bound itself to form and clung to an unthinking tradition in the effort to find something that could justify a claim to its uniqueness—liturgically repeat something often enough, and it sounds natural.

3. An illustration of one kind of religious superstition comes from an article from *The New Yorker Magazine* ("Reflections," Ap. 23, 1990, pp. 45ff.) on Jim and Tammy Bakker. Its author, Frances FitzGerald, offered a number of insights into their minds. For instance, Jim Bakker read some writings of one of the influential figures in the Pentecostal movement, Oral Roberts, while attending a Bible college and learned that Roberts had a revelation

while reading a verse from the third Epistle of John: God wanted His children to prosper and be healthy; He was a good God—not a God of endless suffering and sacrifice but a God who wanted His children to find comfort, happiness, and material rewards in this life. The revelation was liberating to Roberts, and his message came as a huge relief to many Pentecostals, for it meant that poverty and self-deprivation were not a part of God's plan for good Christians (p. 70).

Pentecostal tradition, Bakker's inheritance, allowed him to embellish Roberts's thought of "a God who wanted ... comfort, happiness, and material rewards." God's plans were to be manifested in all aspects of life, especially its materialistic configurations. With this theology in mind, Bakker went forth with new bride, Tammy, to preach the gospel of God's favor on those who believe in Him and serve Him. Certain episodes in his life confirmed him in this faith.

[I]t was not that the supernatural was mundane but, rather, that the material world had a miraculous, God-filled quality; the chandeliers were spiritual chandeliers, and the burgundy camper that came in answer to prayer was a sign of His presence in the world. That was what Bakker's supporters meant when they described Heritage USA as "Heaven on earth." ... That gospel was not entirely new: it had always been a matter of Pentecostal folk theology that if your car broke down or if you were behind on mortgage payments you might pray for a miracle (p. 74).

FitzGerald argued that Jim Bakker and his followers were practicing their faith—there was nothing disingenuous about it. Bakker believed God answered prayer. His own opulent style was proof enough of God's material blessings. Other explanations appeared to him not to have the directness of "God answered my prayer." The analysis of the psychological events surrounding these "miracles" wouldn't reveal the divine hand; and the logical difficulties of evil in human affairs requires the invention of *ad hoc* forces of evil—the devil.

The interesting consequence of this sort of belief in super-natural forces at work is that were it true that God answers prayer, then Bakker was not a crook. If it is true that "God" refers to a being with the psychological properties of wanting things for his children, planning events in everyday experience, then that Bakker prayed and got results demonstrates God's nature and causal activity in the world. To the unwashed it looked as if Bakker were guilty of fraud: he oversold the condominiums of Heritage USA and used the excess money for his own enrichment. To Bakker and his defenders, he prayed and was blessed by God.

4. In the *Future of an Illusion* (p. 32) Freud argues that the philosophical adjustment of religious language are dishonest. Philosophical theology turns concepts of God into the merest semblance of the anthropomorphic divine power of religious life. Such philosophers shroud themselves in piety pretend to be believers. However, says Freud, their claim of an elevated sense of God

is makes God an "insubstantial shadow" when compared to the personalities of genuinely religious gods.

5. *Op. cit.*, p. 25.

6. See for example, Rudolph Bultmann's opening article, "New Testament and Mythology," in *Kergyma and Myth: A Theological Debate*, ed. H. W. Bartsch, tr. F. Reginald (London: SPCK) 1957.

7. Indeed, only in recent times has philosophy grappled with the logic of meaninglessness, and it finds itself in foreign territory, straining to deal with something which is essentially religious in its bearing. It seems to me that the writings of Jacques Derrida are a case in point.

With Derrida there is a play of possibilities in hermeneutical procedures which shows that texts cannot be said to have a fixed sense. Because of their interpretative abilities, persons seem to have a sovereignty over texts and language. If so, religious language has no force because the being it purports to address (human existence) in the final analysis was its creator. Yet, religious language is the expression of a person's confrontation with finitude. It is the probe for the limits of human understanding. If so, confession rather than interpretation is proper to the understanding of religious language.

Derrida is noted for his methodology of "deconstruction," which continues the theme of continental philosophy that it is a prejudice to insist that our experience is structured by the contrast between subjectivity and objectivity. Rather, the intellectual life is rooted in human creativity; the notion of an objectively fixed truth is a prejudice. Thus with the other continental philosophers he avows "the death of philosophy" (see "White Mythology" in *Margins of Philosophy* (University of Chicago Press, 1982 [orig. 1971]) as it has been practiced heretofore, and the new treatment of language mentioned above continues as a centerpiece in this avowal—but with the following exception. Derrida sees hermeneutical procedures opening a play of interpretive possibilities. His concept of the playfulness of language—the capacity of words to draw thought beyond one determinative sense—opens up and draws one to interpretation. The supplementary senses which the written word invites renders useless the idea that a text has one meaning. Texts shine differently in different lights, so much so that it is disingenuous to think that a text has a necessary meaning.

The speaking subject brings the sense of a world alive; religious language brings the senselessness of our being to light. Religious language is talk about our nothingness. If Derrida is correct about language, it becomes impossible to speak of the nothingness of human being. Language isn't the "house of being" (a phrase coined by M. Heidegger in "Letter on Humanism" in *Martin Heidegger: Basic Writings* [Harper and Row, 1977]); it doesn't give us (prescribe the limits of) the world we know. Texts are the opportunities for the stirring of imagination. Though the intent of deconstruction in philosophy is on target (it aims at severing philosophy's Aristotelian metaphysical biases), Derrida's way of reaching the goal leaves us with words—disembodied, decontextualized expressions about which one can be "playful"—and not worlds. Derrida may be participating in a philosophical spirit which finds its reincarnation "at the margins."

In contrast to Heidegger for whom the "de-struction" of philosophy involved a study of contexts for living and thinking and for whom speaking and interpretation would be bound to the earth and a person's everyday dwelling in tradition and culture, Derrida could be caught by a misidentification of understanding with interpretation. The hermeneutical underpinnings of the "death of philosophy" do not depend on Derridian deconstruction but on an account of the senselessness of human existence, made explicit in religious language. An ultimately unjustifiable human existence has its own logic which changes the direction of our approach to truth.

8. John A. Hutchison, *Paths of Faith* (New York, McGraw-Hill, Inc., 1991).

9. *Ib.*, p. 5.

10. *Ib.* p. 3. Italics deleted.

11. *Ib.*

12. There is a misunderstanding on Nietzsche's part in accusing Christianity of the transvaluation of all ancient values. In seeing the values of strength or power set aside in favor of weakness and humility, Nietzsche sees that something treacherous for the meaning-creating activity of persons has transpired. He is correct in seeing that Christianity must regard "pity" as a part of Christian life. What he doesn't see is that so-called "pity" is not a *value*. The confession of meaninglessness leaves even Nietzsche's romantic notions of man proper and "the will to power" in the reality of despair. It's not the ancient values of strength which are replaced by the new values of "pity." It's that the idea of value is itself supplanted in favor of meaning created in living out a sustaining relationship with the other person. See Yodar's last chapter in *The Politics of Jesus* for an account of what the subversion of value comes to in Christianity.

13. Christianity's expansion into the 'gentile' world encountered the flourishing religions of gnosticism. Their Platonistic origins framed a cosmology of Being as matter and spirit, and their attendant machinations. Here, the rationality of causality (what gods caused what, the implications of things' natures, and so on) resulted in a kind of knowledge (gnosis) whose purpose was to lead one to a divine life. As early as the writing of St. Paul (e.g., Rom. 8:38-39) but especially the Gospel of John, gnosticism became a focal point for these writers' concern about this Hellenistic world view.

John tries to tailor aspects of a gnostic sense for causality to suit Christian faith. Thus Jesus is made to be "one with the father" from the beginning in order to assure his divine authority (Jn. 10:30; also 1:1-18), becomes a spiritual substance having overarching knowledge—he knows from whence he comes and the divine plan for his own dying at the right time (Jn. 8:14), is capable of choosing the hour of his death, and has the right words of knowledge—is "the way, and the truth, and the life" (Jn. 14:6). In the doctrine of incarnation the writer of John may have attempted to make adjustments in theological emphasis which articulate God's *agape*, but his commitment to a gnostic language which is grounded in causality drives him to a metaphysical inventiveness which it is fair to call "religious superstition."

14. The Gospel and Letters of John can be read as attempts to mediate gnostic ideology. However, in their attempt to show how *agape* dissolves the gnostic world view with its separation between God and mankind, its effect is to sustain this same outlook in its protest. Value elements are contained in the gnostic ideas of "this world" and "the divine realm" as one strives after supreme rationality and eschews the material order. Though saying that "God is *agape*" in the First Letter or developing the notion of incarnation in the Gospel of John the gap between this world and the divine is bridged, the rationalistic context for discussion remained in place. Thus light and darkness, this world and the other world, height and depth, a knowledge that saves, introduce "value" into a discussion which then sustained the very force it sought to neutralize.

15. The degree to which the early Christian church is affected by its intellectual culture explains why we receive Christian dogmas and doctrines in the form we have them. A number of accessible books are available for filling out the historical detail, including Edgar Goodspeed, *A History of Early Christian Literature*, Robert M. Grant, *Early Christianity and Society*, Jaroslav Pelikan, *The Christian Tradition*, and Walker Williston, *A History of the Christian Church*.

16. Thus the Gospel of John opposed the metaphysical dualism of Gnosticism with the expression: "The Word was made flesh and dwelt among us" (Jn. 1:14).

17. G. W. F. Hegel, *Reason in History* (New York: Macmillan/Library of Liberal Arts, 1953), p. 13.

18. Hutchison, *op. cit.*, p. 8.

19. It is the "blik" of the Flew/Hare debate, in *New Essays in Philosophical Theology*, "Theology and Falsification," eds. Flew and MacIntyre, (New York: MacMillan Co, 1955, 1964), pp. 96ff, esp., p. 100f. In a different vein of argumentation about prayer one can play havoc with metaphysical conceptualizations of God. Were one to argue that the effect of praying invokes divine intervention, God then loses necessary self-consistency. The mere logical possibility of contravening the established order of being through prayer threatens the general harmony of nature with intrinsic unpredictability. By being able to intervene in natural events, prayer could be answered; but then there could be nothing to differentiate divine activity from divine inactivity, in which case one could not in fact know whether God answered prayer. Prayer loses its power,

and so arguments from causal relationships render praying a superstitious practice. Rejoinders offered in behalf of the idea that God answers prayer would have to show how one could pray and still preserve scientific causality in the order of being.

20. Freud, *op. cit.*, p. 30.

21. See *ib.*, p. 54.

22. See *ib*, p. 55f., where he argues the point respecting the evolutionary adaptation of the brain to the structure and physical presence of the natural world.

23. Kierkegaard, S., *Concluding Unscientific Postscript, op. cit.*, p. 182.

24. A notion of rational perfection is characteristic both of the god of reason and of mystic intuition. In the Allegory of the Cave, Plato provides a model for both positions. As the sun can be looked at only for a brief moment after a struggle to ascend from the cave, so the vision of god likewise takes a lifetime of preparation to achieve the fleeting glimpse. The rationality of the divine nature is captured in St. Anselm's 'that than which nothing greater (more perfect) can be conceived'; and Descartes speaks to the origin of ideas in us for which there can be no empirical explanation—infinity and God. The notion of revelation is more difficult to sustain because of its unpredictability (non-rationality). There is no reason to think for instance that Jesus was God incarnate. He looked like any other person and was psychologically vulnerable as are we all. Yet though Jesus was fully man, according to traditional church theology, 'God was in Christ reconciling the world to himself.' This claim appeals to revelation.

25. *Summa Theologica*, I, Q. 2, Art. 2.

26. For Freud the question was: Why should people remain religious in a time where its superstitious quality was exposed? One might see psychological components of religion as lending themselves to superstition. The human susceptibility to sentimentality, cultic ritualism, aesthetic excess (or depravation), parapsychic musings, and generally, what Sigmund Freud calls "the universal obsessional neurosis of humanity" are certainly apt candidates for investigation under the idea of "superstitious religion." In view of the more fruitful human tool of scientific inquiry, Freud wanted to purge religion in toto from human affairs. If in any form religion pretended to inform us about reality, it either faltered in the presence of more scrupulous scientific procedures, or it outright failed for lack of referent for its words. In contrast, my argument subsumes superstition under the more fundamental ontological and hermeneutical rubrics of "causation" and "referentiality."

27. Freud, *op. cit.*, p. 24. Here he cites his work in *Totem and Taboo*.

28. Conceive of language as referential, and "the determination of the being of an entity as presence" (to cite a concept developed in Jacques Derrida's, *Of Grammatology*) is presumed to be the proper philosophical commitment to exploring the nature of reality. Derrida calls this idea "logocentrism." A

logocentric attitude naturally requires referentiality as its point of departure. See Jacques Derrida, *Of Grammatology*, (tr. G. C. Spivak [Baltimore and London: The Johns Hopkins University Press, 1974, 1976, orig., 1967]), p. 12. In his section titled "The Signifier and Truth" (pp. 10ff.) the idea of logocentrism is more fully developed.

29. God's invisibility creates speculation about God's existence which leads people to think that there is something of religious significance in such speculation. However, suppose god were *known* objectively to exist. Would anything of religious significance result? The objective presence of God might have a force like the presence of moral responsibility—the moral law within may equate with the starry universe above. But as with moral duty, religious life would be merely one more episode in life's alternatives. The lesser certainty of proofs for God's existence wouldn't then hold greater promise of impacting one's life.

30. Freud, *op. cit.*, p. 32f.

31. *Ib.*, p. 54.

32. See *ib.*, p. 56.

33. See *ib.*, p. 55.

34. In the language of Christendom, for example, these "elements" might include the Trinitarian God the Father, God the Son, and God the Holy Spirit. Thus to speak of God the Son appeals to the person of Jesus as its object, but the language which surrounds the person of Jesus ("the Christ," "the Son of the Father") is itself theological. What shall these words refer to, if Jesus (as an ancient creed states) "is fully man"?

It should also be noted that the traditional theological formulae (God the creator, Jesus born and died, the resurrection of the flesh, and so on) were responses to the Platonized versions of Christianity, especially as found in Gnosticism. This was the language they had in which to carry on the fight. The key is to see what the point of the fighting was. In this regard, see Nygren's *Agape and Eros, op. cit.*

35. In the first century B.C., Publilius Syrus said, "As men, we are all equal in the presence of death." Christianity likewise recognizes a fundamental equality of all persons: they come to nought—they die. In this way, both Judaism and Christianity take human existence to be intrinsically meaningless. The particulars of this claim are argued further on, but I offer a clue as to the direction this thought follows in the following scriptural citation:

> Two men went up into the temple to pray, one a Pharisee and the other a tax collector. The Pharisee stood and prayed thus with himself, 'God, I thank thee that I am not like other men, extortioners, unjust, adulterers, or even like this tax collector. I fast twice a week, I give tithes of all that I get.' But the tax collector, standing far off, would not even lift up his eyes to heaven, but beat his breast, saying, 'God, be merciful to me a sinner!' I tell you, this man went down to his house justified rather than

the other; for every one who exalts himself will be humbled, but he who humbles himself will be exalted (Lk. 18:10-14).

36. Ps. 22: 6-11. The Psalm is open to various interpretations. The early Christian church used it as the literary model for the crucifixion of Jesus. In one sense, the passage has merely a local urgency; a more optimistic viewpoint on life could as well be cited. However, the religious force of the passage is to be centered on how the concept of "God" is employed in locating the finitude of human existence.

37. (New York: Crossroad Publishing Co., 1986, English trans. 1975, orig. 1960), p. 4.

38. The theory sounds plausible until one asks how one could recognize something as experience that was independent of a capacity to see it as such and mark it. It seems rather that the capacity for speaking presumes a primacy of language over experience. The capacity for speaking, coextensive with the capacity for thinking, establishes context and whatever subsequently is to be meant by experience. Experience gains its meaning in originary acts of persons. This is Gadamer's point in saying "The experience is not wordless to begin with and then an object of reflection by being named...."

Other sympathetic forms of this view of language have been developed by various thinkers in continental philosophy. Heidegger's "Letter on Humanism" (in *Martin Heidegger—Basic Writings*, Harper and Row, 1977, pp. 189ff.), Merleau-Ponty's chapter "The Body as Expression, and Speech" (in *The Phenomenology of Perception* [tr. C. Smith, Routledge & Kegan Paul/Humanities Press: New York, 1962, pp. 174ff.]), or Georges Gusdorf's *Speaking* (tr. P. T. Brockelman, Northwestern University Press, 1965) are cases in point. Anglo-American followers of Ludwig Wittgenstein's *Philosophical Investigations* (New York: Macmillan Co., 1953) echo these same concerns.

39. *Concluding Unscientific Postscript*, tr. Swenson/Lowrie, (Princeton: Princeton University Press, 1941) esp. pp. 71f. and 182f.

40. Unreflectively, I exist in a center of self-generated importance. Those who pass by become for me objects—to be depreciated, ignored, reckoned with. It is not until I see *myself* in the image of an insignificant passerby, which also for them I am, that I can recognize that my self-assessed meaningfulness is a fanciful self-deception. I was once walking the dog in a cemetery in Santa Rosa, California (a city whose history harks back to early Spanish mission times in that region) looking at the inscriptions on the grave stones. For California, it was an old cemetery with graves dating back into the mid-nineteenth century. I came to one weather-beaten headstone, its crown almost hidden by tall weeds which had thrived there. Pulling back the growth to reveal the inscription of the man's name and the nineteenth-century dates, I read "That so and so may never be forgotten"—and I released the weeds, once again to obscure the epitaph.

41. *Postscript*, p. 521. "For Christianity is a fine belief to die in, the only true comfort, and the moment of death is the appropriate situation for Christianity."

42. The imagery of religious language lends itself to both causal and referential thinking. For instance, the Jewish story tells of the Jews receiving God's law as a gift. Through the language of myth, we see God on the mountain promising Moses to rectify the unhappy plight of the Jews, interceding for them against the Egyptians. For the Jews' part, they entered into this agreement with the hope that obedience to God's law would redeem an otherwise empty and meaningless existence of slavery. Submission to God instead of man was to create a fully meaningful life.

This way of speaking and this way of utilizing the "God" concept holds the finitude of human existence before the speaker. Only life lived in obedience to God's law, a meaning which was above anything human, would make life meaningful. Thus, mythically, the promises of God remind the existing individual of his own helplessness and finitude. The task remaining is one of obedience, which sets aside notions of self-importance.

As a Jewish sect, Christianity's formulation is not *ab ovo*. It continued in the context of a Jewish world view but (it seems to me) with the addition of a relentless realism. Given the Jewish task of obedience to God's law as the condition for redeeming life's meaninglessness, failure to achieve the requirements of the divine law was a failure not only of human existence but of being itself. Obedience to God became an unrealizable hope; and if so, there was no commutation of the sentence of meaninglessness in life, unless (once again in the mythical language at hand) it were to originate outside of things human. In this regard, St. Paul spoke of the redemption of all existence (independent human contributions to the matter) in the coming kingdom of God. This way of speaking likewise maintained the essential condition for religious self-understanding, that of the meaninglessness of one's existence. The force of this mythical thinking still presumed the state of human meaninglessness and found God creating meaning (including his acceptance of persons) where there was none.

Language reflected one's being in a world, and it took different forms. There was the language of objectivity as well as that of subjectivity. In this regard, Freud received religious language as teachings. But the mythical language of religion was properly uttered on the occasion of probing one's subjectivity.

43. *Postscript, op. cit.*, pp. 99ff.

44. Here I reflect a passage from the *Postscript*: "If one who lives in the midst of Christendom goes up to the house of God, the house of the true God, with the true conception of God in his knowledge, and prays, but prays in a false spirit; and one who lives in an idolatrous community prays with the entire passion of the infinite, although his eyes rest upon the image of an idol: where

is there most truth? The one prays in truth to God though he worships an idol; the other prays falsely to the true God, and hence worships in fact an idol" (*ib.*, p. 179f.).

45. Besides the synopsis of Christian mythology found in Rudolph Bultmann's lead article in *Kerygma and Myth* (Hans-Werner Bartsch's, ed., London: SPCK, 1972) titled "New Testament and Mythology," see also Bultmann's *The New Testament and Mythology and Other Basic Writings* (Philadelphia: Fortress Press, c. 1984).

46. Jacques Derrida's challenges to the metaphysics of presence and logocentricism contained in works such as *Of Grammatology* (Baltimore, Johns Hopkins University Press, 1976, orig., *De la Grammatologie*, 1967), *Dissemination* (Chicago, University of Chicago Press, 1981, orig., *La Dissémination*, 1972), or *Margins of Philosophy* (Chicago, University of Chicago Press, 1982, orig., *Marges de la philosophie*, 1972) are cases in point.

47. *Postscript, op. cit.*, p. 182.

48. Cf. Merleau-Ponty's *The Phenomenology of Perception*, tr., C. Smith (London: Routledge & Kegan Paul [New York: The Humanities Press], 1962), p. viii f.

49. The early church became consumed by Christological speculation about the nature of Jesus in part because the ontological speculations of Gnosticism required that Jesus be a divine creature of pure spirit and no flesh. In the competition for the intellectual loyalties of people in the early church, the thinking of Jesus, which itself grew in the soil of Judaism, had to be given divine authority. Some sort of imprimatur was sought in a world populated by spiritual forces and realities. To me, what is interesting is that in places Jesus himself seems to reject the signs of authority, which is quite in keeping with the idea of *agape*.

When I speculate what might have shaped Jesus's own outlook, I think that it might in part have been due to his father, Joseph, who accepted him as a son. The Gospel of Matthew reports Joseph's astonishment about Mary's pregnancy. Jewish gossip of the time likewise questions Jesus's parentage:

> The Talmud contains many statements that are wholly polemical—for example, that Jesus was the illegitimate son of an adulteress by a Roman soldier named Pandira or Panthera.... (Howard C. Kee, *Jesus in History* [New York: Harcourt Brace Jovanovich, Inc., 1977], p. 51).

Were there truth in the gossip, Jesus's questionable parentage would have given pause to anyone in that culture. Mary would have to have been seen as having disgraced herself; for Joseph to marry Mary, he would have had to have rejected a normative moral stance toward Mary's indiscretion and, correspondingly, to her illegitimate child, Jesus. What characterizes his attitude is openness and acceptance toward both Mary and Jesus, the persons whose lives were "stained." This position as well seems to have been adopted by Jesus.

Although appealing to the Holy Spirit to cause Jesus's conception would have cultural precedent, the fact remains that these remarks came long after the fact of the circumstances which immediately surround Jesus's birth. In a fundamental way, then, Joseph may have been the founder of Christian faith.

50. Anders Nygren, *Agape and Eros* (tr., P. S. Watson [Illinois: University of Chicago Press, 1953 {orig., Bk I: 1932, Bk II: 1938,39}]). The book provides a synopsis of the idea of *agape* through a contrast with *eros*—Book I is a conceptual analysis of the two ideas of *eros* and *agape*; Book II shows how *agape* and *eros* vie with each other in church history. Reproduced here is a summary chart on p. 210. An exposition of his rather persuasive but involved argument transcends the objectives of this essay.

51. Jean-Paul Sartre in his play "Dirty Hands" (*Les Mains sales*, found in *no exit and three other plays* [New York: Vintage Books, 1949]) investigates this theme through his principal character, Hugo. At a point Hugo's wife Jessica asks him: "And you have to kill the people who don't think your way?" He responds: "Sometimes." A bit later he has in interchange with another major character, Hoederer, in which Hoederer makes this remark: "With us others, it's not so easy to shoot some chap for the sake of a theory, because we're the ones who cook up the theories and we know how they are made. We can never be entirely certain that we're right." Then turning to Hugo, he asks: "Take you: are you sure you're right?" As events reveal, Hugo's affirmative answer is betrayed. Yet in order to be on the side of truth, Hugo must judge and act on the truth of the judgment. *Agape* requires no such commitment.

52. The administration of the sacraments have wide-ranging authority in Christendom. Some churches, the Society of Friends (Quakers), for instance, find communion administered by a clergy disruptive of the religious life. "High" churches administer sacraments only by way of qualified sacred authority—and for Roman Catholics, not one drop of the sacred wine (blood) can be allowed to spill for fear of desecrating the sacred, not that Protestants are less punctilious. A manufactured holiness shrouds the eucharist, with proper gesture and pose. (The earliest celebrations of The Last Supper weren't invested with such sanctity.)

Led by a referential theory of language in which the words possess divine authority, superstition invades the religious. Infants are baptized to alleviate parental fears about what might transpire in the event of the child's untimely death, and with some sects, the baptism can only take a certain form, or else it isn't effective. Presumably, one pays the consequences when one violates the sacred; and although a case can be made that the sacred ritual can have an authentic religious sense, I fear that many of the participants in ritual are superstitious.

53. An implication of this view is that there might be religious language which was not institutionalized in the language of the world's religions and yet would qualify as "religious" language.

54. *Postscript, op. cit.*, p. 523.

55. Notice a parallel with secular occasions in which we honor accomplishment, posture before life's unavoidable realities, give homage to the matters of living and dying, and moralize about good things which are well suited to their purpose. In good conscience one participates in rituals of state—attending graduation ceremonies, singing the national anthem, addressing dignitaries in formal terms, sending cards of congratulation or sympathy, even pontificating about 'the dignity of man' (in the absence of confirming evidence)—without these being accompanied by superstition. All of these things can be understood as establishing a context for sealing or moving forward in the affairs of civil life.

# Chapter VIII

## Conclusion—The Dwelling That Words Among Us[1]

### The End of Philosophy

Religious thinking is absorbed in a philosophical culture. Christendom was especially vulnerable. From its beginning it baptized unrepentant philosophical concerns into the faith. However, the essence of philosophy is unrelenting, critical analysis; it leaves nothing sacred, even to the extent that it challenges its own grounding in the long tradition of commitment to absolute objectivity. Philosophy as it has been practiced is being undone, and the ideal of a universal philosophy is all but abandoned. Historically, Christian thinking echoed philosophy's objectivity. It is now set adrift. No longer does the idea of "God" make objective sense. Contemporary philosophy forces Christianity (and religion generally) to reexamine its own being.

Purged of philosophical tradition, what will be required of religion? The Christianity which continues to depend on traditional philosophy will become even more unconvincing—unless a philosophically unadorned religiousness can renew itself out of its own resources. As contemporary philosophy dislodges itself from its misdirected history,[2] religion must likewise investigate its own genesis, to see itself in its own light, independent of philosophy.[3]

When Martin Heidegger (1889-1976) took up Kierkegaard's challenge to pay attention to being, he undid the sorts of philosophies on which Christianity had come to rely.[4]

> Only epochs which no longer fully believe in the true greatness of the
> task of theology arrive at the disastrous notion that philosophy can
> help to provide a refurbished theology if not a substitute for theology,
> which will satisfy the needs and tastes of the time. For the original
> Christian faith philosophy is foolishness.[5]

The religious unmaking of its foolishness means that it cannot rest in
philosophical theories. One begins the process of religion's renewal by
turning attention not to "God" but to the searcher for God, there to see
a person who perpetually exists in his/her own thinking. The purge of
philosophy from religion anticipates its renewal in a sphere of concern
proper to it.[6] Otherwise, religion's deterioration will parallel that of
the philosophical traditions which sustained it.

Philosophy provided answers to questionable questions: Why was
there something rather than nothing? What ultimately is real? Under
what conditions can we know the truth? Where empiricism was
reckoned a legitimizing source of meaning, "God" became a religious
reality with intuitive, psychological or emotive import. Divine reality
was sustained by wonder and awe, fixed in the aesthetics of logical
perfection, augmented by a sense of well-being prompted by a moral
ordering of life, "felt" as the moving of the Holy Spirit. Where reason
was deemed ultimate, metaphysics about the "spark of the divine within
every human breast" or "the inherent dignity and worth of every
human person" (both sentiments of the Enlightenment's ethical and
religious musings represented in Kant) were made to flower into
religious doctrines. By making *thought* an aspect of the divine mind,
Descartes, Malebranche, Berkeley, Hegel each found ways to make
"God" a solution to the philosophically created problem of sub-
ject/object dichotomy. Religious people were satisfied by philosophical
theories as they searched for a referent for "God." Whatever the word
"God" gained in its philosophical associations was likewise a gain in
its overall legitimation.

Grounding the word "God" in the familiar, something arguably
objective, something rational, was to give vitality to an otherwise
vacuous concept. The idea "God" was infused into a philosophical
articulation of what (surely) must count as divine. One used the word
"God" in the belief that one might even produce the "divine god-
thing," were it not for the mere detail that human finitude imposed its
limitations. Like all genuine ideas, "God" was to be grounded in an
objective state of affairs. Religious language became the shadow of an

objective reality. Its words, sounds, were signs *referring* to the independent world of objective things.[7] Both Christian liberalism and fundamentalism remain outside parochial religious confines and are caught up in a philosophical urge to uncover an objective divinity which arguably establishes or authenticates religious faith. They each seek a state of affairs, the truth of which (in one way or another) is discernible and which allows access to the mind and will of God. To sustain the hope promised by objectivity, both ends of the Christian spectrum reach beyond the territory of humble religious matters to broach far-ranging metaphysical issues: the meaning and purpose of the universe (at least this particular corner of it), the machinery and paraphernalia needed to make "God's will" (should there be such) prevail, the inexorable requirements of moral law. The prospects are seductive.

Lessing's imagery of God coming to someone with the offer of objective truth in his right hand, and in his left "the lifelong pursuit of truth" is clear: choose the right hand and make oneself the equal of God. Choose the left and remain human. The right hand allows one to defend truth, assured that one is correct. One is bathed in purity. Knowing truth, one could be guiltless in its vigorous prosecution. One metes out justice by truth's demands. Its victims are deservedly so. Possess truth; judge others; be God's earthly advocate; assume God's role. Failure to judge and pronounce marks both shortcomings in the intellect and perversity of character for one who knows truth.

However, if the traditional view of language is askew, and the word "God" does not refer to a thing to search for; if proofs for God's existence (as Immanuel Kant argues) only tell us about the relations between concepts, not about God, how should we understand religious language? Failure to show how the word "God" might refer to something, if not actually justify atheism, would bury "God talk" in the graveyard of failed ideas, a place governed by indifference. If the search for objectivity is not relevant to religious life, what is?

Lessing's chooser picked the left hand. Here "truth" functioned as a perpetual human striving. God's Truth was closed to persons. This vignette recast our understanding of truth. It became something that functioned within the pragmatics of living, a perpetual quest that directed one's life, although its results remained provisional and evasive. With God's truth closed to human scrutiny, there was no unshakable foundation on which to rest one's life. Truth's final, objective formulation lay perpetually over the horizon, rendering tentative the claims made on its behalf. Attention returned squarely to the person, the striver, whose life itself remained without ultimate justification. This is a particularly bitter result. Kierkegaard's analysis of "objective truth" made answers to the consuming issue of human existence—its meaningfulness—a matter of ultimate indifference.

> The way of objective reflection makes the subject accidental, and thereby transforms existence into something indifferent, something vanishing. Away from the subject the objective way of reflection leads to the objective truth, and while the subject and his subjectivity become indifferent, the truth also becomes indifferent, and this indifference is precisely its objective validity.... The way of objective reflection ... leads away from the subject, whose existence or non-existence ... becomes infinitely indifferent.[8]

There is no *objective* sense of human meaningfulness people can dwell in. The intellectual edifices of philosophy were not reports on Absolute Truth with the thinker a reporter in their service. Ideas were human inventions lived within a horizon of human interests. Philosophers, caught up in an earnestness to make philosophy absolute, were simply "forgetful" of their existence as *human* beings. They overlooked "the existing individual" who brings forth those ideas in whose terms life is lived. This dwelling in finitude created an existential notion of truth in which "truth is subjectivity," founded in the meaning of being a subject. Subjectivity becomes the context for religious life.

Religious language—a language of subjectivity, a language of human existence—is formed by the recognition and expression of one's finitude. It is used in the context of confession, not representation. The truth of religious language is to be found in its capacity to frame and unfold human existence, not in whether its propositions are objective enough to be believed. To think of religious language as depicting objective truths about the universe disguises, hides, sometimes obliterates the world of human experience which genuine religious language is meant to address. One's being comes into focus through religious language. To make religion serve other purposes distorts it—religious language addresses human finitude and explores the limits of human existence. Differing responses to finitude become fixed in the variety of religions.

Only superficially do philosophy and religion exist in the same arena. Philosophy's fundamental concern with issues of meaning originated in positive theories about ultimate reality. All existence and its meaning was an extension of the general theory of reality. In contrast, coming as it did from a confession of the inner depths of human finitude, religious language's articulation of human meaninglessness was disinterested in the nature of things. How meaninglessness became expressed imparted unique properties to each world religion. But when religious thinkers also possessed a passion for coherence in ideas, where they decreed that what would be meaningful must be objectively sanctioned, they turned to philosophy to authenticate religious claims. Religious motives became subverted by philosophical theorizing. It is this point—the point of a "natural," philosophical attitude—which I have attacked. Insistence on the facticity of religious claims is a murky form of scientific thinking and has no religious merit. The authentic religious thinker is unconcerned with an objective knowledge of God and the world. Religious life begins with what it means to be a subject.

## Speaking a Wor[l]d

Like all language, religious language finds its context in human concerns. Religious language begins with "dwelling that words among us." Person's don't simply live and survive; they "dwell." Speaking establishes that sense of "world" which transcends its indexical words. It creates presence, so that dwelling and speaking become inseparable. Speaking permits dwelling, creates presence, engulfs existence with the meaning of temporality. Things lose mere spatiality. As a function of human presence, they are invested (contaminated, infected) with meaning. In an objectivist account something becomes meaningful in its being noticed, as if "noticing" could be a wordless abstraction. However, one simply doesn't come into something's presence unarmed (a requirement of a representational theory of language). To recognize the possibility of something's being meaningful, one's sense for "context" makes oneself and world be present. Though context is inconceivable in the absence of things, it is likewise true that thing and thought are conceivable because of speaking. Heidegger touches this theme in "Building Dwelling Thinking"[9] when he says:

> When I go toward the door of the lecture hall, I am already there, and I could not go to it at all if I were not such that I am there. I am never here only, as this encapsulated body; I am there, that is, I already pervade the room, and only thus can I go through it.
> Man's relation to locations, and through locations to spaces,

> inheres in his dwelling. The relationship between man and space is
> none other than dwelling, strictly thought and spoken.

Our speaking is filled with and fills out the context of our living, our
dwelling. Our dwelling words among us.

The world we live is unfolded as a human project, forged (constructed, built, intensified, shared) out of the activities of life which
engage speaker and hearer. Caught up in expression, bound by the
engagements and entangling of souls, individual words drop out, and
the gestures and articulations of persons, present in different ways,
erupt in speaking. Verbal gestures become the intricacies of life and
world. Discourse is a mutual effort of speaking in a manner appropriate
to what we intend and of hearing what the other intends. Just these
words must be uttered if a world is shared. We come to understand one
another because we participate in a common effort to consummate a
world. One person speaks, crystallizing a world. Another hears and in
hearing grasps the intentions found in lives shared. Thought and things
are not independent; word and meaning are not different. Though we
live and breathe on terra firma, there is no thing, no world for persons,
until it is said. It is not as if a person's mind were imbued with a
heavenly vision of the absolute for which names are learned, or as if
one's eyes are innocently informed by the etchings of experiences
which commute meaning to the mind's theretofore imageless slate, or
as if things in the world are prepossessed by those meanings consciousness merely recognizes, or even that words learned go in search of
their meanings. Traditional analyses of language pass over the
phenomenon of speaking.[10] Speaking is the activity of living; it is a
participatory and enlivened thinking which stands outside analysis.

Were an analogy to be sought, one might suggest that speaking is
something like performing music. A passage of music is enjoined by
the previous one and invokes what is to come. Individual notes are not
especially heard except as the music deliberately focuses on them.
Musical context—harmony, dynamics, meter, silence, a sense produced
in melody—creates musical meaning. There are musical cliches,
musical jokes, musical surprises.[11] Analogously, when speaking, what
we say is enjoined by the context being created; silence punctuates
meaning, settled thought nests in cliches, and we call attention to
individual words in puns. As individual notes have no musical sense
(context), so autonomous words and sentences only portend meaning
and, independent of context, make no statement. In our verbal

"singing," we constitute ourselves in meaning; things emerge, "ready-to-hand," meaningful; they come into view through life activities established within speaking. After we speak, analysis shows us morphemes and phonemes, grammar, style, logic (instead of thinking). Analysis transforms our understanding of the event. When one focuses on language, the dwelling which words disappears and rhetoric emerges. We analyze musical structure with music theory, compose according to rule; and as the notes disappear in a melody, so the sounds of the words spoken disappear to favor meaning.[12]

We speak, and this creative power of a living *logos* which marks human existence suspends subject-object distinctions. We speak, not to identify meaning but to bring it about. We are not using signs to refer. We "create a world." We speak, sharing a common interest to make ourselves present in some way to the other. An openness to others is sought. Utterances become promises which evoke a sense of life. The established language reflects the ordering of past successes. In speaking we simultaneously live out and evoke context—ways in which persons become present for one another. It is living in this mutually shared presence by which self-expression and communication—the human context—become what they are. It is this view Martin Heidegger summarizes: "It is in words and language that things first come into being and are."[13]

## Agape's Creative Power

Philosophy presupposed the intrinsic meaningfulness of existence; religion arose in the recognition of the finitude of life and the confession of its ultimate meaninglessness.[14] Meaninglessness is offensive to our philosophical pronouncements on our inherent dignity and worth. Christianity's history is a recitation of philosophical efforts to overcome the offense. Thus it is that primitive Christianity flirted with gnosticism and its account of an ultimate meaningfulness. The later theological works of Augustine and then Thomas Aquinas accommodate a philosophical affirmation of meaningfulness, respectively, in the work of Plato and Aristotle, though simultaneously they also saw conflict with the Pauline insistence on an essential human fallenness and sin. Finally, no longer willing to endure the indignity of meaninglessness, Christian thinkers of the Enlightenment abandoned themselves to a belief in glorious mankind's basic goodness and its fundamental meaningfulness, a philosophical spirit culminating in Nietzsche's espousal of the *Übermensch*.[15]

Rejecting both the Christian presumption of human meaninglessness and (equally) the Enlightenment accounts of meaningfulness, Nietzsche's pronouncements about the human capacity to produce meaning lifted the human spirit beyond a dependence on philosophical theories to give meaning. We preface our understanding of how the life of *agape* addresses human meaninglessness by spending a moment on Nietzsche. His contrasting account of human existence sharpens *agape's* radical insight.

Nietzsche's *Übermensch* completed the idea of human meaningfulness. Instead of searching for meaning in an objectivity found in a philosophically contrived "elsewhere," the *Übermensch* exercised his own meaning-creating activity as a will to power. The evocation of meaning was a human project. Those who shuddered at their humanity and did not recognize or could not bring themselves to act on the singular power persons have to create meaning "shall be given every possible assistance" to perish as worthy candidates for the human race. Nietzsche called for frank honesty, a turn to that state of being in which persons understand they are without excuses. Such an individual humanizes existence. Says Nietzsche,

> With the help of custom and the social strait-jacket, man was, in fact, made calculable. However, if we place ourselves at the terminal point of this great process, where society and custom finally reveal their true aim, we shall find the ripest fruit of that tree to be the sovereign individual, equal only to himself, all moral custom left far behind. This autonomous, more than moral individual ... has developed his own, independent, long-range will, which dares to make promises; he has a proud and vigorous consciousness of what he has achieved, a sense of power and freedom, of absolute accomplishment. This fully emancipated man, master of his will.... Think how much trust, fear, reverence he inspires ..., and how, having that sovereign rule over himself, he has mastery too over all weaker-willed and less reliable creatures! Being truly free and possessor of a long-range, pertinacious will, he also possesses a scale of values. Viewing others from the center of his own being, he either honors or disdains them. It is natural to him to honor his strong and reliable peers, all those who promise like sovereigns: rarely and reluctantly; who are chary of their trust; whose trust is a mark of distinction; whose promises are binding because they know that they will make them good in spite of all accidents, in spite of destiny itself.[16]

For Nietzsche, strength of will created meaning. The capacity to will defined human existence, not an abstract metaphysics of objectivity nor deference to a God projected out of the fears and insecurities of human existence. Christianity distorted human existence when it pronounced blessings on the poor in spirit, those who mourn, the meek, those *thirsting* for righteousness, the merciful, the pure in heart, the peace makers. These are the human failures who substituted the life of finitude and its "values" for a strength of human resolve to make its own principles. Understanding what *agape* involved, Nietzsche called for its eradication. There could be no blessedness for those who possessed a sense of their *lack* of value. The values of strength would overcome expressions of weakness. Repulsed by a life of forgiveness, care, endurance, suffering, the *Übermensch* existed as something asserted, created from one's willing it. The proper stance for one who lives in values' truths is to judge. Forgiveness is inappropriate for that which demands total commitment. And yet the Nietzschean person might forgive. For Nietzsche forgiveness implied strength of character. It was a noble act marked by generosity. Because of a magnanimous temperament, one forgives. Forgiveness expresses one's own intrinsic value. In the sphere of objectivity where value is central to human existence, judgment becomes possible regarding other human acts and lives. The transgressor, though undeserving, becomes the fortunate recipient of forgiveness. The *Übermensch* is one who could pardon because of a positive self-assertion. For Nietzsche, that one might forgive was an expression of one's own intrinsic worth, a noble act. Nietzsche proclaimed life's humanization. He called for a return to a self-generated, self-imposed ethics. No further demand to justify the rightness of its claims was needed; for such rationalizations were themselves rooted in the will to power, and to succumb to them represented philosophical chicanery. Where resistance against life was overcome by "the unconquerable soul,"[17] *there* was authentic human existence. This unconquerable soul, this person undiminished by the foibles of humanity to embrace philosophy and religion, was Nietzsche's *Übermensch*. He created his own blessedness by overcoming resistance. Nietzsche's *Übermensch* thus stood in awe of its God-like capabilities to define a world. Enlightenment philosophers sought power in philosophical truth. Nietzsche's *Übermensch* would stand beyond the imagined objectivity of philosophy and religion. Instead of ideal philosophical abstractions in the absence of which being could not be, we are given an equally abstract but romantic *Übermensch* at the center of meaning's possibility.

> What is good? Everything that heightens the feeling of power in a man; the will to power, power itself.
> What is bad? Everything that is born of weakness.
> What is happiness? The feeling that power is *growing*, that resistance is overcome.
> Not contentedness but more power; not peace but war; not virtue but fitness....
> The weak and the failures shall perish; first principle of *our* love of man. And they shall even be given every possible assistance. What is more harmful than any vice? Active pity for all the failures and all the weak: Christianity.[18]

The triumph of Man portended God's death. Pride was the proper effect for a well-lived life instead of a debilitating Christian humility.

Humility is antithetical to Nietzsche's account of human nature. Humility results when values are an impossible measure for one's own authenticity and the authenticity of others. What conceptual structure leads to this conclusion? As the pride of an *Übermensch* was both natural and proper in Nietzsche, so likewise, persons who abide in the uncertainties of finitude find humility manifesting itself as their state of being. The issue is thus one of self-understanding;[19] and here no philosophical necessity can prevail to shape one's choice. The meaninglessness of one's being comes as a confession generated from attempting to take one's life seriously. Failure to achieve a hoped for meaning by incorporating value into life is attended by a sense of humility in the presence of one's resultant meaninglessness. Nietzsche views "humility" as if it were a value, something created from human will. However, Nietzsche was mistaken. Instead of a value, humility is a confession of what is implicit in human finitude, in subjectivity.

The contrast lingers between the values of the *Übermensch* and *agape's* rendering of human existence. It is as if somehow Nietzsche could escape the void of the human frailty by which he produced his ideas. Nietzsche's hope in the will of the *Übermensch* was naive and gratuitous, an adolescent fantasy sustained in self-congratulatory words of assurance—words uttered from the individual's perpetual possibility of error. The *Übermensch* becomes an intellectual fiction, a seductive confusion steeped in pathos.

The Sermon on the Mount presumes thought's failure to produce life's meaning. With realism it accepted meaninglessness as a person's state of being. Persons who lived in terms of finitude expressed their self-understanding through the images of weakness, of human finitude.

> Blessed are the poor in spirit, for theirs is the kingdom of heaven.
>
> Blessed are those who mourn, for they shall be comforted.
>
> Blessed are the meek, for they shall inherit the earth.
>
> Blessed are those who hunger and thirst for righteousness, for they shall be satisfied.
>
> Blessed are the merciful, for they shall obtain mercy.
>
> Blessed are the pure in heart, for they shall see God.
>
> Blessed are the peacemakers, for they shall be called sons of God.
>
> Blessed are those who are persecuted for righteousness' sake, for theirs is the kingdom of heaven.
>
> Blessed are you when men revile you and persecute you and utter all kinds of evil against you falsely on my account. Rejoice and be glad, for your reward is great in heaven, for so men persecuted the prophets who were before you (Mt. 5:3-11).

The blessed individuals were not directed by the spirit of the *Übermensch*. The sovereignty implicit in striving and the autonomy of self-assertion succumb to an insurmountable finitude which no will to power can address. Despair over life's meaning is transformed by the gift of *agape* whose underlying assumption is finitude. Concerns with the metaphysical issue of meaningful or meaningless existence were set aside. There was neither sovereignty nor self to defend.

> ... if any one strikes you on the right cheek, turn to him the other also.
>
> Love your enemies and pray for those who persecute you....

Values are submerged in the larger issue of how those who have recognized their subjectivity can live.

For Christendom, the formulation of this sense of being is initially given in Jewish religious language and traditions. Thus, what individuals could not gain for themselves, God offered as a heavenly gift: life redeemed from meaninglessness. It was a kind of forgiveness which made openness in relationships possible. The forgiveness which characterizes *agape* emerged from finitude, not self-assertion. In the world view of first century Jewish beliefs, our lives would be justified (blessed) only by God's redemption of life in his coming Kingdom.

Through the giving up of self (an act of *agape*) *agape* penetrated even the value structures of life, overcoming them with a life-giving care. The life at risk itself becomes meaning-giving. The philosophical legacy of value is threatened when the truth of value is suspended and enemies are recreated as persons. In "turning the other cheek" or "loving enemies," values are suspended, set aside. It is in this light that the primitive church defined the concept of God in the symbol of the Cross. Instead of the images of might and power utilized in the defense of truth, it developed the image of one who in his suffering forgives.

In his mythic voice, St. Paul gives expression to finitude's thoroughness by seeing God alone as capable of redeeming existence.

> For the creation waits with eager longing for the revealing of the sons of God; for the creation was subjected to futility, not of its own will but by the will of him who subjected it in hope; because the creation itself will be set free from its bondage to decay and obtain the glorious liberty of the children of God. We know that the whole creation has been groaning in travail together until now; and not only the creation, but we ourselves, who have the first fruits of the Spirit, groan inwardly as we wait for adoption as sons, the redemption of our bodies. For in this hope we were saved. Now hope that is seen is not hope. For who hopes for what he sees? But if we hope for what we do not see, we wait for it with patience (Rom. 8:19-25).

Embedded in this eschatological language is the recognition that nothing of human proportions could redeem existence from its emptiness. A religious language arose to express the human condition. Even if uttered from a mythological perspective, the language captured the fundamental stance of human dependence. Nygren's account was in terms of *agape's* 'coming down,' being from God, specifically, "God's way to man," an act of grace, and so on. As noted by Nygren, the structure of Jewish religious thinking as developed in first-century Christianity required that God initiate *agape*. God need fit no philosophical demand that He take cognizance of human value. The meaning of human existence could not be effected by its own design. No circumventing of finitude was possible. Only God could redeem life. The religious perspective insisted that no human guile could effect *agape*.

Yet the fact remains that even this religious sense of "world" is a human effect. This indefinite, passive voice by which "love is brought down" is also a creature of some person's understanding what sort of language finitude must sustain in order to reveal itself. As all language comes out of the sensitivities of human existence, *agape* was a Greek word turned to religious purposes. It framed a redemptive power, a holy presence, which made itself real in its being lived. Human finitude presented in a religious language suppressed self-assertion as this was expressed through forgiveness, humility, *agape*; and the facticity or objectivity of what was proclaimed was silenced in favor of that mythological language which provided context for finitude, thereby capturing the religious sense of life. Where one fails to understand what makes the language religious, where one assumes that language is bound by causality and referentiality, the person is given up to religious superstition and idolatry.[20]

That language emerges as the expression of human existence leads to a conclusion which becomes controversial to those who persist in the objective hermeneutics of causality and referentiality. The conclusion is this: the idea of *agape* deployed as the shaping force in the articulation of one's being requires no concern with the reality of divine or ultimate being. *Agape* is implicated solely as an aspect of human finitude; or put the other way, a fully understood finitude leads to the life of *agape*. It is the hermeneutic of finitude by which *agape* makes sense. However, since we live in our ideas, the conceptual framework which generates *agape's* expression (the "machinery" of *agape's* delivery) is a language which locates the meaninglessness of human existence by placing it within the larger idea of a sovereign God. The imagery of "sinful man in the hands of an angry God" is an effective "placement" language, although its literalness is unessential to *agape's* expression. Myths, images, or sayings that capture the experience of people in the articulation of their subjectivity have religious validity. Thus the juxtaposition of dependent persons and the sovereign God reiterates an understanding of human existence in which one is dependent on God—in death as well as life. Human existence is given a structure, a context. This is the function of "placement" language. The contextual placement of life for the writers of the synoptic gospels (Matthew, Mark, Luke) was the Jewish apocalyptic hope for the coming Kingdom of God. This myth exposes an underlying notion of human dependence with the sense of Being vested in God. In the present time, existence remained essentially barren of meaning. God's kingdom where meaningful life was established is brought to those for whom the love of neighbor (Mk. 12:28ff) was the unavoidable expression of their being.

By default the failure to understand religious language's existential function of placement leaves one in the grip of philosophical objectivity. Philosophy seeks decisiveness and certainty, not the uncertainty intrinsic to religious language. "God" is projected as a thing in the universe, and statements about God appear descriptive and objective. The door opens to a non-religious (metaphysical) understanding of God. Religious language is drained into blatant superstition and idolatry where collusion with the supernatural (a human conspiracy with "God") arranges existence to human purposes. Yet metaphysically designed meanings that were proposed to render life significant suffer from the same uncertainties that human existence itself does. Meaning derived from a purely human source (for the ancient Jews, the stuff of false religion and idolatry) would be insufficient to redeem life of its emptiness. As Jewish mythology presumed, only God's word could authenticate human existence. If *God* offered life, then persons shall live. Human existence remained meaninglessness prior to God's life creating word in which intrinsic meaninglessness—sin and death in New Testament terms—were overcome. God's word created a wholeness to life which could not have been gained otherwise.

The human finitude addressed by the idea of Christian *agape* draws "God" into its conceptual delineation and reflects the way persons structure their understanding of their meaninglessness. The realism of *agape* sets aside philosophical beginning points that proposed to bring objective meaning to light. The familiar Christian "command" to love one another occurs in the context of religious desperation, a context where the essential meaninglessness of one's life is realized. One utters "God" in the context of life's uncertainties and misapprehensions, vacillations and indecisiveness. "God" is uttered from the context of finitude, from the interpretative force that dwells in one's consummate helplessness in the face of one's inexorable death. In this context God is no Santa substitute nor a lucky rabbit's foot for wishful thinking. Superstitious uses of "God" which are bound by human longings and explanatory placebos are to be set aside in favor of a religiously authentic use of "God." One lives as faith.

In contrast to the perspectives on human existence of a philosophical culture where Being is deciphered as having intrinsic value, recognition of the essential state of meaninglessness was possible in the religious world. Thus, for instance, as part of the conceptual tapestry of *agape* it extends its caring to that which exists in meaninglessness. Love which sacrificially gave, which upbuilt, which "created value in its object," became possible when there was no self to enhance and defend. From this state of being, no judgment was forthcoming regarding conformity to metaphysical ideals. Rather, *agape* presumed that meaning was effected in the manner in which one was present for another person. It was not eternal value which became an individual's primary concern but the task of bringing lives together.

## Revelation

Where one gives expression to the sphere of subjectivity, the idea of "revelation" becomes an expression of resignation to the consequences of finitude. But as with other religious concepts, revelation also operates under the influence of philosophy. One characteristic formulation of revelation is to make it a form of knowledge which has no need for further justification. "Revealed truth" stands above criticism. Philosophical criticism emerges to ask whether any idea can possess a privileged standpoint. Revelation may be a religiously useful way to assert an idea, but when viewed as a source of knowledge, all ideas still remain within human capabilities to produce them. Ideas are produced by persons. Thus, from the perspective of philosophy's objectification of knowledge and a representational language to express it, the appeal to revelation is chicanery. If religious language were to see its function as providing knowledge, revelation would become a sneaky way of giving authority to a claim without needing to be held accountable for it. The revelation of the unity of the Trinity is a case in point. It is to be believed through the authority of revelation—a scheme devised to meet epistemological objections to the dogma itself. However, the view of revelation which intends to counter philosophy's demands for rationality fails if revelation retains an authentic *religious* sense, namely that it address subjectivity.

Revelation is part of a placement language that reinforces the general idea of human helplessness. Revelation isn't an alternative source of knowledge about God, His will, and Being. It is rather the confession of the impact of something in a person's life in terms of which one's being becomes fully uncovered. One speaks of the revelation of God's *agape* in the person of Jesus only to see there a person who establishes relationships in a life-giving forgiveness, who in this meaning-creating activity gives the other himself in relationship in the face of human hopelessness. St. Paul provides a case study in finding a language to address the reality of human finitude. His confession of his inability to overcome an underlying meaninglessness (Romans 7) finds its context in his Jewish religious life which promised a redemption from meaninglessness through obedience to God's law. He confesses that he languishes in the impossibility of giving his life meaning in his striving. There was no deliverance. It was at this point of revelation where a new language came forth, one centered in the redemptive power of *agape* as the life of Jesus. The meaning said to redeem life came from its bestowal by one person on another. This way of living in the presence of others had a redeeming effect which was put in terms of being from God. For St. Paul, the redemption of all life in a coming Kingdom of God remained at the horizon, an eventuality which kept the sense of human finitude perpetually at hand until "the day of resurrection."

From within the context of the Christian Jewish community of the first century—and this context is rich with complexities both in cultural milieu and religious heritage too involved to explore here[21]—the writers of the synoptic gospels regarded the life and person of Jesus from within a general scene of other competitors to prophetic or messianic leadership. One who was struck by his teachings would see the story of Jesus's life and death as displaying what the redemption of life through *agape* meant. The later gospel writer who gave us the Gospel of John (c. 100) attempted to bend the idea of *agape* to a philosophical account of Christian life when he moved from religious to philosophical concerns exemplified by the words he used. He saw Jesus as part of a pre-existent "logos," where, as the bearer of "truth," the salvation Jesus brought depended on what is known. These historical entanglements still leave visible the principal religious concern to address an essentially meaningless human existence. The language that evolved to grasp and inform human meaninglessness issued forth in an *agape* made visible in Jesus's creation of meaning in life. *Agape* was not the effect of recognizing and appreciating values intrinsic to being. The religious language that captured the sense of *agape* was not spoken in the sphere of an objective search for truth or even of useful fantasy. In *agape* virtue is turned from meaning recognized to meaninglessness confessed. The contrast is striking. On the one hand, if one achieves virtue (a process which in some measure presumes a structure of reality first envisioned by Plato), one rightfully can be proud of one's accomplishment. One is qualified by one's knowledge of virtue to judge its appearance in others. On the other, where one recognizes one's essential meaninglessness, humility becomes one's way of being; forgiveness becomes the stance one takes in relationship to others. The gift of forgiveness creates meaning.

The linguistic ties between the concept of "self" and that of "God" come to parallel one another. For instance, the formula 'to love one another as God first loved us' (1 Jn 4:19) presumes on the part both of God and man an openness which is passive respecting its own being. The self is forsaken for the benefit of the other—an image sealed into the accounts of Jesus's crucifixion where Jesus becomes the personified revelation of God's love. In other words, the formulations of religious life require a language suitable to the task, a language which remains entirely within the sphere of human existence. The language is not that of cause-and-effect relationships nor of words referring to things in a metaphysical world. With the individual's confession of a meaninglessness which only s/he can testify to in her/his own experience, the religious language needed to address meaninglessness appeals to the *agape* of God made concrete and religiously focused in the person of Jesus.

## The Silence of God

The response of *agape* to the meaninglessness of human existence sets an emotionally charged *philosophical* issue in motion: that of God's factual existence and the divine nature. The question: does God exist? is not a religious issue and is irrelevant to religious life. Worse—it destroys *religious* concerns; and the philosophical question of God's nature misdirects the religious task. Questions bearing on God's existence intimate discovery, the effect of which creates plausible grounds for the word "God" referring to something which in turn can be further examined—and perhaps even esteemed. Persons endowed with the thinker's perspicacity and judgment stand at the center of the inquiry—the thinker whose own existence is without justification. It is this state of being that unfolds a religious life in which "God" envelops the sense of one's being in the world. Religion is a sphere of existence rather than the effect of discovery. It confronts nothingness. The Western religious context for creating the requisite language of existence was Jewish religious language and tradition. In this context, *agape* became Jesus's unfolding of the senselessness of human existence. Earliest Christianity articulated the working of *agape* in Jesus's life in the image of a self-sacrificing God.

So if there is any encouragement in Christ, any incentive of love, any participation in the Spirit, any affection and sympathy, complete my

joy by being of the same mind, having the same love, being in full
accord and of one mind. Do nothing from selfishness or conceit, but
in humility count others better than yourselves. Let each of you look
not only to his own interests, but also to the interests of others. Have
this mind among yourselves, which you have in Christ Jesus, who,
though he was in the form of God, did not count equality with God a
thing to be grasped, but emptied himself, taking the form of a servant,
being born in the likeness of men. And being found in human form he
humbled himself and became obedient unto death, even death on a
cross (Phil. 2: 1-8).

The idea of incarnation was not an infusion of metaphysical divinity
into life but God's divesting himself of divinity. The image of rational
perfection that marked philosophical divinity could not logically
transform itself into a self-sacrificing God. It is precisely this impossibility which led St. Paul to speak of foolishness.[22] The religious
language that produced the life of *agape*, which embodied subjectivity,
divested God of the prerogatives of rational perfection and involved
God in the affairs of human existence, shrouded in finitude. T  h  e
existence of God need not be established as a condition to unfolding the
life of *agape*. In fact, philosophically, what is meant by "God"
becomes problematic. Philosophy's bias toward objectivity led church
thinkers to reject the Biblical rendering of God with the categories of
subjectivity found in *agape*. The more accessible proofs for God
appealed to meaning and purpose. Values were authenticated by
positing divine being; and alternatively, the presence of value pointed
to God. None of these ratiocinations are relevant to a religious language
that expresses subjectivity. For the religious person, the existence of
God is not something of philosophical curiosity. "God" is not a thing
nor even the condition for the being of things. God is neither an
assumption nor a conclusion. God is not an object for discovery,
argument, or reason.[23] It is precisely this state of being from which
*agape* arises—in a silence wherein God exists. One's manner of
existence is framed in the silence of God.

## Notes

1. The title plays with the scriptural phrase "the Words became flesh and
dwelt among us" (Jn 1:14). It seems to me defensible to think that both
expressions are after the same thing.

Georges Gusdorf's little book *Speaking (La Parole)* (Paul T. Brockelman, tr., Evanston, Northwestern University Press, 1965) is a background against which the following reflection occurs. He introduced his remarks (p. xxix) with a series of definitions—I'd call them "warnings" or "clues"—which have a bearing on the present topic. After indicating the objective features of "language" ("a collection of anatomical and physiological potentialities") and "tongue" ("the system of spoken expression peculiar to a human community"), he turns to an activity of persons—speaking.

> *Speaking* denotes human reality as it evolves, from day to day, in expression. It is no longer a psychological function nor a social reality, but an affirmation of the person in the moral and metaphysical order.
>
> Language and the tongue are abstract data, conditions for the possibility of speech, which incorporates them, assuming them in order to actualize them. Only speaking men exist—men capable of a language and situated within the horizon of a tongue. Thus, there is a hierarchy of signification. It stretches from the simple vocal sound, which is stylized into a word through the imposition of a social meaning, to affective human speaking which bears particular intentions that are the vehicles of personal values.

His analysis of human existence as this is formed in speaking is one way of giving context to religious life.

2. The history of one aspect of what is here called "contemporary philosophy" can be found in books such as Robert C. Solomon's *Continental Philosophy Since 1750: The Rise and Fall of the Self* (Oxford/New York: Oxford U. P., 1988). The names of this movement include Edmund Husserl, Martin Heidegger, Jean-Paul Sartre, Maurice Merleau-Ponty along with their heirs.

3. I see this work as a continuation of reformation in Christian thinking. Second century Christian orthodoxy lamely fought against Platonic mysticism through the Gospel of John and its theological culmination in the Council of Trent. The Reformation doctrine that God's redemption of life was to be by God's grace, not by man's striving to enter into union with God, was the mainstay of Luther and Calvin's thinking. They harked back to St. Paul's insistence on 'salvation by faith alone and not by works.' Striving after God was denied as a form of human authentication. The absence of God as an object of fulfillment (as this is suggested by the striving itself) left one within the state of faith. In this regard Kierkegaard stated that

> The truth is precisely the venture which chooses an objective uncertainty with the passion of the infinite. I contemplate the order of nature in the hope of finding God, and I see omnipotence and wisdom; but I also see much else that disturbs my mind and excites anxiety. The sum of all this is an objective uncertainty. But it is for this very

reason that the inwardness becomes as intense as it is, for it embraces this objective uncertainty with the entire passion of the infinite.

But the above definition of truth [viz., an objective uncertainty held fast in an appropriation-process of the most passionate inwardness] is an equivalent expression for faith (*Concluding Unscientific Postscript*, p. 182).

The religious point is this: for one to "have" God belies the finite stature of human existence. But doesn't Kierkegaard also say that "the ideal of a persistent striving is the only view of life that does not carry with it an inevitable disillusionment" (*op. cit.*, p. 110). Persistent striving holds one in one's humanity, avoiding the disillusionment of *not* being able to lay hold of the divine.

Kierkegaard's initial questioning of philosophy's presumption of access to objective truth focused on "what it means to be human." It does not seem to me that he fully understood the Christian "resolution" of the problem of human meaning. Kierkegaard's "persistent striving" (occasional or persistent is the contrast Kierkegaard makes) inappropriately enters the religious picture of Christianity, for implicit to striving is a deafness to the creative power wrought in speaking, delineated in Christian *agape*. *Agape* uniquely marks the Christian insight.

4. In his difficult way, Heidegger gets at the matter of a misdirected philosophical history through the ancient philosophical question: "Why is there something rather than nothing?" Plato and Aristotle's philosophical turn to the "something" in this question is to be contrasted with Heidegger's return to the "nothing." In *The Introduction to Metaphysics* (*op. cit.*) Heidegger asks what does the phrase "rather than nothing" add to the question? From the viewpoint of objectivity, the "nothing is useless, nonsensical, not making the slightest advance toward the knowledge of the essents [things and meanings]" (p. 23). However, Heidegger continues,

this "rather than nothing" is no superfluous appendage to the real question, but is an essential component of the whole interrogative sentence, which as a whole states an entirely different question "Why are there essents [things and meanings]?" With our question we place ourselves in the essent [meaning] in such a way that it looses its self-evident character as the essent. The essent begins to waver between the broadest and the most drastic extremes; "either essents—or nothing"—and thereby the questioning itself loses all solid foundation. ... Our questioning only opens up the horizon, in order that the essent may dawn in such questionableness (p. 29).

It is not surprising that the concept of "nothing" was dismissed from ancient philosophy's inquiries. The scientifically dismissed "rather than nothing" undermines the commitment to things implied in the idea of objectivity. Things and their fixity offer a security not available in the uncertainties of subjectivity. In this regard Heidegger writes,

> The man who wishes truly to speak about nothing must of necessity become unscientific. But this is a misfortune only so long as one supposed that scientific thinking is the only authentic rigorous thought, and that it alone can and must be made into the standard of philosophical thinking. But the reverse is true. All scientific thought is merely a derived form of philosophical thinking, which proceeded to freeze into its scientific cast (*ib.* p. 25f.).

Heidegger uses the "nothing" to separate the objectification of experience from a sense of Being, of world, which is established by personal engagements in the context of everyday existence. Philosophy denied everyday existence. It divided our ordinary dwelling into subject and world, objectifying each. Persons (the "subjects" or "agents" of philosophy) were made to exist in the privacy of their thoughts, the world conjoined to thought as an alien substance, an object, against which thought reacted. The denial of everyday existence created philosophical perplexity: how was the subject to know the truth of the object?

5. *Introduction to Metaphysics, op. cit.*, p. 7.

6. One way Heidegger pried the philosophical mind loose from our understanding of human experience was through his analysis of language. Traditionally, Platonic ontology created a perspective on being which separated subjective and objective reality. One effect of Heidegger's work was to reject this starting point. He probed the sense of the pre-Socratic world, specifically, Parmenides and Heraclitus, both of whom (for different reasons) rejected the subjective/objective dualism. As scant as their writings are, Heidegger turned them to his favor, arguing a return to pre-Socratic perspectives. He stated:

> The thinking of Parmenides and Heraclitus was still poetic, which in this case means philosophical and not scientific. But because in this poetic thinking the thinking has priority, the thought about man's being follows its own direction and proportions (*Introduction to Metaphysics, op. cit.*, p. 144; the book reworked a 1935 course and was first published in 1953).

Poetry yielded a power to touch existence. No science reached here, and though poetry may inform human existence with its insight, it seems to me that rather than poetic language, religious language more realistically addresses human existence. Heidegger does not investigate religious language maybe in part because the Occidental religious edifice is built from the scientific prejudice he challenges, or maybe because he does not understand religious discourse in the context of "speaking." Heidegger does insist meaning begins with human existence. He puts the matter this way:

> The question of who man is is closely bound up with the question of
> the essence of being. But the definition of the essence of man required
> here cannot be the product of an arbitrary anthropology that considers
> man in basically the same way as zoology considers animals. Here the
> direction and scope of the question of being-human are determined
> *solely* through the question of *being*. In accordance with the hidden
> message of the beginning, man should be understood, within the
> question of being, as *the* site which being requires in order to disclose
> itself. Man is the site of openness, the there. The essent juts into this
> there and is fulfilled. Hence we say that man's being is in the strict
> sense of the word "being-there." The perspective for the opening of
> being must be grounded originally in the essence of [Dasein] being-
> there as such a site for the disclosure of being (*ib*. pp. 204f.).

How is one to speak of man, that being which is "the site of openness," "the
there"? I respond: with the language of human meaninglessness; but to uncover
and elaborate a completed language of nothingness has been difficult in the face
of the triumph of "thingness." It is the contention of this book that religious
language (those ways of speaking associated with the world's great religious
traditions) is a completed address reflecting its foundation in the meaninglessness of human existence, the "nothing."

7. The objectivity of different languages lead some to think of words as
signs. The argument is that the irreducible things of human experience each can
be presumed to have a constant meaning. Persons invent a sound, a word, to
represent these meanings. Since there is one thing but many signs of that thing
in the sounds of the different languages, words are arbitrary and when spoken
to communicate, are fuzzy representations. Nevertheless, despite "the problems
of communication," some sign is required for the thing's identification and a
communication about it.

This theory presumes a subject-object dualism in which the meaning or
sense of the "world" is recognizable in the absence of language. It's as if there
were an unknown, hidden language of "what we know" behind the language
of "what we say." There is no reason to posit such a language, and there is no
reason to accept the analysis of language and thinking through the convenient
idea of "signs."

8. *Concluding Unscientific Postscript, op. cit*, p. 173.

9. In *Poetry, Language, Thought*, tr. A. Hofstadter (New York: Harper
and Row, Publishers, 1971) from a lecture delivered in Aug., 1951. I take it
that the absence of punctuation in the title of this essay is meant to indicate the
inseparability of being, of life. Subject-object distinctions becomes intellectu-
alizations. The quotation is from p. 157.

10. See Hans Gadamer's *Truth and Method* (New York: Crossroad, 1975), especially Part III, "Language and Truth"; or Theodore Kisiel's introduction to Werner Marx's *Heidegger and the Tradition* (tr. T. Kisiel and M. Greene, [Evanston: Northwestern University Press, 1971]); or Richard E. Palmer in *Hermeneutics, Interpretation Theory in Schleiermacher, Dilthey, Heidegger, and Gadamer* (Evanston: Northwestern University Press, 1969). Kisiel writes:

> Being and man meet and are held together in the medium of language, which itself points to something immediate. For Being and man are not related as two substances but belong together and appropriate each other in a unique occurrence which is simplicity itself, in which Being is nothing but the claim that addresses man, and man is nothing but the repose to this appeal (p. xxxi).

Palmer echoes this theme in saying that

> language shapes man's seeing and his thought—both his conception of himself and his world.... His very vision of reality is shaped by language (p. 9).

The persuasiveness of this motif regarding speaking and language forces religious language to be cast in a different light.

The battle is mounted on several fronts. Two mid-twentieth century names come to mind: Ludwig Wittgenstein and Maurice Merleau-Ponty. With different styles and intentions but to the same point, they demonstrate that the sense of meaning depends on the way persons (both as individuals and in community) exist. Here the word "exist" suggests that persons are involved in the activities of life in such a way that meanings arise or appear in conjunction with the interests and contexts generated in living.

11. E.g., the "music" of "P. D. Q. Bach" is a case in point.

12. Consider the proposition "Bill sold the car to Ed" by individually emphasizing the four principal words. With each emphasis one imagines different situations in which the inflection makes sense. Context is provided. Though at one level the sentence describes a business transaction, in each case of inflection, different meanings are generated.

13. *Introduction to Metaphysics, op. cit.*, p. 13. Another way of looking at the matter of speaking is suggested by Maurice Merleau-Ponty in *The Phenomenology of Perception* (tr. Colin Smith, New York: The Humanities Press, 1962), the notion of "gesture" informs both pointing and speaking. As the speaker, I find myself using words as if there were gestures arising in the soul. (See chapter 6, "The Body as Expression, and Speech.") Merleau-Ponty says:

> Here the meaning of words must be finally induced by the words themselves, or more exactly, their conceptual meaning must be formed by a kind of deduction from a *gestural meaning*, which is immanent

in speech.... I begin to understand the meaning of words through their place in the context of action, and by taking part in a communal life (p. 179).

It is a common theme in existential continental philosophy to affirm the intrinsically human quality of speaking and its derivation, language, in contrast to seeing meanings as discoveries with attendant signs in words. Much like gesticulation which is never the result of a self-conscious effort to teach it, our speaking is not exactly taught and learned by systematic procedures, either. The gesture—the wave of the hand, a recoil, a raised eyebrow—is the incarnation of sense captured in bodily movement. Pointing is a gesture which has been regarded as establishing the meaning of words. Because of context engendered by speaking, sense is made of pointing. Pointing could not be the definitive source of meaning, because we still have to know what is pointed at, exactly, when a word was uttered in conjunction with the pointing. The terminal end of "the point" is always indecisive and vague, but the context enjoined by the hearer in listening to what is said gives precision to the gesture of pointing and generates its meaning.

14. In *Being and Time* Martin Heidegger portrays one's confrontation with one's death as essential to understanding authentic living. That religious language does this seemed to escape him, perhaps because he saw only its philosophical bent as this evolved in history.

15. The simple-minded English translation of "superman" doesn't touch what Nietzsche is after. "Mensch" is a human being or person. "Über" is over. The Übermensch is a person who expresses the highest of which persons are capable. The text that follows unfolds the sense of this idea.

16. *The Genealogy of Morals*, p. 190f.

17. See William Ernest Henley's poem, *Invictus* (1875).

18. *The Antichrist*, #2. In *The Portable Nietzsche*, W. Kaufmann, ed. (New York: The Viking Press, 1968), p. 570.

19. Albert Camus's monograph, *The Myth of Sisyphus* (New York: Vintage Books, 1955 [orig., 1942]—see pp. 88ff) opens this concern for meaning in the following way: "There is but one truly serious philosophical problem, and that is suicide. Judging whether or not life is worth living amounts to answering the fundamental question of philosophy." The effect of existence is itself a matter for philosophical speculation. Camus ends on a Nietzchean note of optimism where "One must imagine Sisyphus happy" (p. 91). This is too much to hope for, especially for one who would labor pushing boulders. Instead of happy, I imagine Sisyphus with hemorrhoids due to the strain of interminably pushing the boulder, with sharp gravel caught in his shoe mercilessly tormenting his foot. He can't sit down; he can't stand up. With this fate, Sisyphus can have no "silent joy."

20. Rudolf Bultmann articulates the involvements of "demythologizing." See for instance his *Jesus Christ and Mythology* (New York: Charles Scribner's Sons, 1958) or *Primitive Christianity in its Contemporary Setting* (New York: Living Age Books [Meridian Books], 1956).

21. For instance, Richard A. Horsley's (with John S. Hanson) *Bandits, Prophets, and Messiahs: Popular Movements in the Time of Jesus* (San Francisco: Harper & Row, 1985) recounts the social conditions and religious assumptions characteristic of Jesus's Palestine. From within the historical context developed by Horsley one can understand why certain emphases and language were relevant to writers of the New Testament scriptures. Suffice it here to say that early New Testament writers did not tailor a newly designed language to fit a unique Jesus.

22. "For consider your call, brethren; not many of you were wise according to worldly standards, not many were powerful, not many were of noble birth; but God chose what is foolish in the world to shame the wise, God chose what is weak in the world to shame the strong, God chose what is low and despised in the world, even things that are not, to bring to nothing things that are, so that no human being might boast in the presence of God (I Cor. 1: 26-29).

23. Regarding God's existence and Christianity, the word "agnosticism"—the denial of the possibility of knowing God's objective reality—best expresses a Christian position. "Christian agnosticism" moves away from the voice of philosophical objectivity to a recognition that no determination of God's being will be established by one understanding finitude's judgment on the intellectual enterprise.

# Index